MAKE YOURSELF
A MILLIONAIRE

MAKE YOURSELF A MILLIONAIRE

How to Sleep Well and Stay Sane on the Road to Wealth

Charles C. Zhang

with Lynn L. Chen-Zhang

McGraw-Hill

New York Chicago San Francisco Lisbon
London Madrid Mexico City Milan
New Delhi San Juan Seoul Singapore
Sydney Toronto

The *McGraw·Hill* Companies

3 4 5 6 7 8 9 0   DOC/DOC   0 9 8 7 6 5 4 3

ISBN 0-07-140982-3

This publication is designed to provide accurate and authoritative information in regard to the subject matter covered. It is sold with the understanding that neither the author nor the publisher is engaged in rendering legal, accounting, or other professional service. If legal advice or other expert assistance is required, the services of a competent professional person should be sought.

> —*From a Declaration of Principles jointly adopted by a Committee of the American Bar Association and a Committee of Publishers.*

McGraw-Hill books are available at special quantity discounts to use as premiums and sales promotions, or for use in corporate training programs. For more information, please write to the Director of Special Sales, McGraw-Hill, Two Penn Plaza, New York, NY 10121-2298. Or contact your local bookstore.

 This book is printed on recycled, acid-free paper containing a minimum of 50% recycled, de-inked fiber.

Library of Congress Cataloging-in-Publication Data

Zhang, Charles C.
    Make yourself a millionaire : how to sleep well and stay sane on the road to wealth / Charles C. Zhang and Lynn L. Chen-Zhang
        p.   cm.
    ISBN 0-07-140982-3 (hardcover : alk. paper)
    1. Finance, Personal. 2. Investments. 3. Portfolio management. I.
    Chen-Zhang, Lynn L. II. Title.
HG179.Z47 2003
332.024'01— dc21   2002011402

*To our children, our all-time best-performing portfolio,
Mitchell and Alex.*

DISCLAIMER

While the information in this book is believed to be accurate, distribution of this material should not be considered an endorsement of any particular investment strategy, product, or service described herein. This information is being provided only as a general source of information and is not intended for use as a primary basis for investment decisions, nor should it be construed as advice designed to meet the particular needs of an individual investor. Please seek the advice of your personal accountant, attorney, or tax and financial advisors regarding your particular financial concerns.

In addition, please note the following:

- Mutual funds are offered by prospectus only. For more information about individual mutual funds, including fees and expenses, ask your financial advisor or product provider for a prospectus. Read the prospectus carefully before you invest or send money.
- Loans and withdrawals from an insurance contract may generate income tax liability, reduce available cash value, and reduce the death benefit. Negative performance in the underlying subaccounts of variable insurance products may impact the death benefit. Refer to your individual contract for applicable provisions. Guarantees issued by insurance companies are based on the claims paying ability of the issuing insurance company.
- Stocks of small or midsized companies are generally subject to greater price fluctuations than large-cap stocks.
- International investing involves some risks not present with U.S. investments, such as currency fluctuations and other economic and political factors.
- Interest received from investments in Municipal Bond Funds may be subject to Alternate Minimum tax (AMT).
- Variable Annuities and Insurance Products are subject to fees and expenses that may impact performance.
- Most annuities have a tax-deferred feature. So do certain retirement plans under the Internal Revenue Code. As a result, when you use an annuity to fund a retirement plan that is tax deferred, your annuity will not provide any necessary or additional tax deferral for you retirement plan.
- Options are not suitable for all investors. Ask your financial advisor for an options risk disclosure booklet and read it carefully before investing in options.

CONTENTS

ACKNOWLEDGMENTS

We owe a debt of gratitude to many people for this book. But our deepest gratitude goes to Jennifer Eritano, our assistant and friend, who devoted her time and talent to make this book possible. Without her, this book would have never been completed!

A big thank you goes to our editor, Steve Isaacs of McGraw-Hill, for his guidance and patience, and to Sally Glover for her great editing work. Our undying gratitude also goes to the leaders and staff at American Express, especially Ken Chenault, Jim Cracchiolo, Brian Heath, Mark Regnier, Rhonda Schwartz, Guinero Floro, Paula Swanson, and our compliance and legal department, for their invaluable support and suggestions. We would like to thank our wonderful assistants, Kerrie Peterson, Tricia Watkins, and James Walsh, for their dedication through all of this. Their unfailing loyalty is appreciated from the bottoms of our hearts. Our families and friends have been very supportive through this process. To our parents, we give them our deepest appreciation.

MAKE YOURSELF
A MILLIONAIRE

1

THE FIRST STEP

IT'S NOT AN EASY OR A QUICK PROCESS, to become wealthy. Actually, it takes a lot of discipline and hard work. However, recent history has shown us that becoming wealthy can indeed happen overnight. Over the past few years, we've seen many people strike it rich through the stock market. Internet stocks, IPOs, and stock options—it seemed that everywhere we looked there was someone else, and usually a young someone else, who had just suddenly become worth millions of dollars. Every week or so there was another initial public offering of a company whose stock price would soar into the range of hundreds of dollars. People were quitting their jobs to become day traders, all in the name of money and riches.

But counting on the stock market to make you a lot of money very quickly is not only risky, it's also highly unlikely, especially now. Plus, if you had known then what you know now (i.e., when to buy and sell Yahoo! or Microsoft), would you have done what it takes to become rich off the stock market? Probably not. Buying low and selling high go against human nature. Just ask the man who bought Yahoo! at more than $150 per share and watched the share price plummet to around $12 per share. The meteoric rise of the stock market in the 1990s was an abnormality. Will the stock market continue to go up? Sure, historically speaking over the long term it will. (See Figure 1.1) But the markets will continue to rise and fall all the time. Will it skyrocket the way it did in the 90s? No one can say. Investors today are smarter, younger, and have more time to wait to make the returns they want. For those who are trying to make their first or their umpteenth million, today's market serves as a lesson of hurry up and wait. This is a road that the average investor just shouldn't travel alone. Here's the first secret that many wealthy people know: Hire a financial advisor to do some of the worrying for you.

WHAT IS A FINANCIAL ADVISOR, AND DO YOU NEED ONE?

"A financial advisor? I don't need one. My cousin Tony is a whiz with investments and finances." If this is something you find yourself saying, stop. Unless your cousin Tony has taken classes and passed comprehensive exams, like the CFP™ boards, and works as a financial advisor, chances are you don't want to trust your retirement to him.

Cousin Tony is probably not going to be able to help you decide if you need to invest in a traditional IRA or a Roth IRA. Nor will he be able to advise you on what the possible benefits of investing in an annuity would be for you. The best answers to these questions, and others like them, come in the form of a financial advisor.

A financial advisor is there to keep you educated and invested for the long term when the market goes down, as well as when decisions are to be made. Put simply, he can be your best friend. Financial advisors, or planners, work with clients to find the best fit between the client and different investment vehicles. Some advisors are affiliated with national firms, while others work as independents.

The last time you paid your car insurance, did your insurance agent offer you the chance to purchase a Roth IRA through him?

The historical growth of stocks

Through good times and bad, the stock market has moved upward, although there have been peaks and valleys along the way.

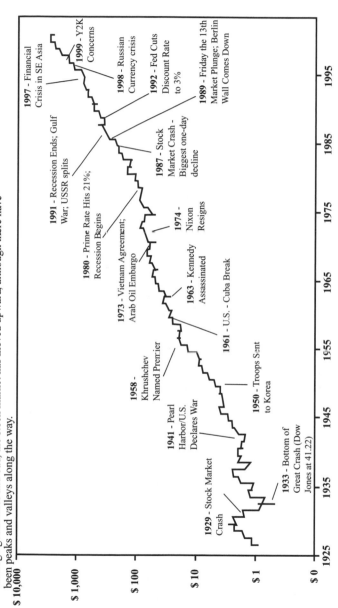

Figure 1.1 Hypothetical value of $1 invest at year-end 1925 has grown to $2587 by year-end 2000; assumes reinvestment of income and no transaction costs or taxes. This is for illustrative purposes only and not indicative of any investment. Past performance is no guarantee of future results.

Source: S&P 500, which is an unmanaged index group of securities and considered to be representative of the stock market in general, and American Express Funds.

3

More and more insurance agencies, banks, and even Certified Public Accountants are getting into the investment business. Many of these people only promote and sell certain products. You may like the Oppenheimer Global Growth and Income Fund, but that doesn't mean that you should invest in every Oppenheimer fund. There are, perhaps, other mutual fund companies that would better fit your needs. Every investor's portfolio benefits from having choices available. Financial advisors have many different investment vehicles at their fingertips that help their clients achieve their goals. Advisors focus on these goals and needs to decide which investment is best, rather than applying a cafeteria plan to each client.

At some point in time, everyone will need the help and expertise that only a financial advisor can provide. They offer a well-balanced approach to your finances. Let's face it, you may be too emotionally involved with your money to manage it properly. You have worked hard for you money and don't want to lose it. A financial advisor is the third party to your financial situation. Just like you wouldn't perform surgery on a family member, why should you perform surgery on your money?

Recognizing the need for a financial advisor is the first step to taking control of your finances and increasing your wealth. Selecting the proper advisor is a harder task. This is a very important challenge. You need to find the right advisor for your situation. Receiving referrals from friends or family members is a good place to start. If they are willing to share the name of their advisor, that means that they trust him. However, if you are uncomfortable asking or don't know anyone who uses an advisor, then you will be starting from scratch.

There are a few things to keep in mind when selecting your advisor. First, don't be afraid to interview your potential advisor or shop around. Most planners offer a free initial consultation. This will give you the chance to sit down with advisors and ask questions. Second, make sure you feel comfortable with your advisor. During your initial meeting, gauge how you feel. Did the staff make you feel welcome? Do you feel comfortable discussing the most intimate details of your financial situation with this advisor? Do you think you can trust this person? If you answer "no" to any of these questions, then you should probably continue to look for an advisor. Third, make sure that any potential advisor is qualified. Nowadays, almost everyone can call themselves financial advisors. But those same people could be delivering pizzas during the evenings. To make sure advisors are thoroughly knowledgeable, look for designations following their names: i.e., Joe Smith, CFP™, ChFC, CLU. These designations mean that they have passed rigorous examinations.

QUALITY COUNTS

The CFP™ mark identifies financial advisors who have met the stringent education, experience, and ethics standards set by the Certified Financial Planner Board of Standards, Inc. The CFP™ Board not only owns the certification mark, it also licenses the qualified individuals to use it. Any advisor using the CFP™ mark has passed the Board's certification and relicensing requirements. Only those licensed to use the CFP™ mark are allowed to represent themselves as Certified Financial Planners. In this country, there are more than 700,000 people who represent themselves as financial planners. However, only about four percent, or 30,000, of those individuals are Certified Financial Planners.

Among the requirements to become a CFP™ is a two-day, 10-hour certification exam that covers the financial planning process, retirement planning, tax planning, investment management, and insurance and estate planning. CFP™ candidates must also prove that they have the required work experience before being certified and then must adhere to the rigid CFP™ Board's Code of Ethics and Professional Responsibility. Additionally, there is an ongoing continuing education requirement that must be met in order to continue to use the CFP™ designation. Although other professional designations exist, the CFP™ is the most difficult, prestigious, and comprehensive designation available.

THE ChFC AND CLU DESIGNATIONS

Two common certifications that financial advisors earn are the ChFC and CLU designations. Both the ChFC, Chartered Financial Consultant, and CLU, Chartered Life Underwriter, can help you analyze your financial needs and choose the right course for maintaining and increasing your assets. They have studied the many areas of insurance and financial services and can assist with life and health insurance, estate conservation, etc.

Both designations require comprehensive curriculums of 10 college-level courses. The ChFC designation also requires an additional three courses. Extensive education, experience, and ethics requirements must also be met. These designations are granted by The American College, a fully accredited institution in Pennsylvania.

YOUR ADVISOR—GOOD OR BAD?

You've gone through the interviewing process with a number of advisors and have picked one. This person seems very knowledgeable, and you feel like this is a good fit. However, the time may come when you decide that your financial advisor is just not the right one for you anymore. That's okay; it's perfectly alright to switch advisors if you feel that your advisor isn't doing the right thing for you. Here are some guidelines to help you make your decision:

Do You Understand What Your Accounts Are Doing and What They Are Designed to Do?

Although no one expects you to become an expert on every aspect of your portfolio, that's what your advisor is for, you should have some understanding of its components. If your advisor recommends investing in an annuity, make sure you are familiar with what an annuity is. Don't be afraid to ask questions; it will make you feel better. Be sure you are comfortable with the answers your advisor gives you, as well as with each individual product.

I have a client who invested $20,000 in a real estate investment trust. At the time he purchased it, I explained how they work and the pros and cons of investing in one. I made sure he understood the product. Since then, he has asked me a number of times to reexplain the REIT. While other advisors may become irritated at having to explain the same things time and again, I don't. I'm glad my client wants to understand his investments.

Does Your Advisor Have Your Best Interests at Heart?

When you review your portfolio, do you think your advisor is promoting his or her own agenda? Or, does your advisor recommend investments that are suited for you? If you understand your investments, then the answer to this question will be easy. This also includes whether or not your advisor is following his or her own instincts, or if that person is basing recommendations on analysts' predictions. While it's important for your advisor to have a solid opinion of today's market, your portfolio shouldn't be solely based upon what one person thinks. Just because your advisor thinks it's a good time to invest in commodities doesn't mean that you should sink your entire retirement fund into that sector. Analysts' predictions can be right, but they can also be wrong. Rather, your accounts should be based upon your age, risk tolerance level, and circumstances.

Is There a Lot of Activity in Your Accounts?

Many advisors earn their money through commissions, not only when you purchase a product, but also when movements are made within your accounts. Your risk level should determine account rebalancing, not whatever is good for your advisor's pocket. If you feel there are excess transactions in your account, talk to your advisor about it. The only transactions that occur in your account should be done at your discretion and with your input.

I meet with my clients at least twice per year. This doesn't mean, though, that I am changing things in the portfolio at least twice a year. I rebalance their portfolios only if they need to be. Changing around your investments more than necessary defeats the purpose of investing, and may actually cause your portfolio to decrease in value.

What Kind of Investments Are You Involved With?

This relates to your understanding of your investments. Many brokers push certain products known as "proprietary products." These are investments that are managed by the firm the advisor is affiliated with and, thus, will get paid more for. Take a look at your account statements. Do you see a lot of securities that all have the same name (i.e., the XYZ Value Fund and the XYZ Growth Potential Fund)? If so, ask your advisor why you are invested in these funds. They may be excellent funds, but there may be other, similar funds that are better suited for you.

Does Your Advisor Know You Financially?

Have you been asked to show your tax return to your advisor? Is he or she in contact with your CPA? Does your advisor ask about your 401(k) at work? A good financial advisor needs to know everything about your financial life. If your 401(k) at work is heavily weighted in technology stocks and stock funds, your portfolio with your advisor shouldn't be. Make sure your advisor knows everything he or she needs to know in order to make the best possible recommendations to you. If your advisor doesn't seem to care, or isn't listening when you bring it up, it's time to find someone else who will.

Who Are You Making Your Checks Out To?

There are always stories in the newspapers about unknowing clients getting bilked out of thousands, even millions, of dollars by some financial advisor. Always be sure that you are writing your checks out properly. For payment of consultation fees, it's okay to write a check directly to your advisor. If the advisor works as an independent, then it may be alright to write the check out to him or her personally. However, if the advisor is the agent of a registered investment firm, then do not make your check payable to the advisor personally.

Who Controls Your Portfolio?

Some firms allow what is called discretionary power. This means that if you consent, your advisor can make moves within your portfolio without consulting you. For some clients, this is exactly what they want, and they are willing to take the risk associated with having a discretionary account. For most, though, discretionary power is a problem.

A few months ago, I had a man come meet with me for the first time. He was unhappy with the performance of some of his accounts at another firm. He asked that we transfer his assets so that I could be his advisor. This man was out of the country quite a bit for business, and had given his advisor at the other firm discretionary control over his accounts. When we liquidated his holdings at the other firm, he discovered that one of his poorest performing assets was a Unit Investment Trust—an investment he didn't even know he owned! His advisor had purchased it using discretionary power while the man was out of the country.

Although this isn't a complete list of questions, these are the most important. If you find yourself in doubt about switching, trust your gut feeling. That will be your best guide.

A WORD ABOUT FEES

There's an old saying that goes, "It takes money to make money." In other words, in order to make some money, you need to be willing to spend some money. I have had many people come into my office and ask my advice. While I am more than willing to help my clients and potential clients, I find it troubling that many people expect financial advice for free. Financial advisors, myself included, charge a fee for the services we provide. However, I have encountered people who are adverse to paying any type of fee for financial planning. They would rather have the advice up front for free. Would you go to your doctor or dentist, ask them what needs to be done, and then expect not to pay? Of course not. Financial planners are professionals just as doctors and lawyers are. There is a fee for service.

That being said, if you find that you are fee-adverse, think about it this way. Many financial advisors charge their planning or retainer fees on an account-balance basis. For example, let's assume that Mike Advisor, CFP™ charges a one-percent retainer fee to his clients. He bases the fee on their account balances. You, his client, have an account balance of $875,000. The annual retainer fee you would pay is $8750. As your account balance goes up, so does his fee. But, if your account balance were to decrease, his fee would also. Therefore, the more money you make, the more money your advisor makes. It's really a win-win situation for both of you because your advisor is going to want to see your account balance increase. He's going to do everything he can to see that you make more money. And what's wrong with that? What you don't want to see is your fee being increased while your account balance is decreasing.

It's understandable to look at the fee amount in the above example as a large amount, but often that money can come straight out of your account, rather than out of your pocket. Plus, the fee may be deductible on your federal income taxes. Financial planning fees pretty much boil down to this: Either you pay or you don't. Chances are, if you don't pay for your financial advice, you're not going to get the quality advice that you need.

MONEY AND FEAR

Many people are afraid of money, especially their money. Think about it, when was the last time you were at a dinner party and everyone was talking about how much money they had, or didn't have? Probably not very recently. While we as a society have discovered that it's permissible to talk about the neighbor's divorce, your sister's therapy sessions, or your grandfather's bout with cancer, no one feels it's alright to talk about their financial situation. And, sure, maybe it's not the best idea to brag about how much money you've saved in your company 401(k), or that you have thousands of dollars in outstanding credit card debt, but you'd be surprised at how many people feel the same way or are in the same situation.

Facing your fears about money is probably the hardest thing you'll ever do. But what exactly are you so afraid of? Losing all your money? Not being able to afford those material things your friends can? Not having enough? And how much is enough money, anyway? In order to get control of your money and realize your goal of being rich, you need to know where you are starting from, and get hold of your fears.

Sometimes our fear of money is directly linked to a past action that drives us. For instance, when you were young did you get an allowance? What did you do with this money? Save it or spend it? Does your reaction to your allowance connect with your reaction to your current salary? In other words, do you still find it hard to part with your money, or are you spending it the minute you get it? By identifying your money habits, it becomes easier to change the bad habits. Of course, fear may drive you away from even looking at your financial habits.

The only way to eradicate your fear is to replace it with positive thoughts. Think about what your goals are. Then think about what your deepest financial fear is. Do you want to retire early, but are afraid that if you do you will run out of money before you die? Or perhaps you want to have a second home, but feel that if you buy one you are being selfish and that you don't deserve it. No matter what your goals are, your fears can override them to the point that you become too paralyzed to try and achieve your goals. Ultimately, you need to overcome your fears to realize your dreams.

Money is also deeply tied to our emotions and is a prime motivator of our behavior. Our self-images are directly affected by the amount of money we have or don't have. Try to become aware of your attitudes toward money. Once you have ascertained how you react to money, and what drives you, you will be able to increase your chances of becoming rich. Your personal money management style will dictate the way you handle money now and in the future. You need to realize what your style is so that you may better harness and use it.

Ask yourself some questions about your actions and feelings. Is money important to you? How important? Do you feel guilty when you spend money? Do you find that you spend money until your credit card is rejected, or until you have no more money in your wallet? Are you a risk taker? When you look at your bank account balance, how do you feel? How much money do you think you need to feel secure? How much money do you spend on a monthly basis? By asking yourself these questions, you will be on the way to achieving your goals.

However, the next step is to answer the questions honestly. That's where our fears come back into play. Take the last question, for instance. I ask all my clients to prepare a cash flow statement for me. (This is discussed more in depth in Chapter 2.) If you were to estimate how much money you spend monthly, and then compare it to the actual amount, which number would be bigger? You may find that you are spending more money each month than you thought. How does that make you feel? Are you afraid that you won't be able to cover your bills? Or, do you feel relieved that you now know what you are truly spending?

Write down what your goals and fears are. Come up with a positive statement about how you will reach your goals, thus crushing your fears. Although much has been said about the power of positive thinking, the effects cannot be denied. The more positive your outlook, the more good will come your way. Think about it. The last time you were in a bad mood, did you affect those around you so their moods turned sour, too? Similarly, when you smile at people, the more likely they are to smile back at you. The more positive your thoughts are about money, the more good things will happen.

One more thing, it's important to remember that fears come in different forms than just self-doubt. Many times family members or loved ones will instill doubt in us. This may come in the form of, "Why do you think you can do that?" or other statements along those lines. Whatever the reason for these statements, don't let them discourage you. Only you can change the way you think. Keep a smile on your face and a glint in your eye, because you can become as wealthy as you want to be. By having a more positive outlook, you may see a change in them, too.

THE FINANCIAL PLANNING PROCESS

Personal financial planning is the process through which you, along with your advisor, determine how to meet your financial goals. Financial planning distinguishes financial planners and advisors from other professional investment advisors who focus solely on individual products.

Now that you have selected your financial advisor, he or she should address these six key areas:

1. Understand what your financial goals are.
2. Gather all essential financial information.
3. Analyze this information.
4. Make recommendations to help you achieve your goals.
5. Take action on these recommendations.
6. Review your progress.

Your advisor's job is to listen to your concerns and objectives. Do you want to provide financially for your children or grandchildren's college education? Or is buying a vacation home in Florida your main priority? By telling your advisor what you hope to gain, that person will be able to guide you along the best path to help you reach your goals. An advisor's job, however, is not to make the decisions for you. He or she merely suggests what should be done. You are the decision maker. It's important to have realistic goals. Perhaps you can't afford to have your vacation home in Florida just yet. That doesn't mean you should give up the idea, you just have to work with what you have. Your advisor will be able to put you into investments that will have the potential to make enough money to get your vacation home.

For example, a married couple comes in for an initial consultation. They are in their 40s and say that they want to have $3 million in performing assets in five years. A look through their assets reveals that they currently have $1 million total. But, that figure includes their house, the surrounding land, and some other land they own. Their investable assets total $400,000. In this case, it's great that they had this goal, but while their net worth was very good for a couple their age, $3 million in performing assets in five years was just not realistic. In order for this to happen, they would need nearly a 50-percent return every year for the next five years.

It wasn't that the $3 million in performing assets was the unrealistic part; it was the time frame in which they wanted to work. Your advisor will help you decide what goals should be short term and which ones should be long term. Most importantly, though, he or she will continue to provide client service. This means that as your needs change, your advisor will change with you to make sure you are still on track to achieving whatever your goal may be. Anyone can sell you an investment product; it takes a committed financial advisor to provide ongoing client service to ensure that you are heading in the right direction.

ESTABLISHING A FINANCIAL PLAN

Smart investors know that they must know where they are currently, what they want to accomplish, and they know that they need to have a game plan. A financial plan is just that: a financial road map. A sound plan should cover a broad range of topics that relate to your present security, as well as to your future well-being. It should include an analysis of your net worth, investable assets, commitment to goals, and a time frame. The successful plan is balanced, pinpoints your particular needs and goals, creates an integrated strategy to help meet them, and encompasses these six cornerstones:

Examine Your Present Situation

In order for your financial advisor to guide you along the path to achieving your goals, he or she needs to have a clear understanding of where you stand presently. This means figuring out your net worth and liquid net worth, examining your cash flow, and determining your cash reserves.

Cash reserves are a vital part of your financial well-being. For instance, let's say you have $50,000 in your savings account and $3000 in your checking account. You want to invest the $50,000 so that it potentially earns more than it does in a regular savings account. Now, I recommend keeping three to six months worth of expenses as a cash reserve. Therefore, if you find that your monthly expenses, after taxes, are $2000, then the $3000 in your checking account isn't going to cut it. You should have at least $6000 as a cash reserve.

By analyzing your current situation, your advisor may find ways to help you save money and reach your goals faster than you may have known. Redirecting some of your money could help you put money away for retirement, or achieve another goal, without it seeming like you are spending any more money than you currently are.

Have Adequate Protection

Protecting yourself from the unexpected is a vital element in financial planning. As time goes by, you change, and so do your protection needs. Having adequate protection means a number of things, such as providing for your family after your death or replacing earning power after a disability. Protection means insurance, and while many people dislike the thought of insurance, it is terribly important.

Many of my clients are already retired and older. They don't need any disability insurance since they aren't working, and for many of them, life insurance really would be a waste of money. However,

long-term care, or nursing home insurance is perfect. These are people who have multi-million-dollar net worths. To see all of their hard
work, money, and possessions decimated by having to pay for a nursing home is sad and unnecessary. Many of my clients have opted to
transfer the risk of paying for nursing homes, rather than trying to
self-insure or rely on family members.

However, you may find that you don't require any type of insurance. Protection analysis looks at the different types of insurance and
the most economically efficient ways to manage the different types
of risk.

Investment Planning

Do you enjoy sitting at your computer, trying to figure out which
mutual fund is the best option for you? Chances are, you don't.
Today, there are so many different types of mutual funds, stocks,
bonds, and investment choices, that it would make your head spin.
An advisor's job is to sort through all these choices and match specific investment vehicles with your goals, needs, and time frame.
Whether you are investing for the long term or short term will determine what kind of product your money should be invested in. You
don't want your money tied up in an illiquid investment if you are
planning to use the money in the next couple of years.

Before investing any money, it's important that you communicate
to your advisor how much risk you want to take. I give my clients a
risk tolerance quiz. The quiz is six questions long, and it gauges how
aggressive my clients wish to be. I've had more than a few clients
come to see me and tell me that they are aggressive risk takers. Sure,
we all are when the market is soaring to new highs and everyone is
making money. But not many people are aggressive when the market
starts to come back down, people are losing money, and stocks are
hitting all-time lows. The truly aggressive people are the ones who
are buying when the market is low. Many people want to become
more conservative at that time. It's human nature.

That's why I give them the quiz. Once I score them as conservative, moderately conservative, moderate, moderately aggressive, or
aggressive, I can suggest investment vehicles that match up with
their risk factors. It's the quiz that helps determine the mix of invest-

ments so that the clients can concentrate more on their lives, rather than worrying about the market's performance.

Tax Planning

Proper tax planning can be a powerful element in protecting and building your wealth. There are certain tax breaks that usually only the wealthy employ, and then there are the tax breaks that aren't tax breaks and are actually illegal. Financial planning can help identify the impact that taxes will have on you in the future. While we can't predict tax increases or decreases, we will have a good idea of how to minimize the taxes you pay, both now and in the future.

There are a number of different tax-exempt and tax-deferred investments you can buy that will help reduce your tax burden. Virtually all tax-exempt investments are free from federal income tax, and many are exempt from state and local income taxes when purchased by residents of those states.

The income paid on investments in certain tax-deferred products, like deferred annuities and universal life insurance, is not immediately taxable. Unlike tax-exempt income, tax deferment simply postpones the payment of taxes until receipt of this income at a later date. This helps reduce your tax bill in that by the time you receive the income from these investments, you may possibly be in a lower tax bracket, thus reducing the tax due. I explain all of this more in a later chapter.

Retirement Planning

It's never too late to start planning and saving for your retirement. If you have already begun, it will be helpful to review what you have achieved so far and what you need to do to get you to your retirement goal. If you have already retired, you will want to look at allocating your resources so that they may provide income for your entire retirement.

Initially, you and your advisor should consider how much money you think you will need to live the kind of retirement you want. Into that equation, you will need to factor in any Social Security or pension benefits you are planning to receive.

Your financial plan will tell you if there is an additional need for income, and at what age you should be able to retire. From this plan, you will also know what additional savings are needed, if any. Since we can't predict what the stock market will do, it's important to update your plan fairly regularly, especially once you get close to retirement. Knowing your financial situation in regard to your retirement is essential to achieving the kind of retirement you desire. It's better to know sooner rather than later what you need to do to make sure that you can live the way you want.

Retirement planning also addresses any job changes you have had or are planning to have. If you think you will be leaving your job, or already have, you will have to make a decision about what to do with your retirement benefits from that employer. Since for many people this is the largest amount of money they have handled, it's essential to consult with your advisor, who will help you choose the right investment vehicles and tax strategies for your retirement money. Your financial plan will address your specific concerns and help you pave the road to a successful retirement.

Estate Planning

You may be thinking that you don't need any type of estate planning because you don't have that much money. If that's the case, then you would be mistaken. Estate planning isn't just for the extremely wealthy. You may have a potential estate large enough to require the special information that your financial plan can provide. Besides, don't your goals include having enough money and assets to make your estate very large?

It's important for you to know what will be available to your heirs when your estate is settled. Additionally, you want to make sure that estate transfer costs and estate taxes are as low as possible. Estate planning is a highly specialized area that your financial plan will cover. Your advisor will help you plan to ensure that there is enough estate liquidity to meet estate settlement costs, as well as address any other key estate planning concerns.

IS A FINANCIAL PLAN REALLY WORTH IT?

People neglect financial planning for a number of reasons. Feeling that they have insufficient assets or income is one reason. Another is that people feel that their finances are already taken care of, or are in good shape. While that may be true, everyone can benefit from hiring a financial advisor and having a plan. However, humans tend to procrastinate, often putting things off so long that it becomes too late. Plus, planning encompasses certain life experiences that may be unpleasant. While planning for retirement may be a positive experience, planning for a disability or death might not be. Then there is the financial cost of planning. Professional financial planners charge a fee for their services. All of these factors can be deterrents to planning.

In regards to financial planning fees, these may be deductible from your federal income taxes. The current tax laws permit the deduction of expenses caused by the management or maintenance of property held for the express production of income. However, there are limits to deducting these fees.

While planning for uncertain events, such as unemployment, a disability, or a nursing home stay, may be uncomfortable, certainly planning for these events would be preferable to not being prepared for these occurrences. Being caught off guard could then cause the rest of your financial world to go into a tailspin. However, planning and being prepared for such events would make their happening less stressful. Think about it. If you were injured and unable to work, wouldn't you like to know that you will have money coming in because you purchased disability insurance for yourself?

Death is an eventuality that we all must face. If you want to leave as much of your estate to your heirs as possible, it's necessary to plan. This way, you will have an idea of what will go to your heirs and what will go to the government in estate taxes. Failure to plan may cause your heirs to fall behind and lose most of their inheritance to the IRS.

WHAT IF I DON'T DO ANY FINANCIAL PLANNING?

In addition to the possible situations of not being prepared when a disability occurs, or when a death happens, there are other costs of not doing any planning. Failure to plan may result in higher than necessary income, gift, and estate taxes. There may not be enough money for further education or retirement. You may find yourself unprotected in the event that there is a car accident, unemployment, disability, a prolonged hospital stay, a nursing home stay, home care needed, etc.

Perhaps the most devastating cost of not planning is the loss of your personal goals and objectives. How many times have you heard someone say that they wanted to retire at age 55 but were stuck in a job that they hated until 60 or 62? That's seven years later than they wanted! Not planning can cause you to work longer than anticipated.

Having an advisor and having him prepare a financial plan for you will help keep you on track to meeting your goals. However, this *is* just the beginning. Your plan and advisor won't instantly make you more money, nor will they show you any get-rich-quick schemes. Things like that just don't work. But there are a few tricks of the trade to help you.

2

AN INVESTOR'S
BEST FRIEND—
ASSET ALLOCATION

THERE ARE A NUMBER OF WAYS to pick how to distribute your money across different investments. You could pin the stock pages onto a dartboard and throw darts to pick stocks to invest in. You could stay hunched over your computer, researching every different mutual fund. Perhaps you've decided that you like real estate, and therefore you're going to sink all your money into land. Or, you could employ all three different investments, along with a few others, and follow what is called "asset allocation."

ASSET ALLOCATION

I structure all my clients' portfolios based on the asset allocation model, a Nobel prize-winning theory developed at the University of

Chicago. The tenet of asset allocation is to identify a mix of different types of investments with the highest potential return for your level of risk tolerance, consistent with your goals and the time frame in which you have to reach them.

It's very simple to pick out the "hot" investments—those that have performed very well over a short period of time. Let's consider an example of someone who keeps a fair amount of money in a cash position. Each time she receives recommendations, she says that she would like to think about it before acting. She then calls and says she has picked out a few funds on her own. As a financial advisor, I pick mutual funds based upon past performance over 10 or more years. I look at track records, fund managers, and the makeup of the funds. This woman, though, only looks at 1-year returns. Even though she knows better, she continues to chase returns. Purchasing funds at their 52-week high isn't the smartest reason to invest in a particular mutual fund. This is something I caution all my clients against.

What isn't so easy is to pick the proper mix of investments that will perform well over a long period of time because investments fluctuate throughout various market conditions. Purchasing mutual funds because they are at, or near, their 52-week highs is not a good reason to buy. The key to successful investing is to recognize that no single investment will provide consistent, high returns that will allow you to reach your financial goals. By diversifying through different types of investments through asset allocation, you increase your chances of long-term, positive portfolio increases. (See Figure 2.1.) It's important to have your investment dollars spread across many investment vehicles to help protect your money against the performance of one single investment.

Different investments provide different levels of returns. For example, some stock prices tend to rise and fall with the economy, while the values of variable fixed-income securities generally change with the interest rate. Then there are investments that strictly earn interest and are not subject to the ebbs and flows of the stock market or the interest rate. Even though separate forces may affect different investments, the change in one may trigger a predictable movement by another. While asset allocation doesn't

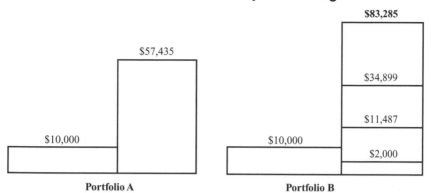

Diversification: The Key to Investing

Figure 2.1: Portfolio A and Portfolio B each have $10,000 to invest. Portfolio A is invested 100 percent in an investment earning 6 percent. Portfolio B is equally split between five higher-risk investments. Two of these investments earn 10 percent, one earns 6 percent, one earns 0 percent, and one loses 100 percent. After 30 years with this mix, Portfolio B has earned nearly $26,000 more than Portfolio A. Diversification does not guarantee a profit. These values are hypothetical and do not indicate any type of future results. The value and return on most investments will vary. (*American Express Funds literature.*)

assume that you'll make a profit or insure against a loss, it may help temper any loss you may sustain.

INFLATION AND TAXES—HIDDEN DANGERS

The asset allocation approach also considers how other factors may affect your investment. Both inflation and taxes can wreak havoc on your investment accounts and may inhibit your ability to make more money. No proper financial plan should fail to take these things into consideration. For example, if you have a 10-percent return on your overall portfolio in a given year, your actual return may be 4 to 5 percent less because of federal, state, and local taxes.

Additionally, if you believe you will need $75,000 per year (in today's dollars) to live on during your retirement, and you will be retiring in 10 years, you will need to factor in inflation. The purchasing power of $75,000 now could be drastically different 10 years from now. Based upon an inflation rate of 4 percent, in 10 years you would need about $111,000 per year! That means that in a decade you will need nearly 50 percent more in income just to keep up with the rising cost of living.

With my clients, once we have identified and prioritized their objectives and goals, I create an asset allocation model that compares their current portfolio to a proposed portfolio. It shows over a given number of years what happens if they stay invested in the same mix they are currently in, versus the proposed mix that I will follow. (See Figure 2.2.)

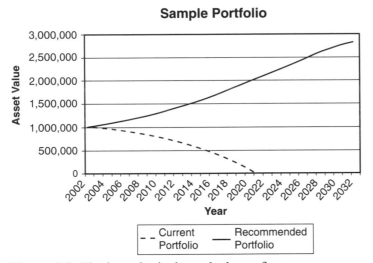

Figure 2.2. The hypothetical graph shows future asset value, with the current line representing the client's present mix. The proposed line shows following the investment strategy in asset allocation. The x-axis is the year and the y-axis is the dollars. Hypothetical clients retire in year 2002 at the age of 55. Mr. and Mrs. Client have $400,000 in their 401k plans and will receive a lump sum pension of $600,000. We assumed they would withdraw $40,000 after taxes per year, and that their average tax rates would be 20 percent for federal and 4.1 percent for Michigan. The proposed investment strategy is using a moderately aggressive risk approach.

Years of intensive studying of market trends and financial theory development have gone into this model. Therefore, I have at my fingertips the ability to put together the best possible portfolio for all of my clients based upon their risk levels and goals. We then discuss different types of investments within each of the proposed investment categories. The asset allocation model encompasses all the different classes of investments, including real estate; international stocks and bonds; tax-deferred investments; large, medium, and small company stock; and low-grade and high-grade bonds.

THE IMPORTANCE OF DIVERSIFICATION

Diversify, diversify, diversify—it can't be said enough. History has shown us, very recently in fact, how vital it is to diversify our investments. When a stock, mutual fund, or even a sector is hot, it can be tempting to think about investing a good portion, or all, of your money in it. However, this is the riskiest thing you can do. Smart investors know that in order to make consistent positive returns over the long run, your portfolio must reflect different types of investments and different sectors.

I have many clients who came to me with large holdings in their companys' stocks. It's very easy to accumulate a lot of stock in the company for which you work. Many companies only give their 401(k) match in company stock. It's then up to the client to diversify that stock across different funds within his or her 401(k). I personally caution my clients about holding more than 5–10 percent in one stock or holding, although diversification alone is no guarantee that the overall return will be profitable.

One client of mine works at Johnson Controls. The company's stock has done reasonably well over the past year or so, and my client had amassed a 401(k) worth more than $1,300,000. She watched the stock prices daily and was actively managing it herself. However, the entire amount was invested in Johnson Controls stock. This meant that whenever the stock price dropped even a little bit, her portfolio took a hit.

When we first met, she explained to me that she felt very comfortable leaving her money in Johnson Controls because she worked for the company, watched the stock price every day, and was confident that her 401(k) was stable. I discussed the importance of diversification with her. As is the case with every meeting, I left CNBC on so that I could stay constantly informed about what's going on in the market. During our meeting, a trade for Johnson Controls came across the bottom of the screen; it showed the stock down by a few cents. Now, a few cents is not a big deal when the stock price is as high as Johnson Controls was at the time. However, my client's entire 401(k) had just dropped noticeably during our meeting. I used this as reinforcement of my point about diversification.

At our next meeting, my client brought her husband in with her. She was still keeping her money in the Johnson Controls stock, which I again told her she should reconsider. I discovered that I had a very strong ally in this: her husband. He was very nervous about the fact that everything was in one stock. Though she wasn't convinced to diversify totally, leaving only a small portion of money in Johnson Controls stock, she did move a portion of her 401(k) to different funds within her retirement plan. At our subsequent meeting, both she and her husband confided that they felt much more comfortable having money spread across different asset classes, rather than in just one stock.

Another client came to me recently because he was having problems with his 401(k). He had retired two years earlier and had rolled his 401(k) into an Individual Retirement Arrangement at an investment firm. He was now self-directing his retirement money. When he retired in 1998, his 401(k) totaled nearly $1 million. Following the advice of friends, as well as his own research, he spread the whole amount over five different individual stocks and one mutual fund. By the time he came to see me, his accounts were nearly $350,000.

When we met, he was just sick with anguish. Not only had his accounts lost more than half their original value, but also he hadn't told anyone about this. His entire family still thought there was close to $1 million. He also told me that a few of his friends (already clients of mine) had recommended coming to see me when he retired, but he thought that he would be able to manage his money better. He believed, as I'm sure many do, that since he cared more about his money, he would do a better job.

The mutual fund he had picked was a highly sectorized fund that had performed poorly. While other mutual funds were making money during 1998 and 1999, this fund had continued to lose value and underperform. The stocks he picked fared poorly as well. Two were health care stocks, two were Internet stocks, and the fifth was a small cap stock. All the stocks were valued at less than $3 when we met.

He knew that he needed to do something, but was so upset that he didn't know what. Together we discussed diversifying his portfolio to help stabilize it. I put together a financial plan for him and showed him the different asset classes that were recommended. We were able to liquidate a couple of the stocks he held, as well as the mutual fund. We then invested the proceeds across different sectors, including international stock funds, high- and low-grade bond funds, and large company stock funds. Fortunately, we were able to preserve a lot of what remained. However, we had to keep some of the stocks he held because there wasn't a big market for them. We are continuing to sell these off over time, as they continue to make the value of the portfolio jump around wildly.

Diversification into international funds may also be suitable for you. We have become a global-based economy, with countries becoming very connected. Staying invested in just one economy also remains risky. Each of the world's largest markets has experienced a decline of 30 percent or more over the past two decades. Most notably has been the fall of the Japanese market. In just 10 years, the Nikkei dropped from 38,915 in December of 1989 to 13,406 in September of 1998. In July of 2001, it hit 11,609, its lowest point since January of 1985. Being invested in just the Japanese market would have spelled doom for that investor.

Likewise, I try to make sure that each of my clients has some sort of fixed investment that helps stabilize the portfolio when the overall market is down. While diversification won't totally protect a client's portfolio from losses when the market is down, it will help preserve most of the portfolio's value. After analyzing a client's current holdings, time frame, goals, and comfort level, I will recommend one or more investments that I believe will help them. In the past, I have recommended fixed annuities, which grow at a certain rate of interest and aren't subject to market fluctuations; money market funds, which don't vary with the market; or real estate investment trusts, which pay the client quarterly dividends.

One last point about diversification: beware of overlapping individual securities within different mutual funds. You may feel that you want to stay as light in the technology sector as possible, and think that you are invested in mutual funds accordingly. Ask your advisor to do some research to make sure that is the case. Many funds invest in the same, or similar, individual stocks, thus making your portfolio heavier in certain sectors than you may want it to be.

DIRECTLY OWNED ASSETS—PROS AND CONS

Where you own your assets is as important as what asset classes you own. Certain investments have tax benefits that may be lost if owned in a retirement plan, whereas there are distinct advantages to holding directly owned investments.

There are many advantages to holding directly owned assets. There are also limitations. With directly owned investments, capital gains aren't realized and taxable until the asset is sold or exchanged in a taxable transaction. For example, you hold 100 shares of Microsoft stock that you bought at $89 per share. The ups and downs of the stock price won't affect your taxes until you decide to sell. Should you sell the stock at $85 per share, you will realize a $4-per-share capital loss. However, if you were to sell at $95 per share, then you would be taxed on a $6-per-share gain. Depending on how long you have owned the asset, you will be subject to capital gains taxes. If you held the stock for less than one year, the gain will be taxed as a short-term gain, which is at your ordinary income tax rate. However, if you held the stock more than one year prior to the sale, then the gain is taxed at the long-term capital gains rate, which, as of 2002, is at a 20-percent maximum. This 20-percent maximum is an advantage for all taxpayers who are in the higher tax brackets. For those in the lower brackets, the maximum long-term capital gains rate is 10 percent.

Another advantage to directly owned assets is called a "step-up" in basis at death. While the original cost is usually the starting point when calculating basis, when a directly owned capital asset, such as stock, is inherited, the value at the time of the owner's death becomes the starting point. For instance, you inherit 1000 shares of Schering-Plough stock. The original cost basis for the stock is $20 per share. However, when you inherit it, the cost of the stock is $57 per share. You decide you will sell the stock at $60 per share, which you then do. Your gain on the stock is $3 per share, not $40 per share because of the step-up in basis.

If you were to sell your holdings for a loss, you would be able to use that capital loss on your taxes to offset any capital gains you may have had, plus offsetting some of your ordinary income. Up to $3000 of a capital loss may be used per year. Any unused portion of the loss may be carried over to subsequent years. Financial planning may help reduce your tax burden due to capital gains and you may be able to postpone or even avoid capital gains taxes through proper planning.

The limitations of holding directly owned assets are fewer than the advantages. However, they should be considered just as seriously. Each year that you receive taxable interest and/or dividends on an investment, they are taxable to you. Likewise, any capital gains you receive are taxable. This is generally found with mutual funds through fund turnover that occurs throughout the year. At the end of each year, mutual fund companies are required to declare their dividends and capital gains, which are then passed on to the shareholders. You, the shareholder, receive a 1099-DIV form from the company and you must declare it on your tax forms. Also, capital gains may be triggered when your advisor rebalances your portfolio. Any selling or exchanging of an asset for a gain will be taxable to you on your taxes. Whether it's a long-term or short-term gain depends on how long you have held the asset.

TAX-ADVANTAGED PLANS—PROS AND CONS

Tax-advantaged, or qualified, plans include qualified retirement plans (i.e., 401(k)s), traditional IRAs, variable annuities, and variable life insurance policies and the like. (See Chapter 6 on annuities.) While each type of tax-advantaged investment has its own pluses and minuses, the following advantages and disadvantages apply to each.

With qualified plans, all investment income, such as capital gains, dividends. and taxable interest, is deferred until the owner takes distributions from the plan. At that time, the money is taxed at ordinary income rates, regardless of how long the asset has been held by the owner. Any dividends, taxable interest, or capital gains that would normally be *currently* taxable under directly owned investments isn't. The distributions from these plans may be stretched out over many years, thus delaying the payment of taxes and allowing the tax-deferred feature of the investments to continue.

Any changes that are made within the tax-advantaged plan are done so tax free. This means that any selling or exchanging of investments can be done without triggering any capital gains taxes, as long as it is done within the qualified plan. The advantage here is that any asset that has appreciated in value may be sold or exchanged tax free, so as to fully realize the gain. However, any assets that would be sold for a loss are better to be sold outside of the tax-advantaged plan (as a directly owned asset) in order to use the capital loss for tax purposes.

Unfortunately, there are some limitations to holding assets in these tax-advantaged plans. For starters, there is no step-up in basis at death for these plans. Second, although the gains in the assets may have been through capital gains, the capital gains tax rates don't apply when the money comes out. Plus, participants must follow the guidelines of their particular plan when it is an employer-sponsored plan. The employer is also allowed to make changes to the plan for the future.

There are also tax implications for these types of plans. While deferring the gains on these plans is an advantage, pulling the money out and paying taxes on it at ordinary income rates may be viewed as a limitation. (The exceptions to this are Roth IRAs and education IRAs, where the money comes out tax free.) For many people, when they begin to draw from their tax-advantaged plans, they may be paying more in taxes than if they were pulling money out of their directly owned assets. For example, you take a distribution of $20,000 from your traditional IRA. You will pay taxes on this amount at ordinary income levels. However, if you were to pull out $20,000 from your directly owned asset, and it was viewed as a gain, then you would be paying capital gains tax on it, either at ordinary income tax rates or at long-term capital gains rates, depending on how long you held the asset.

Additionally, the balances of these plans must be distributed at some point. The government has imposed minimum distribution rules, which require the qualified plan owner to withdraw a portion of the money each year beginning at age $70^{1}/_{2}$. (This is discussed in more depth later.) However, you may be subject to penalties for early withdrawal of the money, as well as for failing to take any distribution. In most instances, people are not allowed to take distributions from their tax-advantaged plans until they are $59^{1}/_{2}$ years of age. Failure to comply with this rule results in a 10-percent IRS penalty. If you don't take any distribution, you will be taxed 50 percent of the required distribution for not taking any out. So, if you were to take out $10,000 when you were 50, you would pay ordinary income tax on the whole amount plus $1000 for the 10-percent penalty. Likewise, if you were supposed to take out $10,000 and didn't, your IRS penalty would be $5000.

TAX-DEFERRED INVESTMENTS WITHIN QUALIFIED PLANS

There are both advantages and disadvantages of holding tax-deferred investments inside qualified plans. For example, I'm not adverse to advising clients to hold an annuities within their IRAs. Annuities have the tax-deferred advantage built into them. (All capital gains, dividends, and taxable interest accrue tax-deferred until the owner begins to make distributions.) However, I believe that owning a fixed annuity inside an IRA helps provide stability to the overall portfolio.

This extends to variable annuities. There are situations in which I recommend to my clients to purchase variable annuities within their IRAs. Annuities have a death benefit guarantee as one of their benefits. This means that if you purchase an annuity for $100,000, and at the time of your death the annuity contract is worth $86,000, your heir will receive the $100,000 that you invested. This gives a lot of older, married couples peace of mind because they aren't very aggressive, and are worried about what their spouses will have to live on after they are gone. Plus, within variable annuities, there are a number of fund choices that clients may not otherwise have access to. Inside variable annuities are subaccounts. The money invested in a variable annuity is split between whichever subaccounts the client wants, thus tying the annuity to the stock market. The main disadvantage to holding an annuity inside an IRA is that you lose the annuity's inherent tax-deferred capability. One of the main reasons to own an annuity is that taxes are deferred until you begin to withdraw money from the account, which also is one of the main characteristics of an IRA. By placing an annuity inside an IRA, you don't gain any extra tax deferment.

There are many advantages and disadvantages to owning an annuity, whether it is a fixed or a variable annuity. It's best to consult with your advisor to determine if an annuity is right for you.

Whether you believe in holding individual stocks and bonds, or you like the idea of mutual funds, asset allocation is a method to diversify your portfolio to help work with the ups and downs of the stock market. Being caught in a market downturn is bad enough, but if 100 percent of your holdings are tied to that market, you see that downturn reflected in your account balances. However, by following the asset allocation theory, when the stock market goes down, your portfolio won't be hit as hard because you will have diversified across many different asset classes. (See Table 2.1.)[1] Likewise, the theory of asset allocation proves its mettle when viewed over the long term. (See Figure 2.3)

[1]Source for Table 2.1: Standard & Poor's Micropal.

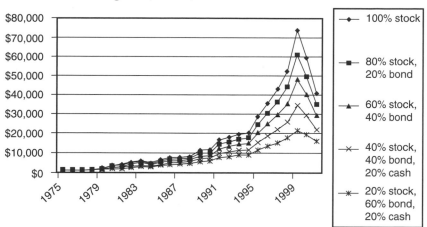

Figure 2.3. This graph shows the historical returns of five different portfolios. The performance of each category was represented by a specific mutual fund that meets the definition of the category. For example, the category of stock was represented by a stock mutual fund.

Table 2.1   Annual Returns by Sector[1]

1987	1988	1989	1990	1991	1992	1993
Foreign Stocks	Small Value Stocks	Large Growth Stocks	Bonds	Small Growth Stocks	Small Value Stocks	Foreign Stocks
24.64%	29.47%	36.40%	8.96%	51.18%	29.15%	32.57%
Large Growth Stocks	Foreign Stocks	Large Stocks	Large Growth Stocks	Small Stocks	Small Stocks	Small Value Stocks
6.50%	28.26%	31.69%	0.20%	46.05%	18.42%	23.86%
Large Stocks	Small Stocks	Large Value Stocks	Large Stocks	Small Value Stocks	Large Value Stocks	Small Stocks
5.25%	24.89%	26.13%	−3.11%	41.70%	10.52%	18.89%
Large Value Stocks	Large Value Stocks	Small Growth Stocks	Large Value Stocks	Large Growth Stocks	Small Growth Stocks	Large Value Stocks
3.68%	21.67%	20.16%	−6.85%	38.37%	7.77%	18.61%
Bonds	Small Growth Stocks	Small Stocks	Small Growth Stocks	Large Stocks	Large Stocks	Small Growth Stocks
2.75%	20.38%	16.25%	−17.42%	30.47%	7.62%	13.37%
Small Value Stocks	Large Stocks	Bonds	Small Stocks	Large Value Stocks	Bonds	Large Stocks
−7.12%	16.61%	14.53%	−19.50%	22.56%	7.40%	10.08%
Small Stocks	Large Growth Stocks	Small Value Stocks	Small Value Stocks	Bonds	Large Growth Stocks	Bonds
−8.76%	11.95%	12.43%	−21.77%	16.00%	5.06%	9.75%
Small Growth Stocks	Bonds	Foreign Stocks	Foreign Stocks	Foreign Stocks	Foreign Stocks	Large Growth Stocks
−10.48%	7.89%	10.53%	−23.45%	12.14%	−12.18%	1.68%

[1]This chart shows the annual returns for the past 15 years divided by sector. Past performance is no guarantee of future results. Figures are for illustration purposes only and do not represent future returns on any investment strategy.
Actual investments will fluctuate.

1994	1995	1996	1997	1998	1999	2000	2001
Foreign Stocks 7.78%	Large Growth Stocks 38.13%	Large Growth Stocks 23.97%	Large Growth Stocks 36.52%	Large Growth Stocks 42.16%	Small Growth Stocks 43.09%	Small Value Stocks 22.83%	Small Value Stocks 14.02%
Large Growth Stocks 3.14%	Large Stocks 37.58%	Large Stocks 22.96%	Large Stocks 33.36%	Large Stocks 28.58%	Large Growth Stocks 28.25%	Bonds 11.63%	Bonds 8.44%
Large Stocks 1.32%	Large Value Stocks 36.99%	Large Value Stocks 22.00%	Small Value Stocks 31.78%	Foreign Stocks 20.00%	Foreign Stocks 26.96%	Large Value Stocks 6.08%	Small Stocks 2.49%
Large Value Stocks −0.64%	Small Growth Stocks 31.04%	Small Value Stocks 21.37%	Large Value Stocks 29.98%	Large Value Stocks 14.69%	Small Stocks 21.26%	Small Stocks −3.02%	Small Growth Stocks −9.23%
Small Value Stocks −1.55%	Small Stocks 28.44%	Small Stocks 16.53%	Stocks Stocks 22.36%	Bonds 8.70%	Large Stocks 21.04%	Large Stocks −9.11%	Large Value Stocks −11.71%
Small Stocks −1.81%	Small Value Stocks 25.75%	Small Growth Stocks 11.32%	Small Growth Stocks 12.93%	Small Growth Stocks 1.23%	Large Value Stocks 12.72%	Foreign Stocks −13.96%	Large Stocks −11.88%
Small Growth Stocks −2.44%	Bonds 18.46%	Foreign Stocks 6.05%	Bonds 9.64%	Small Stocks −2.55%	Bonds −0.82%	Large Growth Stocks −22.08%	Large Growth Stocks −12.73%
Bonds −2.92%	Foreign Stocks 11.21%	Bonds 3.64%	Foreign Stocks 1.78%	Small Value Stocks −6.46%	Small Value Stocks −1.48%	Small Growth Stocks −22.43%	Foreign Stocks −21.21%

3

GUERRILLA WARFARE: YOU VERSUS YOUR PORTFOLIO

What are your financial goals? Do you want to pay for your children or grandchildren's college education? Do you want to be able to go back to school? Or, is having enough money to retire your goal? Having enough money—how much is that? Is this a number you know, or just an idea? Whatever "enough money" means to you, you have to have a starting point. Nowadays, we can't solely rely on the stock market to make us money; we have to create our own wealth. Whether you already have some money put away or are starting from scratch, becoming wealthy means saving money somehow.

SETTING GOALS

There are three types of savings goals you should set for yourself. The first is your long-term goal, the second is your short-term goal, and the third is your actual savings goal. By setting three goals rather than just one, you will be more likely to achieve your financial objectives.

The long-term goal is the amount you will need to save for a certain event, be it your child's college education, a new house, or a new car. Most often, though, the long-term goal is saving for retirement. Through your financial plan, you and your advisor have established just how much money you will need to live the way you want to during your retirement. It's this lump-sum number that is now your long-term goal. However, if you were just to strive for this long-term goal, what would be the chances that you would reach it? If you were told that you needed a lump sum of $750,000 in today's dollars, would you honestly have the ambition to save that much? Probably not. Setting large, long-term goals is great, but they are best met by breaking them down into smaller, more attainable goals.

Your short-term goal is what your long-term goal breaks down to on an annual or monthly basis. Let's say that you and your advisor figure out that if you want to retire in 35 years, you only need to save $15,000 per year, or $1500 per month. That certainly sounds a lot better than any lump-sum amount your advisor will tell you, doesn't it? Smaller numbers are easier to attain because they don't seem so far out of reach. If you have figured out that you are able to save $3000 per month after all your expenses, then putting at least $1500 away each month for retirement shouldn't be difficult.

Your actual savings goal is the amount of money you can and do put away for your retirement on a monthly basis. Just because you say you can save $2000 per month doesn't mean you will do it. Your actual savings is determined by how much money you really do put into your investment accounts. This number may fluctuate a bit in the beginning, but by establishing a systematic savings plan, you will be more likely to stick with it.

Once you have determined your long-term, short-term, and actual savings goals, start acting on them! Most investment firms allow you to invest on a regular basis directly from your checking or savings account. Therefore, you don't have to be responsible for remembering to send in a check every month, or however often you want to invest. Also, since it comes directly from your bank account, you may be less likely to discontinue or skip the saving.

I CAN'T LIVE LIKE THAT!

When was the last time you made a budget? Most people I know make budgets, are very proud of their budgets, and then fail to follow them. Some of my friends don't even last one month on their budgets. Why is that? It's not like they are cutting things out of their lives that they can't do without; they just can't trim the fat off of their monthly consumption. There are some good ways to see where the fat in your expenses lies. First, gather as many of your home expense bills as possible. This means your water, heat, electricity, phone, cable, etc. Then find all the bills relating to your regular car maintenance. Make a list of all the things you spend money on regularly that don't fall into those two categories (i.e., food, credit card payments, auto loan repayments, mortgage, education, etc.). If you don't have this information, make the most accurate estimate possible. Be careful that you don't double count. If you use your charge cards to pay for gas and oil changes for your cars, don't count this twice.

Take all your bills and figures and determine what your monthly expenses are. These are your committed expenses, things that you have to spend money on. Then, figure out how much you spend monthly on things like entertainment and dining out, charitable giving, travel, hobbies, etc. These are your discretionary expenses—things you enjoy but could live without. Add to this figure any systematic savings and contributions to IRAs or employer-sponsored retirement plans (401(k)s) that you make. Don't forget to add in anything that you don't pay on a monthly basis, such as gifts and health club memberships.

Once you arrive at your monthly committed and discretionary expenses, multiply this by 12 to determine your annual expenses. (See Table 3.1.) Now, you will need to figure out how much income you receive. This can be an annual amount. Be sure to subtract how much you pay in taxes from your income. Then subtract your total

Table 3.1   Sample

Committed Expenses	Monthly	Annual
Food	$120.00	$1,440.00
Clothing	$100.00	$1,200.00
Mortgage Payments	$750.00	$9,000.00
Real Estate Taxes		$2,000.00
Telephone/Utilities	$100.00	$1,200.00
Auto Maintenance	$50.00	$600.00
Auto Insurance	$42.00	$504.00
Auto Loan Payments	$200.00	$2,400.00
Personal Care	$100.00	$1,200.00
Total Committed Expenses		**$19,544.00**
Discretionary Expenses		
Entertainment/Eating Out	$100.00	$1,200.00
Travel/Hobbies	$50.00	$600.00
Charitable Contributions		$500.00
Gifts		$2,000.00
Home Improvement		$2,000.00
Total Discretionary Expenses		**$6,300.00**
Savings		
Systematic Savings	$150.00	$1,800.00
IRA contributions		$2,000.00
Qualified retirement plan contributions		$4,000.00
Total Savings		**$7,800.00**
Taxes		
Federal income taxes		$12,000.00
State income taxes		$1,714.00
FICA		$10,000.00
Total Taxes		$23,714.00
Total		$57,358.00

[1]A sample worksheet detailing monthly and annual expenses. Each category is then totaled up, with the final total at the bottom.

annual expenses from your income. If you get a positive number, then this is your discretionary income. However, if you get a negative number, you are spending more than you are earning.

By analyzing your income and expenses, you will see exactly how much you are spending. Most of my clients find that they are spending much more than they thought. If you have negative discretionary income, you need to look at your expenditures to see where you are spending more than necessary. First make sure you didn't double count anything. If you find that the negative number is correct, you will need to curtail your spending, or you may find yourself going deeper and deeper into debt.

If you have a positive discretionary income, ask yourself if that seems right. For instance, you determine that your discretionary income is $6000 per year ($500 per month). Is that right? Do you feel like you have extra money leftover every month after you pay your bills? If so, how much of that money can you save? There still may be extra money that you are spending every month that could be redirected. If you feel that you would like, or need, to save more than what your cash flow is saying you can, take another look at your expenses. Perhaps you can redirect some of the money you are spending, thus saving it without feeling like you are spending any additional money.

Once you have concluded how much money you can save on a monthly basis, start doing it! It will add up much faster than you think it will. It's never too late to start saving for your goals. What you want to be sure of is that you are saving and being proactive in relation to your goals and objectives. The only way you will fail to reach your goals is by failing to work for them.

A WORD ABOUT INCOME AND WEALTH

Many people confuse having a large income with being wealthy. Try not to. A client of mine makes hundreds of thousands of dollars every year. His wife doesn't have to work, and they live a very comfortable life. To look at him, you would think he was a very wealthy man who could buy most anything he wants. However, as his advisor, I see things that others don't. Over the years he has taken out so much money from his accounts that he currently has less than $100 left. Likewise, I have many clients who have never earned more than a quarter of what this man earns in one year who are worth a million dollars or more.

WHEN SAVING ISN'T TRULY SAVING

I have clients who are deceptive savers. They will come to meetings with me and tell me how much they have saved, or that they have X amount in their bank account. Then they ask, "Aren't I saving so well?" On the surface, it sounds as if they are doing a great job. They are retired, so any additional saving on their part would be great. However, the truth is that they aren't doing any saving. The money they have "saved" so well has, in fact, come from their investments with me. They call my office and ask one of my licensed assistants to send them some money from their mutual funds. Then, the money they don't use goes into their bank accounts, where they "save" it. Truly, they aren't saving anything. Rather, they are spending the money they already saved. But these people think they're doing a great job.

Another example of when saving isn't really saving is a sale at a store. Stores always say they have amazing sales going on. Department stores are notorious for this. They'll hold 13-hour sales, or say that everything is 20–50 percent off. People flock to these sales, searching for bargains. Then, after purchasing something, they'll say, "I saved $40 on this shirt! It was only $35." But, did they really save $40?

The only time you save money when purchasing something on sale was if you were going to buy it in the first place. Going to the grocery store and finding out that the dishwashing detergent you need is $2.50 rather than $3.25 is saving 75¢. Going to Marshall Field's and buying a shirt you don't need and didn't anticipate buying for $35 isn't saving $40.

This isn't to say that you shouldn't buy things on sale. Purchasing on sale is a good idea, especially if you find that you need to spend less money. Just be sure that when you buy something, you need it. Passing on the shirt for $35 that you normally would have bought *is* saving $35.

BUYING AT THRIFT STORES

I have read in numerous places that a good idea to help save money is to purchase your clothes at thrift stores. I don't agree with this. Purchasing someone else's castaways may be cheaper, but that doesn't mean you should do it. If shopping at thrift stores is something you enjoy, then by all means, continue. But if it isn't, then don't force yourself to do something you don't want to. It's hard enough to make yourself save, without the added pressure of feeling like you need to start shopping at places you normally would avoid, like buying your clothes at thrift stores.

Don't be afraid to pay a lot of money for quality goods. If you truly can't afford the designer dress that you want, don't buy it. Find something similar that is less expensive. Another good place to look is at outlet malls. If Ralph Lauren is your favorite designer and you feel you just can't live without his clothes, find the nearest outlet store to you and go there. The prices will be lower than in regular department stores or boutiques.

This applies to housewares, luggage, and all kinds of other goods. Outlet stores don't just exist for clothes. Plus, you can compare how much you are spending at the outlet stores with how much you would normally pay because the store prints the savings right on the price tags.

POSITIVE WAYS TO SAVE

The trick to saving is knowing how and making it a habit. There are a number of different ways to save money to help you become wealthy. All you need to do is make sure that saving money becomes a priority for you.

Systematic Savings

I touched on this earlier in the chapter. By saving a set amount on a regular basis, you are more likely to continue saving. Follow the mantra, "Pay yourself first," and you will come out ahead in the long run. (See Table 3.2.) This includes any retirement accounts you have, including your employer-sponsored retirement plan. A good way to make sure

Table 3.2   Bills[1]

Check to myself	$100
Mortgage Payment	$750
Food	$120
Car Payment	$200
Utilities	$120
Charge Cards	$300
Total	$1,590

[1]Incorporate paying yourself first into your monthly budget before you pay out any bills. This will help you increase your savings, as well as help you stick with your savings goals.

you do pay yourself first is to write yourself a check before paying any bills. Another good way is to have your bank account automatically debited to your investment accounts each month.

Maximize your contribution to your 401(k), 403(b), or other employer-sponsored retirement plan. Since this money comes out of your paycheck before you receive your check, you are more likely to stick with this. It is also the easiest contribution to make, since you don't actually see the money. Money grows tax-deferred until you begin to make distributions. These contributions will also help lower your taxes because they come out of your check before taxes are taken out, thus lowering your taxable earnings. But, taxes will be due once you begin to make withdrawals. And, any withdrawals made before you are $59^1/_2$ may also be subject to a 10-percent IRS penalty.

If you are self-employed, consider starting a SEP-IRA. Through this type of account, you will be able to shelter up to 20 percent of your income until you retire. You may want to maximize this account as well, since it will grow tax-deferred.

Set up a traditional or Roth IRA and then maximize your contributions to these. Any money you contribute to a traditional IRA is tax-deductible on your federal income taxes. With the new changes in the tax law, you can contribute a maximum of $3000 per year to either a traditional IRA or Roth IRA. You could split your contribution between the two as well, being careful not to exceed the $3000 maximum. While contributing to a Roth isn't tax-deductible, it grows tax-deferred. Plus, when you begin to make distributions from a Roth, the earnings will come out tax free. There are limits on how much income you can earn and still be able to contribute to your IRA, though. Be sure to talk with your CPA to make sure that you are making the maximum allowed investment for your situation.

Do you get quarterly or annual bonus checks or raises? Consider saving these, rather than spending them. These will help increase your savings at a faster rate. Ignore that raise you just received when you do your budgeting. If you don't increase your consumption habits, but increase your income, you'll be able to save more without skimping on your living expenses.

Manage Your Charge Cards Wisely

Every day my mailbox is overflowing with offers proclaiming, "Preapproved!" or "No preset spending limit!" Sometimes the urge to apply for and use charge cards is overwhelming. Unfortunately, many Americans have fallen into the trap of revolving credit card debt without considering their budgets, how they will pay off the balance, or how the payment will affect their other financial goals. By running up your bills and then only paying the minimum, you will never reach your goal of becoming wealthy.

While debt is a tool that can be used to your advantage, it can also be very dangerous. The more debt you have, the more buying power you have. However, learning when to leverage your debt and when not to is very important. Having a mortgage on your house is alright. It's also okay to leverage your business as long as you can make your payments. What's not alright is to dig yourself so deep into debt that you cannot find your way out. That is, don't use your cards to finance a life that you can't afford to keep. If you find that you are in debt, consider these ways to erase it: Refinance your mortgage, review your budget to eliminate unnecessary spending, use debit cards, pay more than the minimum on debts, or pay charge cards in full.

Think about refinancing your mortgage if interest rates have dropped, especially if you plan on staying in your house for the next few years. By refinancing at a lower rate, you will save yourself a lot of money in interest payments. Also, when refinancing, try to reduce or eliminate any money you would pay on points or fees. Be sure to shop around at a few banks to see what the best rate you can get is.

Many banks now will give you an ATM or debit card when you have a checking or savings account with them. This can be a helpful tool in addition to your credit cards. Because the card is directly tied to your bank account, your spending limit is the amount of money you have in the account. Many stores and restaurants accept these cards as if they were regular charge cards. They also function as debit cards at some stores, enabling you to get cash back if you are short on actual cash. For example, you spend $25.52 at a retail store. By using your ATM card as a debit card, you can increase that total amount to $40.52. You will then receive the other $15 from the cashier as cash. Be careful, though, that you don't spend so much that you deplete your bank account, and make sure you know what fraud protection comes with the card since policies aren't the same as credit cards.

Every month when your mortgage or car payment comes due, see if you can pay more than the minimum amount due. By doing this, you will (over time) significantly reduce the total amount paid because the interest due will be lower. Plus, you will also reduce the amount of time you are paying on your house or vehicle. Just because you have taken out a 30-year mortgage doesn't mean that you have to be paying for the next 30 years.

If you find that you can't seem to get out of the debt cycle, and you have equity in your home, consider taking out a home equity loan. Although I generally don't recommend this, it may help. By taking out a loan on your house, you could use the money to pay off your credit card debt and any other outstanding debt you have. Again, as with refinancing, try to reduce or avoid any fees or points. Check with your CPA to make sure the interest on the loan repayments is tax deductible. This way, you will be replacing your non-tax-deductible debt with tax-deductible debt. However, be sure that you don't borrow more than your house is worth. There are some companies who will let you borrow up to 125 percent of what your home is worth. This is a bad idea and could lead to more trouble.

Shop Around

With the advent of technology, Americans have become more and more impatient. Our Internet connection is too slow, the line at the grocery store is too slow, or traffic is moving too slowly. This attitude has been passed along to the things we purchase, as well. Why should you want to shop around and compare prices when what you want is right there in front of you? The answer is simple: because by shopping around and doing some homework, you will likely save yourself a lot of money over the long run. Ask yourself about your shopping habits. When you need to purchase something, do you buy it at the first place you see it? Are you an impulse buyer? If you answered "yes" to either of these questions, you should consider revising your habits. This is easy; all you need to do is shop before you buy.

One of the best places to shop I've found is at warehouse clubs. I frequent the warehouse club in my town for both home and office needs. I've discovered that by buying items in bulk quantities, not only do I wind up spending less over time, but also I don't have to go shopping as often. Although there is usually a small membership fee for joining, the savings you rack up will more than make up for it. But you don't have to purchase just groceries there. Discount warehouses carry all the assorted toiletries that we need on an everyday basis, plus prescriptions.

Don't confuse shopping with buying. Shopping is a means of comparing the prices on goods that you will purchase at some point. Have you ever decided that you really needed an item, purchased it at the first place you found it, and then saw it at another store later at a much lower price? Shopping would help eliminate this problem because you would become an informed shopper. Do some homework. Is the more-expensive name brand something you really need, or will the less-expensive generic brand suffice? For example, there are many over-the-counter generic aspirins that cost a fraction of what the name brands do. Just like the name-brand bottle, the generic bottle of aspirin that is $2 cheaper must also meet the rigid standards of the Federal Drug Administration.

You may also want to think about delaying the purchase of something that isn't necessary. Are you taken in by the infomercials that are on TV? Did you purchase the Ginsu 2000 steak knife, only to put it in a drawer and never to use it? If you find yourself thinking that you need the newest, latest thing you saw advertised on TV, write it down. Then wait a few days and ask yourself if you still "need" it. Chances are, your "needs" are actually "wants." In just a few days' time, you may decide you don't even want it anymore.

Invest

Putting all the money you are saving into your savings account at the bank may sound like a great idea, but over time you may not be doing yourself any good. Quite simply, although savings accounts are interest-bearing and aren't tied to the stock market and its fluctuations, the interest that you earn on your account won't keep up with inflation over the long run. I base the inflation projections for each financial plan I do on the national average and forecast, as well as on what time frame I'm looking at. Traditional savings accounts don't earn enough interest to keep up with inflation. Plus, if you begin to take out income from your savings account on a regular basis, you will find that you deplete your account much faster once inflation is figured in. The only way to make your money work as hard for you as you did for it is to invest it.

The same is true for Certificates of Deposit (CDs) and money market funds. During a down market, the interest rates on bank CDs and money markets may look attractive, but they may not help you. The best time to invest money is during a down market. Buying low and selling high is the tenet of good investing. However, this goes against human nature.

Think about it, would you rather buy a car for $12,000 or $10,000? How about a gallon of milk for $2.49 or for $3.49? Easy, right? You would rather buy the car and the milk at the lower price. (See Figure 3.1.) Why, then, do people insist upon buying stocks and mutual funds at their high point? They do this because cause of fear—fear of making the wrong decision. People believe that if everyone else is buying the stock, then they should get on the bus, too. However, it's often those who wait who get burned in their investments. By waiting to see who else has purchased that new, hot stock, it's usually past the point where you make money. Therefore, when the stock starts to go down, the first people who lose their money are the ones who were the last to jump on the bandwagon! Don't be afraid to make a wrong decision about

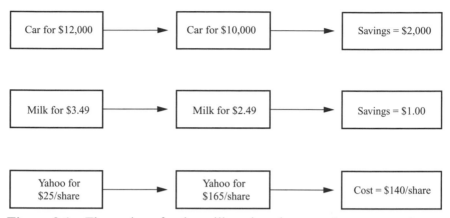

Figure 3.1. The savings for the milk and car increase the consumer's reason for purchasing the goods. However, the greater the stock price, the more inclined people are to purchase shares. This doesn't make sense.

investing. That's what your advisor is there to help you with. It's deciding not to invest that would be the worse decision.

GET EXCITED

By taking this first step to becoming wealthy, you have done what millions of Americans can't or won't do—take control. Be proud of yourself and your achievements. By taking pride in what you are doing, you will be more likely to continue. Above all, don't be afraid to make decisions. Even if you find out that you have made a bad decision, think of it as a learning tool. Always learn from your mistakes.

Some of the wealthiest clients I have are excellent decision makers. They make quick, informed decisions, not hasty ones. Nor do they procrastinate or waffle in their judgment. However, they aren't afraid to ask for help or advice, either. And neither should you. Since you have decided to go this route, you will need to hone your decision-making skills. You'll continue to need them down the line.

4

I OWN THAT COMPANY!

Now that you have started saving your money, the question becomes where to invest it. Although you should have a financial plan from your financial advisor, it's important that you know some things about investing. In this chapter and the following three chapters, we discuss stocks, mutual funds, annuities, bonds, cash, and REITS.

Most people want to make money as quickly as possible. Still, your risk tolerance, time frame, and objectives must be taken into account before deciding which types of investments are right for you. Your objective should also be to get the highest total, after-tax rate of return you can get within your risk tolerance.

INVESTING VERSUS SPECULATING

When people think of speculative ventures, they generally form an unfavorable opinion. But these same people have a favorable opinion of investing. Nowadays, the line between investing and speculating isn't so clear-cut. Speculation used to include investing in a company's stock, whereas investing was reserved for putting money into high-grade bonds. However, now quality blue chip stock is considered an investment. Speculative ventures still exist; junk bonds can be an example.

Generally, though, speculation refers to the purchase of securities, or other assets, by people who hope that the assets' value fluctuations will produce relatively large payoffs over a short period of time. A good example of this occurred in the late 1990s. When the dot.com companies began putting shares of their stock on the market, investors would gobble up as many as they could afford, hoping that the stock price would jump so quickly that they could make a tidy profit in very little time. While many of these investors did succeed in their quest, many became greedy and the highs became not high enough. These people did not profit; rather, they saw their investments plummet in value, sometimes to zero.

One of my clients likes to follow the stock market and invest in stocks outside his portfolio with me. He understands the risks, and takes them in stride. Recently, he decided that he would like to invest $50,000 in a dot.com company. At the time he purchased the stock, it was trading at 50¢ per share, so he purchased 100,000 shares. After a few weeks, the stock was down to 35¢ per share. His investment was down to $35,000 from $50,000. This company is now out of business, and my client has lost his entire investment.

This doesn't mean that speculation is to be avoided at all costs. Smart investors know their risk tolerance and whether they can afford to play with their money this way. Using your son's college money to buy shares of a dot.com is probably not a sound investment, but if you have some money you want to play with, and wouldn't mind if you lost it, then being speculative isn't a bad thing. It's just not for everyone.

STOCKS

Stocks represent ownership in a company. They are traded publicly on stock exchanges throughout the world. Shareholders have the right to vote at shareholders' meetings and review the books of the company. Generally, I don't recommend holding more than five percent of an investor's portfolio in individual stock due to the risk factor associated with stocks. There are two types of stock we discuss: common and preferred.

Common Stock

Common stock can help you accumulate wealth in two ways. First, they provide income through dividends, which are distributed to shareholders from corporate earnings. Second, the stocks can appreciate in value. This is generally the result of successful company management and products, or the prospect of future successes. Common stocks allow the stockholder, as part owner of the company, to participate in the firm's profits.

It is important to remember that the stock value may depreciate as well. A number of reasons may go into why a stock depreciates instead of appreciating. It varies from stock to stock and industry to industry. For instance, Lucent Technologies was trading at around five to six dollars per share during the summer of 2001. This doesn't mean that it's a bad company, or even a poor investment. Depending on your risk tolerance and your outlook, you might think purchasing some shares of Lucent right now is a good investment decision that will pay off in the future.

Stocks traded publicly are easily converted into cash. Because of this, they are considered readily marketable investments. They aren't considered liquid, though, because the sale of the stock could result in a loss of principle. Nonpublicly traded stocks are neither liquid nor readily marketable because they are difficult to sell and the selling price is uncertain.

Publicly traded stocks are exchanged on stock exchanges around the world. The largest exchanges in the United States are the New York Stock Exchange (NYSE) and the American Stock Exchange

(AMEX). Both of these exchanges are located in New York City, but the NYSE is the largest. The NASDAQ (National Association of Securities Dealers and Automated Quotations) is an automated information system that provides stockbrokers and dealers with price quotes for over-the-counter stocks. There are other American exchanges, such as the Philadelphia Exchange and the Pacific Exchange.

Special note: A lot of emphasis is put on watching what the market does every day. It's important to remember that the Dow Jones Industrial Average (DJIA) only comprises 30 companies. The NASDAQ Composite Indes and the S&P 500 are much more representational of what the market is doing because of their size. The S&P is made up of 400 industrial, 40 utility, 40 financial, and 20 transportation stocks, whereas the NASDAQ contains 5000 companies.

The DJIA, as well as the other Dow Jones averages, are price-weighted indices. Throughout every trading day, and at the end of each day, the averages are computed by adding the prices of the included stocks and dividing that number by a specified divisor. This divisor changes all the time, usually daily. No one stock will have a greater influence on the index than another.

The NASDAQ Composite and the S&P 500 are both value-weighted. The value of a given stock will affect the index in proportion to its value.

Common stocks can be segregated into many different categories, and some stocks may fall into more than one category. While it may not always be easy to pigeonhole stocks, here are a few ways to categorize them.

BLUE CHIP STOCKS. These are stocks of companies that have the highest overall quality. Because of the blue chips' high quality, many investors are drawn to them. These companies are known for being financially stable and distributing dividends in both good and bad years. They are usually leaders in their industries or industry segments. All 30 companies that make up the Dow Jones Industrials are classified as blue chip stocks, as well as other utility companies and large, consistently successful companies.

VALUE STOCKS. Companies whose stock is considered undervalued (trading at a price lower than expected) fall under this heading. The stock may be undervalued because of inner company strife (management change, etc.), business operations restructuring, or perhaps that particular industry is currently unpopular. Generally, value stocks have a lower price-per-earnings ratio than growth stocks do, and thus, their price per share is lower.

Many times a value stock may be reclassified as a growth stock. Although growth stocks have dramatically outperformed value stocks in certain years, over time, the returns of value stocks have surpassed those of growth stocks.

GROWTH STOCKS. These are companies that are expected to have dramatic growth rates in business and/or earnings. Generally, stock of companies that are emerging or very young would be considered growth stocks. These companies tend to reinvest their earnings, rather than distributing them to stockholders, to help them increase their business. Therefore, the only income stockholders would see from growth stocks would come in the form of stock appreciation at the time of sale. Growth stocks are also a riskier investment than blue chip or value stocks. Their share prices usually increases much faster than those of blue chips or value stocks, making their potential for appreciation very great. However, the share prices are just as likely to decrease very quickly. Growth stocks also tend to do poorly in down market times.

Depending on your risk tolerance, objectives, and time frame, growth stocks may not be appropriate for your portfolio. If you are willing to assume the risk associated with growth stocks and are investing for long-term potential growth and appreciation, then growth stocks may be a good fit for you.

INCOME STOCKS. Companies that consistently distribute high dividends fall under this heading. Income stock companies are those that are in mature, stable industries. While their dividends are generally a high percentage of corporate earnings, the tendency for their share prices is to hold fairly steady. This is due to the fact they distribute, rather than reinvest, their earnings.

Income stocks are best held by people who look for their investments to provide cash flow. Those investors seeking growth and share price appreciation are typically disappointed with the performance of income stocks. However, if you were to participate in dividend reinvestment programs (DRPs), over time there would be a large capital appreciation of your shares. DRPs are discussed later.

GROWTH AND INCOME STOCKS. This group is really just a combination of the two previous groups. These are stocks that not only pay a reasonable dividend, but also offer the potential for appreciation over time.

CYCLICAL STOCKS. Cyclical stocks generally follow the business cycle. The housing sector is an example of a cyclical sector because as the economy does well, more people are likely to purchase or build houses. Likewise, when the economy is in a recession or depression, people generally don't build or purchase new homes. Investing in cyclical stocks is not without risk. Investors who want to make money from cyclical stocks aim to purchase the shares before a market upswing and sell them prior to a market downturn.

DEFENSIVE STOCKS. In essence, defensive stocks are the opposite of cyclical stocks. They tend to perform better when the market is down and, comparatively, worse when the market is doing well. Defensive stocks are used to help balance the risk in a portfolio because of this. These are companies that produce goods that are still in demand when the economy is not doing well. Food and beverage companies are good examples of defensive stocks.

SMALL TO MIDSIZED COMPANY STOCKS. Small-cap or mid-cap stocks are those from companies that have a smaller market share than their large-cap counterparts. These companies have shown, in the past, to have a better overall performance than the larger companies, but they have also proven to be more volatile.

SPECULATIVE STOCKS. Stocks that present a greater risk to the investor than common stocks in general are speculative. Typically, hot new issues and penny stocks are speculative. While some stocks may be easily qualified as speculative, others may not be so easy.

Over the past few years, we've seen many small companies, particularly dot.coms, release new issues of their companies or take them public for the first time. These offerings found a highly competitive marketplace, thus driving their share prices skyward. Unfortunately for investors, the market for these stocks usually drops just as fast as it rises, sometimes even resulting in the companies going bankrupt.

FOREIGN STOCKS. Although the easiest way for investors to hold foreign stock is through different types of mutual funds, Americans can buy stocks in individual foreign companies through American Depositary Receipts (ADR). These receipts are listed on U.S. stock exchanges and are an alternative to direct investing. Asset allocation usually recommends that a portion of an investor's portfolio be held in foreign stocks.

Market capitalization—The price per share of a company multiplied by the number of outstanding shares.

Large-capitalization stocks—The stock of a company with market capitalization of more than $5 billion.

Mid-capitalization stocks—The stock of a company with market capitalization between $1 billion and $5 billion.

Small-capitalization stocks—The stock of a company with market capitalization of less than $1 billion.

Stocks may sound like the perfect investment choice for you, but remember, not everything is as great as it seems. Until the year 2000, the United States was experiencing unprecedented economic growth. While the stock market, on the whole, soared to new record heights, there were some low points. Throughout the first six months of 1987, the market gained almost 30 percent. However, on October 19, 1987, the stock market suffered its worst crash to date. The Dow Jones Industrial Average dropped 508 points. That day a few new records were set: largest point drop, largest one-day volume of shares traded, and the largest percentage drop. The Dow dropped 23 percent, which was nearly double the previous record. Ten years later, on October 27, 1997, the market dropped precipitously again. This time, it fell 554 points, a new record. However, the percentage drop wasn't as bad due to the value of the Dow at the time. It fell a mere 12 percent. However, within two weeks, the market had regained all its losses of October 27. (See Figure 4.1.) It took the market nearly two and a half years to recover from the October 19, 1987 crash.

This isn't designed to scare you when it comes to investing in common stocks. It's just a reminder of what can happen in the market. In the past decade, this country has seen such unbridled enthusi-

Stock Market Returns 1960–2001

−30% to −20%	−20% to −10%	−10% to 0%	0% to 10%	10% to 20%	20% to 30%	30% to 40%
				1993	1999	
				1988	1998	
		2000	1994	1986	1996	1997
		1990	1992	1979	1983	1995
		1981	1987	1972	1982	1991
		1977	1984	1971	1976	1989
		1969	1978	1968	1967	1985
	2001	1966	1970	1965	1963	1980
1974	1973	1962	1960	1964	1961	1975

Figure 4.1   Although most people remember the recent boom of the stock market, this proves that the ability to predict what's going to happen is unlikely. Note that both 1973 and 1974 had negative returns of roughly −20 and −30 percent, respectively.[1]

[1]S&P 500 and American Express Funds literature.

asm for investing in individual stocks, with ever-increasing returns, it's easy to forget what has happened in the past. When it comes to common stocks, there is no such things as either a safe investment, or a guaranteed thing. This is why I generally don't like my clients to hold more than five percent in an individual stock.

Preferred Stock

Just like common stock owners, preferred stock owners own a part of the company. However, there are more rights that come with preferred stock that aren't associated with common stock. First, preferred stock holders hold the right to be paid their dividends before they are distributed to common shareholders. Second, should the company have to liquidate, preferred shareholders hold the right to receive the par value of their stock before there is any distribution to common shareholders.

Dividends on preferred stock are fixed, much like the interest rates on bonds are. The price of preferred stock also differs from that of common stock, and is affected by interest rate changes. They almost always have a higher dividend yield than common stock does, but preferred stock doesn't have the growth and price appreciation potential that common stock does because preferred stock doesn't participate in the corporate earnings growth of the company.

Other features of preferred stock include more voting rights than common shareholders (either more total votes or the ability to elect more directors), the right to receive more than the stated dividend amount in certain conditions, the right to exchange preferred shares for a fixed number of common shares, and the right to cumulation of dividends. Cumulation of dividends may happen if any preferred dividends have been missed. If this has happened, all prior and current preferred dividends must be paid out before common shareholders receive their dividends.

DIVIDEND REINVESTMENT PLANS

Dividend reinvestment plans (DRPs) are an extremely popular way to increase your holding in a particular stock without any additional out-of-pocket expenses. If the company was good enough to invest in the first time, wouldn't it be a good company to invest in again? That's the premise behind the DRP programs. DRPs allow the investor to reinvest automatically any dividends and capital gains into the stock, essentially swapping the monetary value of the dividends and capital gains for more shares of common stock. These plans are especially good for younger people who are seeking to accumulate capital, or for those people who don't need the income that the dividends would provide.

DRPs are easy to set up, too. You can elect to reinvest the dividends at the time of the initial purchase, or later. The result is a long-term growth of capital, measured in the form of shares owned, as well as in total value. The only difference is that you are investing a little bit of money at a time after a larger initial purchase. In this way, DRPs are similar to dollar-cost averaging a mutual fund.

DRPs do have a couple of drawbacks, though. First, reinvesting your dividends isn't a good idea if you rely on the income that they provide. If you find that you need that money, then you should opt to have the check come to you, rather than be reinvested. Second, finding the appropriate cost basis is more difficult when you participate in a DRP. Should you want to sell your stock, you will want to know what kind of tax consequences you will face. Unless you have kept good records (which I believe is vital), it will be difficult to assess what your true basis is. However, if you don't think you will be selling your stock, or you aren't concerned about your cost basis, then this isn't a concern for you, and a reinvestment program would probably be a good idea.

Essentially, the advantages of DRPs outweigh the disadvantages, depending on your circumstances. The fact that you can consistently increase your holding in a company's common stock without spending any more money out of your pocket is a very enticing way to invest, isn't it? Over time, the number of shares of stock that you own will have dramatically increased, and all you had to do was opt to have your dividends reinvested.

VALUING COMMON STOCK

Several common measures are available for calculating the value of common stock. While most shareholders look mainly for the price per share, it's not the only indicator of a stock's worth. Other factors include: earnings per share, the price-earnings ratio, net asset value per share, and yield.

Return on Equity
Return on equity (ROE) is a very important stock measure because it has a direct impact on the company's growth, profits, and dividends. It shows the overall profitability of the corporation, and seizes how much success the company is having in managing its assets, operations, and capital. The better the ROE, the better the financial condition and position of the firm. Stable or increasing ROEs are good indications. However, stocks with falling ROEs should be avoided.

Earnings Per Share
This is the most commonly referred-to indicator of a stock's value. Whenever you turn on CNBC or look at the stock pages of the *Wall Street Journal*, there are mentions of earnings per share (EPS). The traditional way to compute this is to find the income of a corporation that is available to its shareholders. This is net corporate profit after taxes and minus any dividends to preferred shareholders. This figure is then divided by the number of outstanding common shares of stock.

For example, XYZ Corporation reports that its net corporate profits (after taxes) are $5.8 million. They must pay $1 million out in preferred dividends. The remaining $4.8 million is divided by the number of XYZ's outstanding common shares, which is 1.2 million. Thus, their EPS is $4 per share.

$$\$5.8\text{ m} - \$1\text{ m} = \frac{\$4.8\text{ m}}{1.2\text{ m shares}} = \$4/\text{share}$$

This method of calculating EPS is called the "basic earnings per share." It is also known as "trailing earnings per share" because it is based upon the corporation's reported earnings, which are in the past. Quarterly and semiannual EPS also use this method. However, analysts will also forecast a company's future earnings and base their EPS on these.

Companies also have what are called "diluted earnings per share." These are computed by dividing the available income to common shareholders by the number of outstanding shares of common stock *plus* any shares that would be outstanding if any employee stock options or stock awards outstanding, convertible securities and warrants were considered (dilutive potential common shares). In some cases, the difference between the basic EPS and the dilutive EPS is great, solely because of the number of dilutive potential common shares. Note the difference in the earnings per share in our example when dilutive potential common shares are considered. EPS drops from $4/share to $3.20/share.

$$\frac{\$5.8 \text{ m} - \$1 \text{ m} = \quad \$4.8 \text{ m}}{1.2 \text{ m s} + .3 \text{ m s} = 1.5 \text{ m shares}} = \$3.20/\text{share}$$

Analysts usually place a lot of emphasis on earnings per share. It's important to note that when they discuss EPS, they generally are referring to the diluted earnings per share. They also cite the EPS when discussing the trend for certain companies. However, we can say that the share price will keep up with the earnings per share, either rising or falling. In the past few years, we've seen more of a disregard for EPS when it came to new issues and hot dot.com stocks, which was due, in part, to the fact that these companies had no earnings. But with the market downturn, we've returned to using the EPS as an indicator of how a company is doing.

Price-Earnings Ratio

The price-earnings ratio (P/E ratio) for a common stock is found by dividing the share price of the stock by the current earnings per share. Therefore, from our previous example, XYZ's EPS was $4 per share. If their stock price was $55 per share, their P/E ratio would be 13.75 ($55/$4).

The P/E ratio is also a highly respected method of measuring a stock's value. Generally, the lower the P/E ratio, the better the stock buy. However, a high P/E ratio is all right if the company's earnings are expected to grow. When evaluating a stock, it's a good idea to look at the historical P/E ratio data. Looking at the trends for a particular stock will help you decide if the present is a good time to buy or not. If you find that the present P/E ratio is pretty low when compared to the historical figures, the stock may be a good purchase.

Net Asset Value per Share

Net asset value per share, or book value per share, is the amount of assets a company has working for each share of common stock. It's calculated by taking the net balance sheet values of corporate assets and subtracting the face value of any creditors' and preferred shareholders' claims. This number is then divided by the number of outstanding shares. So, for XYZ Corporation, the company's assets totaled $59 million and their debts and preferred stock claims were $21 million. The remaining $38 million is divided by the number of outstanding shares, 1.2 million. Thus, their book value per share is $31.67.

$$\$59 \text{ m} - \$21 \text{ m} = \frac{\$38 \text{ m}}{1.2 \text{ m shares}} = \$31.67$$

Generally, the book value for a stock is not a widely used indicator of the stock's value. It also isn't as important as the company's ability to generate an earnings stream. For growth stocks, the market value could be many times the book value. Conversely, for companies that are in either static or declining industries, book value may be much greater than market value.

Yields

For common stocks, yields can be measured as "nominal yields" or "current yields." These measure the rates of return for a stock. When considering whether to buy, keep, or sell a stock, it's important to calculate the yields, so you can make an informed decision.

Nominal yields are calculated by taking the annual interest or dividends paid and dividing it by the stock's par value. This is often called the "dividend rate" when applied to preferred stock. Nominal yields really have no meaning for common stocks.

Current yields, though, are a more meaningful measurement for investors. This is found by dividing the annual investment income by the security's current price. Current yields can be applied to common and preferred stocks, as well as bonds. Remember, these yields change all the time due to the fluctuation in stock prices.

XYZ Corporation declares and pays a $2-per-share dividend. Currently, their stock is selling for $60 per share. Their current yield is 3.3 percent.

$$\frac{\$2}{\$60} = 3.3\%$$

Sometimes current yields and historical data on current yields can be misleading. There are companies who increase their dividends on a regular basis, thus increasing the current yield each time. Then there are companies who, while very stable and financially sound, have made a practice of paying little or no dividends. To calculate properly the overall rate of return on a stock, go back and look at the average annual compound rate of gain (or loss) over a period of time, assuming all dividends and capital gains were reinvested. This considers all capital gains and losses on the stock, instead of just dividends.

OPTIONS

Many investors trade options to buy or sell common stocks (calls and puts) as a speculative way of investing. Options are traded on organized stock exchanges. They represent one of the more complex investment strategies because of the different ways to structure your options portfolio. While we don't discuss everything about options here, we talk about put and call options so that you have a better understanding of what they are and how they work.

A call option allows the purchaser to buy from another investor a certain stock or other asset at a predetermined fixed price, the strike or exercise price, at any time during a specified period. A put option allows the purchaser to sell to another investor a certain stock or asset at a set price at any time during the specified period. Options, which are normally around lots (100 shares) of common stock, have standardized quarterly expiration dates. The expiration date is the last date on which the option can be exercised.

Buying Options

Investors can buy both call and put options when they think the underlying stock is going to go up or down. Rather than paying a price per share, as you would with regular common stock, the investor pays a premium for the option. The investor then has the opportunity to hold, exercise, or sell the option. If he or she chooses to hold the option without exercising it, it will expire worthless and the investor will have lost the amount of money that was paid for it. If the investor chooses to exercise the option, he or she will then either buy or sell the underlying stock at the set price, depending on whether it's a call or put option. But, if the investor sells the option, he or she will either have a gain or a loss on the option. It will depend on whether the premium that the investor sold the option for was greater or less than the original premium. For example, if you purchased a call option for $300 and later sold it for $500, your gain would be $200, and vice versa.

Purchase call coptions for	$300
Sell unexercised option for	$500
Net gain (loss)	**$200**

Selling Options

Investors sell, or write, options for the opposite reason that they would purchase them. Usually, the investor has a position in the underlying stock and is looking to make a profit. The increased profit stems from the premium earned by the option writer for selling the option. However, if the option is exercised, the option writer (and usually the stock owner) forfeits the opportunity to sell his or her shares of stock on the common market. Conversely, if the option sold was a put option, the option writer would then wind up paying a higher price for the stock than if it had been purchased on the stock market. The writer would still wind up profiting from selling the option because of the premium he or she would receive.

Those that write options don't necessarily have to have a position in the underlying stock. "Naked options" are those in which the writer doesn't own the underlying stock. They are highly speculative because if the option is exercised, the writer is then forced to cover his or her position. For example, Mark Client writes (sells) a call option for 200 shares of XYZ stock. The strike price on the option is 65. The premium paid for the option is $400. XYZ is currently trading around $72 per share. Therefore, the new owner of the option has the opportunity to buy XYZ stock for $65 per share, rather than at around $72 per share on the open market. The option is exercised, and now Mr. Client has to sell the option owner the 200 shares of XYZ for $65 per share. However, Mr. Black sold a naked call and doesn't own the 200 shares of XYZ. He then must buy the shares on the open market for the market price and then sell them for $65 per share. Let's say he pays $71.50 per share for the stock. He, therefore, has a net loss of $900.

Premium paid to Mr. Black for option	$400
Purchase of stock paid to Mr. Black (200 shares @ $65 per share)	$13,000
Purchase price of stock Mr. Black paid at market	
(200 shares at $71.50 per share)	$14,300
Net gain (loss)	**($900)**

$$\$14,300 - 13,000 - \$400 = \$900$$

Options can be highly profitable for those who choose to invest in them. However, they carry a high amount of risk, as well. Investors may lose the entire amount committed to options in a relatively short period of time. For those whose risk tolerance can handle options, they are a good investment. Be sure, though, that if you decide to try some option trading you can handle the risk. You can obtain a current option disclosure document from your broker or from the Options Industry Council. You can call 1-800-OPTIONS or visit the Options Industry Council's website: www.888options.com.

FINDING INFORMATION ABOUT STOCKS

While there are many different resources out there to help you find information about common stocks, we only touch on a few here. The first place to look for information is the financial pages of your newspaper. These pages will carry a list of stocks, alphabetically, of all publicly traded stocks. On any given day, here is how the information for XYZ Corporation might appear:

52 weeks									
High	Low	Stock	P/E	Vol. in 100s	Open	High	Low	Close	Net Change
66	42	XYZ	14	1500	58½	62	58	59¾	+1¾

Reading from left to right, we see that the highest price that XYZ Corporation's stock has reached in the past 52 weeks is $66, while it has been as low as $42 during that same period. Its P/E ratio (on a trailing basis) is 14, and 150,000 shares traded hands during the business day. XYZ's stock price opened at $58.50, its high price of the day was $62, its low price was $58, and it closed at $59.75. The net change from the closing price on this day as compared with the previous day's trading was $1.75 (therefore, the previous day's closing price must have been $58).

Also listed in the stock pages are the closing marks for the market indices, such as the Dow Jones averages, Standard & Poor's 500 Stock Index, the NASDAQ, and the Russell 2000. There are four Dow Jones averages, which are: (1) 30 industrials, (2) 20 transportations, (3) 15 utilities, and (4) a composite of the 65 stocks.

Some of the financial newspapers and magazines that carry stock information include *The Wall Street Journal, Barron's, Standard & Poor's Outlook, Fortune, Business Week, The Economist,* and *Investor's Business Daily.* However, print isn't the only medium which carries stock information and analyses. A few good places to find stock information also exist online. Yahoo! Finance (*www.quote.yahoo.com*), Dow Jones Market Monitor (*www.dowjones.com*), and Microsoft (*www.msn.com*) are also good places to look. Finally, if you are looking for extensive financial data for just one company, check out their annual report. These will be available in print, and sometimes online at the company's corporate home page.

Many of my clients believe that a good source of information about the stocks they hold is a financial cable station. They think that since this station has different analysts on to talk about what stocks are good and bad, that they should turn there for their financial information. There are two schools of thought on this. First of all, I believe that they do a good job of presenting financial information about various types of stocks, mutual funds, bonds, and other invest-ments. They always have the running stock ticker going across the bottom of the screen so that investors can see what trades have gone through and at what price. They also do a good job at having analysts from different companies come on to discuss the current state of the markets. In that sense, they are a fine source of information.

However, there are also negative aspects of relying on television for your information. Until recently, stock analysts didn't have to dis-close which stocks they held individually. This meant, for example, that Joe Smith from the XYZ Firm could go on television and tell people that the Fly By Night Corporation was a good buy without telling those same viewers that he owned stock in that company. The-oretically, analysts could give out any information they wanted to without publicly acknowledging what their personal positions were in the stocks they were talking about. For the public, that posed somewhat of a danger. How are average investors to know whether the information they are hearing is truly accurate? While I'm not say-ing that this is the fault of the financial television networks, it is something that investors should behold with caution.

One more thing about relying solely on networks for financial information: Do you ever think that instead of just reporting the news, they want to try and shape it? It seems that I am constantly see-ing the financial networks tout some upcoming warning about prof-its or earnings from companies. When you see these, do they affect the way you look at your portfolio? If one of the companies that you are invested in issues a profit warning, do you consider selling? Gen-erally, after a company issues this type of warning, there is a sell-off by investors of that company's stock. The networks then report that, too. Yes, it is their job to report what companies are doing and how they are doing, but sometimes it seems like they are overemphasizing what is really going on, all for the sake of reporting something else later.

As a rule, I recommend that my clients, and others, not rely solely on financial networks for all their financial information. Today, there are so many different places to get information. To ignore these out-lets in favor of just watching television is doing a disservice to your-self and your portfolio. If you like watching these stations and think the information you are getting is good, then continue. But try tempering what you are hearing with something else. Just think of it as double-checking your facts.

NEXT STEPS

Now that we've discussed the different types of stock, stock investing, and stock valuations, it's time to think about what's next. It's easy to say that knowledge is power. What's more difficult is acting on your knowledge. By becoming well versed in the ways of common and preferred stock, you've taken the next step to becoming rich. Now what you need to do is act on your new knowledge.

In the next few chapters, we cover different types of investment vehicles and why they're important. The more you know, the more powerful you become. Believe me, there are people who think that all it takes to pick a good stock is to tack up the stock pages to a dartboard, throw a dart and then see where it lands. If it were that easy, everyone would have millions of dollars. But, it's more difficult than that.

The wealthiest people in the world didn't pick their investments by chance. They became knowledgeable about their investments. They didn't do it alone, though. They hired knowledgeable people to help them, which is what you should do, too. By trying to comprehend everything, you'll wind up studying things so intensely that you'll miss the boat. What I said earlier about making decisions comes into play here. Do some research, hire a financial advisor, and make decisions.

Learning about different investments is important, which is why we're covering it. Just don't try to know everything about everything. In the end, that won't help you. But learn to listen to your gut feelings and trust them.

THE SHOPPING MALL OF INVESTMENTS

Mutual funds are attractive to investors for many reasons. First, they offer the investor the ability to enjoy the benefits of investing in multiple companies. Second, investors may be able to purchase more shares of a mutual fund than of individual stock. Third, mutual funds offer investors the chance to diversify their holdings simply by the type of fund they own.

Mutual funds have become increasingly popular over the past decade and a half. You can't even turn on your television set without seeing an ad for a mutual fund company like Oppenheimer or Janus. But many people don't understand what a mutual fund is, how it works, and what its advantages and disadvantages are.

A good analogy for mutual funds is that they are like shopping malls. If you own one store and it goes bankrupt, you lose everything.

Whereas, if you own a shopping mall and one store goes bankrupt, you still have income flowing from all the other stores within the mall. That's the way mutual funds are. By owning a mutual fund rather than the stock of one company, you are less likely to realize any major loss, should a company go out of business. So, if you own $10,000 of the common stock of XYZ Corporation and it goes bankrupt, you lose your investment. But, if you own $10,000 in the ABC Growth Fund, which has invested in shares of XYZ Corporation, and XYZ goes belly up, the value of your mutual fund decreases. But you won't lose your entire investment because the risk is spread out.

WHAT IS A MUTUAL FUND?

Mutual funds are investment companies. There are three main types of investment companies:

1. Unit investment trusts. (Here the fund invests strictly in a fixed portfolio of securities.)

2. Those who sell face-amount certificates. (Here the company pledges to pay the investor a specified amount upon maturity or a surrender value if sold early.)

3. Management companies. It's the management companies that are the commonly used of the three. While both closed-end and open-end (or mutual) funds fall under the heading of management companies, most people are familiar with the open-end fund.

CLOSED-END MUTUAL FUNDS

Closed-end mutual funds are somewhat similar to corporations because they issue fixed numbers of shares. This doesn't fluctuate, with the exception of when a new stock may be issued. The funds may issue bonds or preferred stock to support the common share-holders' positions. They then use their capital and other resources to invest in other companies' securities. Closed-end funds are not nearly as common as open-end funds.

Closed-end funds' shares are bought and sold at market like other mutual fund shares and shares of stock. Their prices are dependent upon the supply and demand of the market; they're not tied to the net asset value (NAV) per share of the funds. Therefore, when the market price for a closed-end fund's shares is greater than the NAV, the fund is trading at a premium. Likewise, when the fund's shares are trading below the NAV, they are trading at a discount.

Net asset value—The true value of a share of a mutual fund. It is calculated by taking the total value of all assets and other securities of the fund, less any of the fund's liabilities, and dividing that number by the number of the fund's outstanding shares. NAV is valued on a daily basis.

Breakpoint—The dollar amount at which the investor is entitled to a lesser sales charge.

Rights of accumulation—Amount of money already invested in a mutual fund that has a front-end sales load. The sales charge is discounted based upon previous mutual fund purchases within the same fund or fund family.

12-b-1 fees—An annual sales charge taken from mutual funds for sales and marketing costs.

OPEN-END FUNDS

Open-end funds are the most common mutual funds. Unlike closed-end funds, they don't limit the amount of shares. Rather, the number of available shares is constantly changing due to new investors purchasing shares and existing investors redeeming shares. When investors wish to purchase mutual fund shares, they are buying them from the company itself. This means that when investors want to redeem their shares, the company must be ready to buy them back from the individual.

Open-end funds' share prices are derived from the most recent NAV of the shares. Net asset value per share is the total value of all the securities and other assets held by the fund, minus any of the fund's liabilities. This resulting number is then divided by the number of outstanding shares in the mutual fund. The NAV is calculated daily, at the close of the business day. Unlike common stocks, which investors may purchase at any time during the business day, and sometimes later due to extended-hours trading, open-end mutual funds are traded at the end of the day due to the pricing structure of the NAV.

So, which are better: closed-end or open-end funds? The answer is neither. Both have their advantages and disadvantages. Open-end funds are bought and sold by the mutual fund company, whereas closed-end funds are traded on stock exchanges. Therefore, if you want to purchase shares of a closed-end fund, you will need to find an investor who wants to sell his, just as you would with stocks. However, you may be able to purchase shares of a closed-end fund at a discount. Open-end shares are always bought and sold at NAV. Of course, you may also wind up paying a premium price for your closed-end shares. In the end, it matters more what the funds invest in, what their track record is, and what your investment goals and objectives are, rather than whether the fund is open- or closed-end.

LOAD MUTUAL FUNDS

Open-end mutual funds are either load or no-load funds. That means they either have some sort of sales charge, or they don't. However, just because you are investing in a no-load fund doesn't mean that, there aren't any types of expenses. Load mutual funds charged the investor a sales charge for purchasing the mutual fund. Loads may be charged either at the time of sale (front-end load) or when the mutual fund is redeemed (back-end load). There are three different types of load funds, and their share classes differentiate them: A, B, and C

A Shares

When you purchase a mutual fund's Class A shares, you will pay an up-front sales charge. The charge may range between four to eight percent of the public offering price initially, with declining sales charges as you purchase more shares. With the initial purchase, and any subsequent purchases, the investor pays the NAV per share plus the applicable load. Thus, the entire amount of money isn't invested

THE SHOPPING MALL OF INVESTMENTS

because part of it goes directly to the mutual fund family as the sales charge. However, when the investor redeems his shares, he or she will receive the NAV for the shares. There won't be any surrender charge for taking out the money because the front-end load was already applied.

Class A shares are also subject to breakpoints. Mutual funds offer investors these breakpoints to encourage a higher investment. The fund family will set the breakpoints for each fund it offers, and when investors hit a breakpoint, they are subject to a lower front-end sales charge. For example, many fund families set their first breakpoint at $50,000. Let's say you purchase $35,000 of the XYZ Growth Fund Class A. You then pay the highest sales load, which in this case let's assume to be 5.75 percent. This means that of your $35,000, $2012.50 is the sales charge for purchasing the fund. However, let's say you purchased $55,000. The associated breakpoint is at $50,000 at which point the sales charge becomes 4.75 percent. Your sales charge would be $2612.50. Without the breakpoint system, the sales load of 5.75 percent on $55,000 is $3162.50. That's a difference of $550 because of the breakpoint system.

$$\$35,000 \times 5.75\% = \$2012.50$$
$$\$55,000 \times 4.75\% = \$2612.50$$
$$\$55,000 \times 5.75\% = \$3162.50$$
$$\$3162.50 - \$2612.50 = \textbf{\$550 savings}$$

Mutual fund families also offer rights of accumulation to those who invest in Class A shares. Rights of accumulation come into play when you have already purchased some Class A shares and want to make a subsequent purchase. Going back to our previous example, you have purchased $35,000 of XYZ Growth Fund Class A and wish to make another purchase of $35,000. Rather than be charged 5.75 percent on the second purchase of $35,000, you would be charged 5.75 percent on the first $15,000 and then 4.75 percent on the remaining $20,000. Your total sales load for the second purchase of $35,000 would be $1812.50, rather than $2012.50 (saving you $200). This occurs every time an investor makes subsequent purchases of his Class A shares.

Original sales load – $35,000 × 5.75% = $2012.50
$15,000 × 5.75% = $862.50
20,000 × 4.75% = $950
Total sales load for second $35,000 investment = **$1812.50**
$2012.50 – $1812.50 = **$200 savings**

Mutual fund companies decrease the front-end sales load as the amount of the investment increases. The sales load is usually phased out at $1 million. Therefore, if you were to invest $1 million with the same mutual fund family in Class A shares, you would pay no front-end sales load. Some fund families do charge a contingent deferred sales charge (CDSC) of one percent for investments of $1 million or more. For example, the mutual fund company MFS charges a CDSC of one percent when the investment is redeemed within 12 months of the initial investment. After that 12-month period, though, the investment would no longer be subject to any type of back-end load.

B Shares

Class B shares do not have an up-front sales charge; rather, they have a back-end sales charge, or a surrender charge (CDSC). The surrender charges associated with Class B shares are similar to the surrender charge schedules for annuities, which we discuss in the next chapter. (See Table 5.1)

Table 5.1. General Surrender Charges for Class B Mutual Funds

Year	Percentage
1	5%
2	4%
3	4%
4	3%
5	2%
6	1%
7	0%
9	Convert to A shares

When an investor purchases Class B shares of a mutual fund, he or she does so at NAV, thus ensuring that the entire amount of money is invested. However, if the shares are redeemed within the first six years, the investor will pay a surrender charge. The shares will be redeemed at NAV, but then the applicable load will be subtracted. The surrender charge schedule for Class B shares is a declining one. After nine years, Class B shares revert to Class A shares, although no front-end sales load will be assessed at that time.

Table 5.1 shows a sample of the surrender charges for Class B mutual funds. Although this is the standard for surrender charges, some mutual fund companies may charge on a different scale. The time frame will remain the same, but the initial CDSC may be less, and the corresponding years and CDSC rates may be different than what is listed above.

While B shares don't have any up-front sales load, they do tend to have higher 12-b-1 fees inside. These fees, named after the 1980 SEC rule that allowed them, are annual sales fees, which are taken against fund assets to compensate the fund for any sort of distribution expenses, such as broker commissions or advertising costs. The 12-b-1 fees vary in percentage among the different fund families, and usually aren't more than .50 percent per year. However, they may be as high as 1.25 percent.

Although investors are charged a surrender charge for redeeming their shares prior to holding the fund for seven years, if they exchange their shares for shares in a different fund within the same fund family, there is no surrender charge. For instance, you purchase $40,000 of Oppenheimer Global Growth and Income Fund Class B, and a few years later you decide that you want to move $20,000 from this fund to a different fund. As long as you keep that $20,000 with Oppenheimer Funds and in Class B shares, you won't be charged any surrender charge or back-end load. However, if you wish to move that money to another fund family, you will be charged the applicable surrender charge.

C Shares

For many years, Class A shares were the only type of share class that was available. Then fund families introduced the B class and, recently, they have begun offering Class C shares. Class C shares blend the advantages of both Class A and B shares. When purchasing Class C shares, the investor's money is 100-percent invested. There is no front-end sales load, as there is with Class A shares. Plus, as long as you don't redeem the shares within the first year of investing the money, you may pull out all of your money without any type of surrender charge. Therefore, there is no front-end or back-end load. However, your money will be subject to a one-percent surrender charge if you redeem your mutual fund within the first year. The rules for same-fund-family exchanges apply to Class C shares, as they do with Class B shares. Class C shares do not share in the conversion privilege, as do Class B shares. They will remain Class C.

Class A versus Class B versus Class C

There is no clear-cut answer as to which share class is the best. All three have their advantages and disadvantages. For larger amounts of money, Class A shares would probably be the best due to the reduction in the sales charge and since there are no back-end fees. If your money is within an IRA, perhaps Class B shares would be the better option. But if you wanted to invest your money and thought that you may need it within a few years, Class C shares may be the way to go. The share class that you invest in is really determined by your time frame. You may find that a mixture of share classes is preferable.

NO-LOAD MUTUAL FUNDS

No-load mutual funds are those that have no front-end or back-end sales load. Both purchases and redemptions for no-load funds are done at the fund's NAV. Sometimes, the 12-b-1 fees associated with no-load funds have been higher than with load funds since there are no sales charges. In the past few years, no-loads have become increasingly popular with investors because they are easy to move around in. Without any associated sales charges, investors may stay in the fund for as long, or short, as they want.

VARIETIES OF MUTUAL FUNDS

Just as you can categorize common stocks, you can classify mutual funds. Each individual fund has a specific objective or specialty; however, many funds may all have some of the same underlying stocks as their investments. When choosing mutual funds in which to invest, it's important to do some research so you don't wind up buying four different mutual funds that each have the same companies' stock inside. That would defeat the purpose of diversifying your portfolio. Mutual funds don't have to invest just in common stock from corporations; there are many funds that are bond funds, international funds, and hybrid funds.

Equity Funds

These are mutual funds that invest their assets in the common stock of corporations. There are different types of equity funds. Equity mutual funds are the most common type of fund traded and held.

GROWTH FUNDS. Primarily, growth funds hold the common stock of more proven, larger growth-oriented corporations. These funds are akin to growth stocks. The goal of growth funds is to provide the investor with longer-term growth and appreciation, rather than give the investor a sizeable income from dividends and capital gains distributions.

AGGRESSIVE GROWTH FUNDS. Here, the purpose is capital appreciation, rather than income. Aggressive growth funds represent substantially more risk than regular growth funds because they are apt to invest in smaller companies, newer industries, start-up firms, etc. They may also make a practice of holding fewer companies in their portfolios than the average growth fund. Aggressive growth funds may also use different types of equity investments, such as option writing, in the portfolios . They are the more speculative funds when comparing regular growth funds to aggressive growth funds.

INCOME EQUITY FUNDS. These funds are driven to invest in larger, stable corporations that have long histories of sizable dividends, thus providing the investor with the ability to derive income from the fund. Since the goal is not capital appreciation, the associated risk for income funds is relatively lower than that for growth or aggressive growth funds.

GROWTH AND INCOME FUNDS. A mix of the income equity and growth funds, these funds strive to invest in firms that will show positive growth and income (dividends) rates in the future, as well as providing some good dividend income in the present. The risk level for these funds tends to be moderate because of the balance between the growth and income factors.

OPTION-INCOME FUNDS. These funds tend to invest in the common stock of firms that pay reasonable current dividends. However, they also try to increase the income to investors by writing call options on the stock they hold.

GLOBAL EQUITY FUNDS. Global funds invest in the common stock of both foreign and U.S. companies.

> **Special note:** It's important to distinguish between international and global mutual funds. Global funds invest in American companies, as well as foreign companies, whereas international funds invest solely in foreign companies.

INTERNATIONAL EQUITY FUNDS. International equity funds are regular equity funds that invest solely in the common stock of foreign companies.

SMALL-CAP FUNDS. Small-cap funds are made up of smaller, lesser-known companies that the mutual fund thinks show great promise and will grow substantially over a few years. While many people think that small-cap stocks have performed better than other sectors have, small-cap funds, like the underlying small-cap stock, have fewer capital resources, and are known to be more volatile than their larger counterparts.

PRECIOUS METALS FUNDS. Rather than investing individually in companies that produce precious metals, or gold-mining companies, mutual fund companies have come up with precious metals funds. Theses funds can be viewed as alternates to holding gold or other precious metals directly. The prices of the underlying stocks tend to move with the market prices of the precious metals the firms produce, instead of the stock market itself. These funds may be considered sector funds.

SECTOR FUNDS. Sector funds invest in the companies that make up different market segments and industries, such as health care, utilities, natural resources, etc. By investing in these funds, investors can direct a portion of their investments in fields they wish to invest in. For example, if you wanted to concentrate some of your investment dollars in the financial services area, rather than researching and picking a fund that has a high percentage of stock in that area, you could purchase a sector fund.

Hybrid Funds
When comparing a hybrid fund's portfolio with an equity fund's portfolio, hybrid funds are far more diverse.

ASSET ALLOCATION FUNDS. These funds are required to keep a certain percentage spread across stocks, bonds, and money market instruments. By investing in an asset allocation fund, you would be taking advantage of the different types of investment vehicles with the convenience of one mutual fund. Different types of asset allocation funds exist. Some may be more heavily weighted in income-producing investments, while others may be more geared toward growth investments. It's also important to make sure that if you do invest in one of these types of funds, that you don't wind up duplicating your overall allocation through some of the other investment choices you make. For example, let's say your overall asset allocation mix calls for a small percentage to be in growth stocks. Be careful that if you invest in a largely growth-oriented asset allocation fund, you temper that with other, more income-producing mutual funds, rather than an aggressive growth fund. That way, you won't wind up with too many of your investment dollars in one side of the investment spectrum.

BALANCED FUNDS. Balanced funds are similar to asset allocation funds since they hold a substantially equal weighting of common stocks and bonds. However, because they aren't required to have specific percentages, they are their own category, rather than being lumped together with asset allocation funds, The goal of a balanced fund is to preserve the principal, while making reasonable returns, and paying income, based upon dividends. They also seek to achieve long-term growth while keeping the principal preservation and current income values intact. While the percentages of the underlying investments may be changing on a regular basis, the prospectus for a balanced fund will contain the most recent holdings and stock-to-bond breakdowns.

FLEXIBLE PORTFOLIO FUNDS.   Flexible portfolio funds are essentially balanced funds except they change their asset allocation more quickly, and are permitted to hold 100 percent of any one given asset at any time.

INCOME-MIXED FUNDS.   Through investing in government and corporate bonds, as well as common stock that pays reasonably high, consistent dividends, income-mixed funds strive to provide their shareholders with current income at a relatively high level.

Taxable Bond Funds
There are times when investors want the stability of a bond, but don't want to hold it to maturity, nor do they want to bear the risk of the bond being called. (We discuss bonds in depth in Chapter 7.) In order to achieve this, they invest in bond funds. These funds are made up of the different types of taxable bonds, and may be more heavily weighted in one type of bond over another. Since the investor is a shareholder of the fund, rather than an individual bond, there are no fixed maturity dates. The investor, therefore, may hold onto the fund in perpetuity, while the underlying bonds mature and the fund purchases new ones.

U.S. TREASURY BOND FUNDS.   Investors looking for an investment that is relatively safe and income producing, look towards U.S. Treasury bond funds. These funds invest primarily in U.S. Treasury bonds, and are, thus, considered to be relatively safe. The underlying bonds have a variety of maturity dates, and due to the nature of Treasury bonds, they aren't callable. This means that the bond fund will receive the full amount of interest plus principal, which it will then pass on to the shareholders. These funds help provide security and stability for the investor's portfolio.

U.S. GOVERNMENT INCOME FUNDS. These funds attempt to achieve a higher yield by investing in different types of government securities, including Treasury bonds and notes and other federally guaranteed securities.

GINNIE MAE FUNDS. These funds invest primarily in government-backed, mortgage-backed securities. Ginnie Mae is the common name for the Government National Mortgage Association.

CORPORATE BOND FUNDS. Most corporate bond funds try to invest in high-quality bonds issued by diverse companies who are raising capital. The associated risk with these funds is based upon the bonds' issuing companies' creditworthiness. These bonds are normally callable and may have any length of maturities.

HIGH-YIELD BOND FUNDS. High-yield, or junk, bonds try to earn a higher rate of return by investing in bonds with a low credit rating. The lower the credit rating, the riskier the bond is. However, these bonds are known to pay a much higher interest rate than those corporate bonds with high ratings. These bonds often go into default, where the issuer can no longer pay the interest. By investing in higher-risk bonds, high-yield bonds hope to achieve higher returns for their shareholders. The higher the risk, the greater the potential payout.

INCOME-BOND FUNDS. These bonds try to provide current income for their shareholders by investing in a combination of corporate and government bonds.

INTERNATIONAL BOND FUNDS. International bond funds invest in the bonds of foreign governments, corporations, or both. They do not hold any bonds from the United States. These funds are subject to price fluctuations based upon the prices of the underlying bonds, which are expressed in that country's currency. For instance, if within an international bond fund, there is a bond from Great Britain, the price for the bond will be expressed in pounds, not dollars. Thus, these funds have three inherent risks: (1) financial risk, (2) interest rate risk, and (3) currency risk. As the world's different currencies fluctuate against the U.S. dollar, the prices of the bonds, as converted to dollars, will change. These bonds also give the investors the chance to partake, indirectly, in foreign currencies and diversify their portfolios as such. Sometimes, the asset allocation model will recommend some foreign currency investment.

GLOBAL BOND FUNDS. Global bond funds are just like international bond funds, and are subject to the same types of risk associated with international bond funds. However, global bond funds may invest in the bonds of both the U.S. government and U.S. corporations.

Municipal Bond Funds
These funds may provide the investor a stream of tax-free income for both state and federal income tax purposes. I have a number of clients who have benefited from holding municipal bond funds because of their favorable tax treatment.

NATIONAL MUNICIPAL BOND FUNDS. Bonds and other securities that are issued by states, cities, and other municipalities make up national municipal bond funds. The underlying bonds and securities may be from all over the country, or they may be geographically centered. Some of these bond funds invest only in high-quality bonds, while others will invest in lower-quality, or junk, bonds. The bonds may have a variety of maturities. The income from these funds is tax-free for federal income tax purposes.

STATE MUNICIPAL BOND FUNDS. These funds are state specific and are designed to provide the investor with tax-free income for federal, state, and local income tax purposes, provided that the investor is a resident of that specific state. All types of bonds from cities and counties within a state are used in these funds.

Money Market Mutual Funds
One of the more widely held investment vehicles, money market mutual funds, or money market funds, provide the investor with a highly secure, liquid account that earns interest. These funds are gen-

erally used to stabilize a portfolio, as well as be the cash portion of the asset allocation. Money market funds are thought of as cash investments because the mutual fund company usually sells shares for $1 apiece, as well as usually redeeming the shares for $1 each. These accounts may also offer the investor check-writing privileges.

While these accounts do earn interest, it's usually a far cry from what the investor may earn if the money were invested in the stock market or in bonds. However, the interest rates on money market funds are much higher than a regular savings account at a bank. These accounts are designed to be liquid, safe, and convenient. They, therefore, make an excellent choice to hold cash reserve money. Be aware, though, that the mutual fund companies may not redeem the money market funds' shares at par ($1 per share). Look at the underlying short-term securities that the company holds, because this may inhibit the company's ability to pay par value for the shares. Money market funds aren't federally guaranteed, as bank accounts are. However, money market accounts issued by banks are FDIC insured for up to the limit of $100,000.

TAXABLE MONEY MARKET FUNDS. These funds invest in a variety of interest-bearing securities. Some invest in only U.S. government obligations, such as Treasury bonds and notes, while others invest in U.S. government obligations plus securities backed by the federal government. Still others will invest in commercial paper, CDs, and other cash-equivalent investments. Those funds that are invested solely in government obligations are considered the safest. The interest on these accounts would be taxable for federal income tax purposes, and perhaps for state and local tax purposes, as well.

TAX-EXEMPT MONEY MARKET FUNDS. Typically, the interest earned on these accounts isn't counted as part of the investor's income for federal income tax purposes. They may, however, be counted as part of the income for state and local tax purposes. These funds may fall into two categories: national tax-exempt money market funds or state tax-exempt money market funds.

Tax-Managed Funds
Tax-managed funds are a newer type of mutual fund that attempt to help their shareholders minimize the taxes they pay on the fund.

Because dividends and interest earned in mutual funds and capital gains are all passed down to the fund's shareholders, they are completely taxable to the mutual fund's investors. The mutual fund itself doesn't pay the taxes. Therefore, tax-managed funds try to minimize the amount of dividends, interest, and capital gains that are passed down to its shareholders. The funds do this in a number of ways.

First, the fund may elect to concentrate on lower-yielding securities. By choosing investments that aren't focused on providing current interest and dividend income, the funds won't wind up passing that income on to their shareholders, who in turn would wind up paying taxes on it. This means that the funds would then be favoring more growth-oriented securities. Second, the funds may try to reduce the distribution of capital gains. They achieve this by adopting a buy-and-hold stance on the securities, rather than a buy-and-sell approach. This minimizes the turnover in the underlying securities. Third, tax-managed funds may elect a tax-efficient selling policy. This means that when the funds sell some of their appreciated securities, they pick the ones that will have long-term capital gains, instead of short-term capital gains. The long-term capital gains tax rates are more favorable than the short-term tax rates. They will also try to pick the securities that have the highest tax base when selling. Often times when selling, the fund will try to offset any gain with a tax loss, which also minimizes the amount of gain that is passed on to the shareholders. These funds may be appropriate for investors who are in higher tax brackets.

Index Funds

Index funds track whatever unmanaged stock indices the funds follow. There are index funds that follow the S&P 500, the Russell 2000, the Wilshire 5000, and many others. But that doesn't mean that index funds are limited just to common stock indices. They can invest in bonds and other securities, too. These funds are categorized as passively managed funds because the funds' portfolios reflect the individual indices. The other mutual funds we've discussed are considered to be actively managed funds because the fund managers pick the securities they think will outperform the market. They then buy and sell the securities in accordance with their projections. With index funds, the fund managers merely track the index. They don't have to pick individual securities.

PROS AND CONS OF INDEX FUNDS.   One of the advantages of owning an index fund is a tax advantage. Since the funds track the market indices and aren't actively managed, there is little security turnover, resulting in lower capital gains distributions. Thus, really, the shareholder would only have to worry about any interest or dividends that would be declared and passed through. With low turnover of securities, this also leads to lower costs for the fund. There are low transaction costs, as well as minimal research and investment-management fees.

Another possible advantage is that the funds are directly tied to the stock market. Many times, mutual funds that are actively managed will try to beat the market. And while some have done so, many have not. By investing in an index fund, you minimize your chance of being invested in a fund that performs worse than the market. However, that also means that you may miss out on some tremendous performances by other actively managed funds when they outperform the market. Many people believe that actively managed funds do outperform index funds during down markets. According to a recent study by the Schwab Center for Investment Research, over a period of 20 down markets between 1987 and 2000, the average actively managed large-cap mutual fund outperformed the average S&P 500 index fund only half of the time.[1] Therefore, the average index fund outperformed the average actively managed fund half of the time, as well. This, of course, is not a case of one type of mutual fund doing so much better that you should forsake the other type of fund. Rather, sometimes a nice mix of actively managed funds and an index fund may be a good fit for your financial objectives.

As with any type of investment, there are limitations to index funds. One is that because the funds' portfolios mirror the market indices, some of common stocks' better performers' returns may be undermined by other, lesser-performing assets. Since the funds are passively managed, the fund managers wouldn't be selling off some

[1]"Do Actively Managed Funds Outperform in Down Markets?" by Mark W. Riepe, CFA. *Journal of Financial Planning,* July 2001.

of the stock that they don't see as performing well. They would remain in the stock because the fund is an index fund. Also, the shareholders would lose any type of stock selection they desired. Actively managed funds that focus on a certain sector may be more appropriate for those investors who want to concentrate more in one area, instead of the market as a whole.

Index fund shareholders are also subject to market risk. When the stock market is doing very well, so will the index fund. However, when the market is doing poorly, or the country is experiencing a bear market, the index funds will also perform poorly. This is because the portfolios reflect the indices and will remain invested, whereas other actively managed funds may be holding some of their assets in cash or interest-bearing securities during this down time.

VALUING MUTUAL FUNDS

We've discussed net asset value of a mutual fund. But what does this really mean to you, the investor? Net asset value per share is the total value of all the securities and other assets held by the fund, minus any of the fund's liabilities. This resulting number is then divided by the number of outstanding shares in the mutual fund. The net asset value, or NAV, is the price per share of the mutual fund. Just like individual stocks have a price per share, so do mutual funds. Let's assume that the XYZ Growth mutual fund has total assets of $52 million. Their liabilities total $14 million, and the fund has 1.4 million shares outstanding. The NAV of the XYZ Growth Fund would be $27.14 per share.

$$\text{Total fund assets} = \$52 \text{ million}$$
$$\text{Total fund liabilities} = \$14 \text{ million}$$
$$\text{Total shares outstanding} = 1.4 \text{ million}$$
$$\$52 \text{ million} - \$14 \text{ million} = \$38 \text{ million}$$

$$\frac{\$38 \text{ million}}{1.4 \text{ million shares}} = \$27.14/\text{share NAV}$$

The NAV isn't always the price per share the investor pays for the mutual fund. Any applicable sales charge (Class A shares only) will increase the price per share that the investor pays. However, for Class B and C shares, the investor would pay the NAV for the mutual fund.

FIGURING INVESTMENT PERFORMANCE

Wealthy investors may not only be interested in the different types of mutual funds and their asset allocations. They typically are keenly interested in the kind of returns they are making. For many people, it's easy to invest your money and then forget about it. For others, it's vitally important to track investments every day. I recommend a mixture of both. The market is too volatile to watch it everyday and value your portfolio that way. With the ups and downs the market sees every day, it could drive average investors crazy to see their account values rise and fall. In fact, I have more than a few clients who do this and are constantly worried about the state of their portfolios. However, it's healthy to evaluate your portfolio on a fairly regular basis, like quarterly.

A good way to measure how your mutual funds are performing on an annual basis is to calculate their total return. This accounts for any dividends and capital gains paid to shareholders, plus the change in the NAV. For example, let's assume that the XYZ International Fund began the calendar year at $32 per share. At the end of the year, the price per share was $36. They didn't distribute any dividend income, but they had a realized capital gain of $2.30. The XYZ International Fund's total return for that year would be $6.30.

$$\$36 - \$32 = \$4/\text{share increases}$$
$$\text{Capital gain} = \$2.30$$
$$\text{Dividends} = \$0$$
$$\text{Total return} = \$4 + \$2.30 + \$0 = \$6.30$$

But, this whole amount would not be taxable to the investors if the investors didn't redeem their shares. The $4 per share increase would be an untaxable gain because the investors remained invested in the fund. Only the capital gain of $2.30 would be taxable, and depending on how long the fund had held the securities sold, it would be taxed at either long-term or short-term capital gains rates. For this example, the before-tax return would be about 19.7 percent. The after-tax return, assuming the capital gains were long term, would be 18.25 percent.

Before-tax return:

$$\$6.30 \div \$32 = 19.6875\%$$

After-tax return:

$$\$1.84 \text{ (after-tax capital gains distribution)} + \$4 = \$5.84$$
$$\$5.84 \div \$32 = 18.25\%$$

Smart investors don't just look at one-year returns, as they may be somewhat misleading.

Perhaps the particular asset class that one mutual fund was invested in did outstandingly, while another asset class did particularly poorly in a given year. (Refer to Table 2.1 for breakdowns of asset class returns by year.) Therefore, while past performance is no guarantee of future results, investors tend to focus on 3-, 5-, and 10-year returns. Plus, all mutual funds will have a since-inception return. This is the total return since the fund was started. For those mutual funds that are newer, this is important, since they may not have 3- or 5-year returns. However, for all funds, it shows the overall trend of how the fund has done. When figuring the total return for a mutual fund, you may need to adjust the prices per share by the applicable sales load. This could dramatically affect the return for one year, but as you calculate the returns for multiple years, the effect of the sales charge will diminish.

Special note: Try not to make the mistake of holding an investment too long. Sometimes a stock or mutual fund is beyond repair and will not be coming back. By holding that fund and not cutting your losses and selling, you run the risk of losing more of your principal, as well as possibly missing out on a more appropriate investment opportunity.

FINDING INFORMATION ABOUT MUTUAL FUNDS

As with common stocks, there are a number of places to find accurate, reliable information about mutual funds. The best place to look is the mutual fund's prospectus. A prospectus is a legal document prepared by the mutual fund company. It is filed with the Securities and Exchange Commission and lists the most recent information about the fund. These are produced once a year. However, some fund families put out revised prospectuses throughout the year. A prospectus will include an expense summary for the fund, the fund's investment strategy and risks, any minimum purchase restrictions, financial highlights of the fund, and many other useful bits of information. The prospectus will also disclose the different types of securities and assets that the particular fund is allowed to invest in. Each mutual fund has its own prospectus.

Another good source of information is a mutual fund's semiannual or quarterly report. Often times, this is included in the prospectus booklet, but it can also come separately. An annual report should list the fund's top 10 holdings, its long-term performance, an independent auditor's report about the fund, and its portfolio and financial statements, among other things. The annual report will also detail the most recent capital gains and dividend distributions to shareholders. These numbers are important to look at if you are searching for a mutual fund that has favorable tax consequences (i.e., low capital gains and dividend distributions).

Although prospectuses and annual reports include valuable information, because of their infrequent publishing, investors need different resources for up-to-date information. As with stocks, Yahoo! Finance (*www.quote.yahoo.com*), Dow Jones Market Monitor (*www.dowjones.com*), and Microsoft (*www.msn.com*) have information about mutual funds. Magazines such as *Worth*, *Money,* and *Barron's* publish periodic mutual fund performance reviews. Daily financial newspapers, such as the *Wall Street Journal*, will contain the same type of information about funds as they do about stocks, such as the NAV, volume of shares traded, etc. Finally, mutual fund companies update their fund information on a daily basis at their respective Web sites. You may also be able either to download or read the prospectuses on-line, as well.

SO, WHAT'S THE BIG DEAL?

We've spent a lot of time discussing mutual funds, and you may be thinking, why? Well, the reason is very simple: Mutual funds are an easy asset to invest in systematically. Remember the adage, "Pay yourself first." That comes into play here. It's far easier to invest in a mutual fund on a regular, disciplined basis rather than trying to buy stocks or bonds every month. However, it's important to remember that this doesn't assure a profit, nor does it protect against a loss.

They're also important because mutual funds are very prevalent nowadays. Magazines run articles on what funds are currently the best, and which ones to look out for. These articles serve as a good basis for the education you need in order to pick a good mutual fund. If you have taken my advice and hired a financial planner, these articles are still important, because you need to know what is going on so that you may make informed decisions. Remember, your advisor is there to help you make a decision, not to make it for you. An advisor will merely provide the knowledge and experience needed to help guide you to a sounder financial future.

But above all, don't be afraid to jump into the market. We've already talked about how when we go to the store, we look for bargains and enjoy paying the sale price for goods. You should have the same outlook when it comes to buying investments. The less expensive the asset, the greater potential return you could achieve. That's not to say that all cheap investments are worth buying. You have to do some homework to decide whether or not a certain investment is sound and right for you. Unfortunately, many people let themselves be ruled by fear. They don't want to lose money by investing, so they don't even start. That's the worst mistake you can make.

Mutual funds that are suitable for your investment strategy are very powerful tools to help you achieve your goals. You need to have the self-discipline to invest in them and stay invested. The latter of the two actions is the hardest part. Be prepared to ride the waves of the stock market as you would with stocks. Just know that because the mutual fund is invested in several, if not hundreds, of individual stocks, the potential for losing everything may be less than if you held those individual stocks on your own.

6

HELP! I'M RUNNING OUT OF MONEY!

Annuities act in opposition to life insurance. While life insurance protects you financially against an early or unexpected death, annuities protect you from the financial risk of living too long and outliving your money. There are different types of annuities including immediate, deferred, fixed, and variable. Annuities are a special form of investment that is a contract between, the investor, and the issuing insurance company, that states that the insurance company will pay you a series of payments for either a specific period of time or for the rest of your life.

In the past, a life annuity contract consisted of a person paying an insurance company a specified amount of money in exchange for the guarantee that the insurance company would make periodic payments to this person for the rest of his or her life, thus ensuring that this person wouldn't outlive his or her money.

However, individual annuity contracts these days allow the payout of accrued money in different ways. Generally, very few individual annuity contracts are actually taken as life income, or annuitized.

Annuitant—The individual who receives the payout of an annuity

Premium—The amount of money paid to the insurer for the annuity. This can be paid over time or in a single lump sum.

Owner—The individual who enters into an annuity contract with the insurer. This person may differ from the annuitant.

Beneficiary—The person named by the owner who would receive the death benefit from the annuity upon the owner's death.

TAX TREATMENT FOR ANNUITIES

Annuities are very much like IRAs, in that the money grows tax-deferred, and the annuity owners cannot take any distributions from the contracts until they are at least $59^{1}/_{2}$ years old. All money invested in an annuity is done so after tax, and there is no tax deduction for investing in an annuity unless it is done inside an IRA annuity. Then, any tax deduction is subject to the same limits that other IRA contributions are subject to (i.e., $3000 per year). In most cases, those who take money out of their annuity contracts before they are $59^{1}/_{2}$ will face a 10-percent IRS penalty for early withdrawal, plus they will be responsible for taxes on the money that was withdrawn. Taxes are paid at ordinary income rates, regardless of how long the annuity has been held.

For nonqualified annuities (those not within an IRA plan), the annuity owner's investment in the contract is the total premium amount paid, less any nontaxed distributions. Because the contract owner has paid in after-tax dollars, he or she (or the beneficiary, after the owner's death) is entitled to have this amount back tax-free once distributions from the annuity begin. Therefore, hypothetically, if the owner puts in a total of $75,000, once he or she begins receiving payouts from the annuity, the owner will receive a total of $75,000 back tax-free. (Alternative minimum tax, state and local taxes may apply.) If the annuity is worth $87,000 at the time it is annuitized, the owner may only be taxed on the growth, $12,000.

Because the annuity grows tax-deferred, any movement of money within a variable annuity will not be considered for capital gains taxes. For example, you have $20,000 in the Growth subaccount, which is doing very well. You want to protect some of the money you have earned from this subaccount and wish to move $5000 to the Fixed subaccount. The transfer of the $5000 from the Growth subaccount to the Fixed subaccount is done completely tax-free. You won't be taxed on the gain from the Growth subaccount.

IMMEDIATE ANNUITIES

Immediate annuities require the annuitant to pay a lump sum of money, rather than paying a number of premiums over time. The payouts to the annuitant begin as soon as the lump-sum payment is received, or the annuity start date. This date is the first day of the first period (i.e., month) for which an amount is received as an annuity, under the current tax law. A likely use of an immediate annuity is by someone who is about to retire and would like to receive monthly income right away. An immediate annuity can be paid out in either fixed or variable amounts.

DEFERRED ANNUITIES

In contrast to immediate annuities, deferred annuities can have one lump-sum payment by the annuitant, or the annuitant can pay a set of premiums over time. The payouts for deferred annuities typically don't start for at least one year after the purchase payments have ended. Usually, payouts don't occur until many years later. However, just with immediate annuities, the payouts may be either fixed or variable.

Deferred annuities make up the larger segment of annuity contracts that are purchased due to the IRS rules governing annuity payouts, as well as the desire by investors to take advantage of any potential tax-deferred growth.

SPLIT-FUNDED ANNUITIES

This is combination of an immediate and deferred annuity. This approach provides for a portion of the annuity to revert back to the owner as immediate income for a fixed period of time, or for life. The remaining money in the annuity grows tax-deferred, as a regular deferred annuity would. Split-funded annuities act as a good hedge against inflation since the deferred portion can be used in the future as additional income, if necessary.

FLEXIBLE-PREMIUM ANNUITIES

As the name implies, flexible-premium annuities are those in which the annuity owner has discretion over when the premium payments begin. The owner may also decide if, when, and how much the premium payments may change; they may also decide to stop paying the annuity's premium. This type of annuity is only for deferred contracts.

SINGLE-PREMIUM ANNUITIES

These annuities are purchased with one lump-sum payment, rather than premiums over time. The premium may be paid just prior to the annuity's payouts (for an immediate annuity), or it may be paid much earlier (for a deferred annuity). Both single-premium immediate and single-premium deferred annuities may be paid out in fixed or variable amounts.

ANNUITY PHASES

Individual annuities have two different phases: the accumulation phase and the distribution phase.

The annuity owner pays premiums and the contract value grows due to the premiums during the accumulation phase. There is no tax or legal limit to the amount of contributions (or lump sum) that may be made on an annual basis. These premiums are made after taxes, though.

The distribution phase begins once the annuity owner begins to receive the annuity's payouts. There are a few limiting factors to when the distribution period may begin. First, the owner must be at least $59^1/_2$ years old, otherwise he or she will be subject to the IRS's 10 percent early withdrawal penalty. Of course, there are a few exceptions. Second, annuities carry surrender charges. Therefore, you will want to defer the distribution phase until the surrender charges have declined or have been eliminated. Finally, annuity contracts generally stipulate the maximum age at which distributions must start. However, this is usually a quite advanced age, such as 87. There are no tax laws that specify a required beginning date for non-qualified annuities.

FIXED ANNUITIES

Fixed annuities, or fixed-dollar annuities, grow at a guaranteed rate. At the beginning of the annuity contract, the insurance company and the annuity owner enter into an agreement through which the owner will pay a stated amount in premiums and the insurance company will pay a set rate of interest. While the insurance company will lock in a specified interest rate at the beginning, future interest rates will vary according to current market conditions. However, the insurance company will specify for what length of time the interest rate is good. It may be for as short as two months, or as long as five years. Many times, the subsequent interest rates are lower than the initial rate. Generally, though, annuity contracts will have a minimum guaranteed interest rate, below which the insurance company cannot set its rate. The contract may also have a bailout provision designed to protect annuity owners. This provision states that if the insurance company sets its rates below a certain level, the annuity owner has the option of withdrawing all of his or her funds from the annuity, or may exchange the annuity without any surrender charges. Fixed annuities will pay out at a specified dollar amount to the owner for each period once the distribution period begins.

Because the insurance company is paying interest, all the investment risk is borne by the company. The assets behind fixed annuities are invested in the general assets of the insurance company, and are referred to as portfolio products. Should the insurance company become bankrupt, the fixed annuity owner becomes a general creditor of the company.

Investors are attracted to fixed annuities when the interest rate is rising because their investment is guaranteed by the insurance company, and the value won't decline during a period of rising interest rates, as a bond's value would. Plus, since the interest rate is rising, the insurer will be more likely to pay an increasing interest rate to investors.

Conversely, when interest rates are on the decline, investors tend to look elsewhere for returns. As the interest rate declines, so will interest rates on annuities. Although the premium amount will still be guaranteed by the insurer, it will remain static, unlike bonds whose prices will increase.

VARIABLE ANNUITIES

Variable annuities offer a number of different investment choices inside of the annuity, known as subaccounts. When establishing the variable annuity, owners can choose where they want their premiums to be invested each time. They can then change around the subaccount allocation whenever they want. The owner may also move money between the different subaccounts, both with no cost to the owner and with no tax consequences.

The different types of investment subaccounts, or separate accounts, are not part of the insurance company's general assets. These subaccounts and their investment results stand on their own. The performance of the annuity contract as a whole depends upon the performance of the separate subaccounts, most of which are tied directly to the stock market. Therefore, the investment risk lies with the annuity owner, not the insurance company. Since the subaccounts aren't part of the company's general assets, should the company become insolvent, the variable annuity owners would not become general creditors of the company, as fixed annuity owners do.

The available subaccounts are generally managed by or for the insurance company. However, there are companies that offer variable annuities that have a number of nonproprietary funds from other mutual fund companies, such as Oppenheimer or Janus. The availability of these separate accounts typically varies between the different types of variable annuities offered, but annuity owners usually have a wide variety of choices.

The term "variable annuity" also applies when the annuity's payout varies from period to period. Under the general terms of an annuity contract, the owner may stipulate to have the contract pay out a fixed amount of money per period, or he or she may choose to have a fixed amount of units (or annuity units) to be distributed each period. If the owner chooses to have a set amount of units as the payout, each payout will vary because the dollar amount is based upon the underlying subaccounts and their current prices per share. Thus, if the owner elects to receive 100 units per month, one month he or she may receive $550, while the next month he or she may receive $700. Generally, unless otherwise specified, when the payout comes out of the annuity, it will come proportionately from each of the subaccounts that have value.

COMBINATION PLANS

Most individual annuities give the annuity owner the option of investing a portion of the premiums in both fixed and variable subaccounts. This way, the owner will realize some stability by earning a specified interest rate, while also being able to take advantage of current market conditions.

EQUITY INDEXED ANNUITIES

Equity indexed annuities, or EIAs, are a relatively new form of fixed-dollar annuities. They blend minimum insurance company guarantees with linking the annuity's interest earnings to a stock market index, such as the S&P 500. While there are many different designs of EIAs being sold, we use just one as an example.

Let's say you invest $50,000 as a single-premium deferred EIA. The particular policy you purchase will guarantee a minimum value of 85 percent, or $42,500, of your principal amount. The value of the EIA will not fall below the minimum guaranteed value, which is $42,500 in this example. Plus, if it is higher, the EIA will pay a percentage of the increase in an equity index over a specified time period. The percentage paid will vary among the different insurers, and even the different EIAs offered by the same insurer. For this example, we'll use 80 percent. We'll also use the S&P 500 as our stock index and 10 years as our time frame. The percentage of the index increase is called the "participation rate." Therefore, if the increase in the S&P 500 Index over the 10 years were 60 percent, the interest credited for this increase would be $24,000. Therefore, the accumulated value of the EIA would be $74,000, which is greater than the minimum. The annuity could then continue to earn interest in this manner. If the S&P 500, or another unmanaged index, were to decline, the EIA wouldn't fall below its guaranteed minimum of $42,500.

Participation rate = 80%   S&P 500 increase = 60%
Initial premium = $50,000
Interest = 80% × 60% × $50,000
Interest = $24,000
Contract value = $74,000

(All amounts are hypothetical.)

The returns on EIAs may be subject to certain limitations. For instance, there may be a cap on the amount of interest the annuity can be credited with. Plus, there are features that will also limit the return, such as which index is used, the participation rate, how the interest based on the index is calculated, the guaranteed minimum account value, and any possible account charges. Not only are there a number of different stock indices used, there are different participation rates (which may range anywhere from 50 to more than 100 percent) and different methods of calculating the interest.

EIAs are considered to be equity investments because they are tied to stock market indices. However, their returns will perhaps not be as great as other equity investments, such as stocks or mutual funds, due to participation rates being less than 100 percent, possible interest rate caps, and because equity indices usually don't include dividends paid on common stocks in the index. Rather, they are indices of the market prices of stocks.

EIAs are just like other annuities. They can grow on a tax-deferred basis and all interest and gain on the annuity contract is taxed at ordinary income tax rates once distributions have begun. For nonqualified EIAs, the principal amount comes out tax-free to the owner. (Other taxes may apply.) But, all taxes must be paid once withdrawals begin, and for those who are younger than $59\frac{1}{2}$, there may be an IRS penalty of 10 percent.

GENERAL ANNUITY FEATURES

Beneficiaries

Annuity contracts allow the owners to name beneficiaries. One of the reasons that annuities are attractive to investors is because they have a built-in death benefit. Just like the EIA has a minimum guaranteed value, an annuity contract states that if the value of the contract is less than the original premium, minus any withdrawals or loans, the owner's beneficiary upon the owner's death shall receive the original premium amount. However, if the annuity is valued at more than the original premium amount, the beneficiary will receive that larger amount. For example, James Client invests $100,000 in a deferred variable annuity. Four years later, Mr. Client dies. Prior to his death, he hadn't taken any money out of the annuity. His beneficiary for the annuity, his daughter, claims the annuity, which is now valued at $89,000. Because Mr. Client hadn't taken any money out of the annuity, his daughter receives $100,000—the original premium amount.

Original lump-sum premium = $100,000
Withdrawals = $0
Value of death = $89,000
Beneficiary receives = $100,000

(All amounts are hypothetical.)

$$Original\ lump\text{-}sum\ premium = \$100,000$$
$$Withdrawals = \$0$$
$$Value\ of\ death = \$122,000$$
$$Beneficiary\ receives = \$122,000$$

(All amounts are hypothetical.)

If the beneficiary of the annuity owner is the surviving spouse, that person is entitled to treat the annuity as his or her own under the current tax law. The spouse would become the new owner of the annuity.

Recently, annuity issuers have come up with different ways to calculate the minimum guaranteed death benefit, which help out the owner's beneficiary. One example is the reset death benefit, which has a five-year standard. So, using our previous example, if Mr. Client invests his $100,000 in the variable annuity on July 1, 2001, the value would be reassessed on July 1, 2006, again on July 1, 2011, and so forth, for the life of the contract as long as Mr. Client didn't annuitize it. The highest of these amounts, including the original premium, becomes the new guaranteed death benefit. The benefit can always go higher, but not lower.

Another calculation method for the death benefit is a step-up or ratchet basis. The step-up basis works the same way the reset death benefit does, except instead of waiting five years between reevaluations, there is only a one-year wait. Therefore, the value of the contract would be reassessed on July 1 of every year, rather than every five years. Some variable annuities that offer the step-up basis do so on a quarterly time frame, thus increasing the chance of an even higher death benefit.

Finally, some insurers offer a certain escalation of death benefit amounts, which may be three to five percent per year. This type of "roll-up" death benefit works this way: When the annuity owner dies, the beneficiary receives the greatest amount of either the total premium paid, the current contract value, an assumed three percent annual return, or the top death benefit on a specified anniversary date.

"Roll-up" death benefit:

Original premium = $100,000
Contract value at death = $137,000
Assumed 3% annual return on contract = $112,550
Death benefit on July 1, 2003 (specified anniversary date) = $109,000
Beneficiary receives = $137,000

Be sure you know which type of death benefit your contract allows. That way you'll have an accurate concept of what to expect. Plus, the annuity contract may specify that the death benefit not exceed a certain amount, age, or percentage of the original premium.

Loans and Withdrawals

Annuities may also allow for loans or withdrawals by their owners. However, for those owners who wish to take out a loan against their annuity (or just withdraw money) and who haven't reached age $59^1/_2$, there will be the 10-percent IRS early withdrawal penalty. There are some exceptions to this rule, though. Individuals may take substantially equal periodic payments in the case of the owner's disability or death, or for the purchase of an immediate annuity.

Exchanges

The IRS also allows for a tax-free exchange of nonqualified annuities (i.e., those not within an IRA). This is known as a 1035 exchange, and must be from one annuity to another. Should the owner be dissatisfied with the internal subaccounts, service, or performance of the annuity, he or she will be able to exchange it for a different annuity. This works not only from annuity to annuity within one company, but also across different companies. However, there may be some surrender charges for the older annuity.

Many times, the annuity owner differs from the annuitant. I've seen this happen when the wife's trust owns the annuity, but the annuitant is the husband. It's the annuitant whose life expectancy determines the timing and amount of the payouts, should the annuity be annuitized.

Annuities Not Held by Natural People

Annuities may be held by entities, rather than natural people. However, for tax purposes, any deferred annuities would not be treated as annuities and, thus, wouldn't be tax-deferred. Any gain made on the annuity would be taxed to the owner as ordinary income. This includes any annuities held by corporations, charitable remainder trusts, and certain other entities. This doesn't include annuities held by an estate because the owner has died, any annuities held by trusts or other entities acting on behalf of a natural person, annuities within qualified retirement plans, tax-sheltered annuities, or IRAs and immediate annuities.

Expense Charges

Annuities, both fixed and variable, may have a management or expense charge associated with them. This charge is levied by the insurer and is an annual fee, which is usually billed on a quarterly basis. These charges can be contract charges, which generally are fixed for the life of the contract, and operating expenses, which may vary from period to period. Contract charges protect the insurer from excess mortality and expenses charges, which may include administrative and sales costs, risk charge for death benefits, and insurer profits. The operating expense charge covers the cost of investment management fees and administrative costs of managing the particular subaccount funds available. Fees vary from annuity to annuity and between companies. All applicable fees will be disclosed in your annuity contract.

Surrender Charges

Finally, annuities will have some sort of sales or surrender charge. This can be an up-front sales charge or a back-end load. If the insurer deducts a charge when the premium is paid, thus resulting in a lower amount of money being invested, this is a front-end load. However, insurers generally impose a surrender charge, rather than charge the investor up front. Surrender charges are generally charged only if the owner takes more than 10 percent of the annuity value out during a calendar year for the first few years of the annuity contract, like 7 or 10. Many variable annuities allow you to take the earnings out, which may be a larger number than 10 percent. Surrender charges are levied on a declining scale basis. For example, you purchase an annuity for $100,000. This annuity's surrender charge schedule is for 10 years. (See Table 6.1).

Table 6.1   General Surrender Charge Schedule for Annuities [1]

Year	Percentage
1	10%
2	9%
3	8%
4	7%
5	6%
6	5%
7	4%
8	3%
9	2%
10	1%
11	Surrender charges disappear

After the tenth year, you would be able to draw out as much of the contract's value as you wished. This is actually a contingent deferred sales charge, since it isn't levied unless you pull out more than the allowable maximum. More commonly, though, it is called a "back-end load." Back-end loads are designed to discourage the annuity owner from transferring his or her money to a different company, or taking it out altogether. There are some insurers who don't charge any type of sales charge. These annuities are akin to no-load mutual funds.

HOW ANNUITIES WILL HELP

Annuities are great for investing your after-tax dollars on a tax-deferred basis. Think about it. If you could put away money and then not be taxed on the growth, might your overall nest egg grow faster? Annuities help people shelter their money from the government for a

[1] This is the IDS Life surrender charge schedule. Other companies may use a different one.

time, even if it is a limited time. Plus, for annuities outside an IRA, there is no limit to the amount of money that can be sheltered. Annuities inside an IRA are subject to the regular contribution limits.

Annuities also provide a level of comfort for people who are concerned that they may outlive their money. They also provide a good way to help your money grow tax-deferred. Another advantage to annuities is the guaranteed death benefit. The disadvantages associated with annuities are the internal expense charges, surrender charges, and the possibility of limited subaccount fund availability within variable annuities. While annuities sound like a great investment, they're not for everyone. Be sure the annuity you decide on is in line with your financial goals and objectives.

7

THE STEADY STAPLES OF A WELL-BALANCED PORTFOLIO: BONDS, CASH, AND REITS

T here are other types of investments out there besides stocks, mutual funds, and annuities. In this chapter we touch on three other investment vehicles to think about: bonds, cash investments, and real estate investment trusts. While these don't run the gamut of all types of investments out there, they are the most common, and the most commonly referred to. It's important that you have some kind of knowledge about these investments so that if you are advised to purchase one, you will have a better understanding of what your advisor is talking about.

BONDS

Many people think of bonds as an investment for older people. While many older people do enjoy the benefits that bonds offer, such as investment income, bonds aren't just for the older generation. Rather, they are effective investment tools for just about anyone. There are a number of different types of bonds. They include corporate bonds, municipal bonds, U.S. government obligations (i.e., Treasury bills, Treasury notes, and Treasury bonds), U.S. savings bonds, U.S. government agency securities, zero-coupon bonds, and deep-discount bonds.

Bonds are debt instruments designed to help either a company or the government raise capital. When you purchase a bond, you are loaning money to the bond issuer. You exchange cash for the promise of regular interest payments (with the exception of zero-coupon bonds) and the return of the face value of the bond at the time of maturity. Zero-coupon bonds don't pay regular interest; rather, they are purchased at a discount and mature at a higher face value.

Bonds are typically good investments for those who are seeking a steady cash flow or for those who don't have an immediate need for the principle amount invested. Bonds help diversify your portfolio by tempering the amount of risk you are taking with stocks. Plus, they can help fund short- to intermediate-term goals through their interest payments, or you can sync up the maturity dates of the bonds with the time frame of your goals.

Maturity—The date on which a bond comes due and is to be paid off

Face value—The amount for which the bond is, and what is expected at maturity. Also known as "par value."

Coupon rate—The interest rate on a bond.

> **Default risk**—The possibility that a corporation or other bond issuer will fail to make payment on its debt.
>
> **Interest rate risk**—The risk that interest rates will rise, which will lower the market value of earlier issued bonds.
>
> **Original issue discount**—When bonds are issued at a price that is less than their face value.

Usually, the longer the duration of the bond, the higher the interest rate, because you are loaning your money for a longer period of time. It's important to compare the interest rate with the amount of money you will be investing to make sure that they are commensurate amounts. Also, consider who is issuing the bond before purchasing one. The tax status of the interest income you receive depends on who the issuer is, as does the risk associated with the bond.

Then look at how the bond is rated. Two of the institutions that rate bonds are Moody's and Standard & Poor's. They rate the ability of the issuer to pay back the debt plus the interest payments. These companies have financial analysts that study the issuer's creditworthiness at the time the bonds are issued, as well as periodic reviews throughout the duration of the issue. The ratings indicate the bond's investment quality. The first four ratings for both Moody's and Standard & Poor's represent investment-grade bonds, those that are highly unlikely to go into default. Junk bonds are corporate bonds that are characteristically poor in quality, but pay higher-than-average interest.

Bonds are not foolproof, though. They carry with them interest rate risk: the chance that interest rates will rise after the bond issue, and thus, the price of the bond will fall. On the other hand, if interest rates drop, the prices of bonds will rise. The closer the bond is to maturity, the smaller the price fluctuation because (assuming no default) you will receive the full face value at maturity. Conversely, the longer until maturity, the more price fluctuations may occur, and the greater the risk of default.

Table 7.1   Bond Ratings

Moody's	Standard & Poor's	Ratings' Meanings
Aaa	AAA	Highest quality
Aa	AA	High quality
A	A	High-medium quality
Baa	BBB	Medium quality
Ba	BB	Below investment grade
B	B	Low quality
Caa	CCC	Very risky
Ca	CC	Highly speculative
C	C	Lowest quality
D	D	In default

Corporate Bonds

These are bonds issued by private companies that are usually based on how financially sound the issuing company is. They are viewed as less secure than both U.S. government issues and most municipal bonds. Corporations issue bonds for many reasons, but the most common one is to raise capital. By issuing bonds, the firm is borrowing money from the bond's investors. The corporation will then use the money raised to finance different ventures, all the while making interest payments to its bond holders. Then, at maturity, the company will pay the bond holders their original investment.

Some corporate bonds are secured by a claim on all or a portion of the physical property of the issuing company. Examples of these are mortgage bonds and equipment trust certificates. Most corporate bonds, though, aren't guaranteed in this manner, but rather, they are backed by the full credit of the company with no specific lien on the company's property. These are called "debentures," and they generally have first claim on all the company's assets once all specifically pledged property has been distributed. Subordinated debentures have a claim on assets once all older debt is taken care of. These bond issues may also have what is called a sinking-fund provision. These are designed to eliminate a substantial portion of the outstanding debt prior to the bonds' maturity.

While many corporate bonds can be called, or redeemed, prior to maturity, many companies now offer securities that give investors protection against their bonds being called for a specific period of time. Many investors are willing to take a lower rate of interest in exchange for some call protection or even noncallable bonds. The option of call protection changes with the condition of the economy.

Corporations may also have sinking funds established. These are designed to help the company retire its bonds before the maturity date. The firm will put the money earmarked for the bonds' repayment into escrow, which it will then use to retire the bonds a few at a time.

The investment income derived from a corporate bond is fully taxable for federal income tax purposes. It is also taxable for state income tax purposes in those states that have an income tax. The current interest paid on bonds (coupon rate) is taxed to the investor at ordinary income tax rates. If the bond was purchased at a premium (at a price higher than par value), the investor may choose to amortize the premium over the remaining life of the bond. The investor may then use the amount amortized each year to reduce the bond's taxable interest or as an itemized deduction, depending on when the bond was bought. Either way, the amortized amount acts as a way to reduce otherwise taxable ordinary income. It also reduces the investor's tax basis in the bond.

If the investor elects not to amortize the premium, it will be added to the basis and will either reduce the capital gain (if the bond is sold for more than the cost) or produce a capital loss (if the bond is sold for less than the cost).

Municipal Bonds

Municipal bonds, or "munis," carry an important tax feature: the interest paid on these bonds are exempt from federal income tax, as well as state and local income tax in the state in which they are issued. This could mean significant savings in taxes that could otherwise be flowing to the government. Munis are especially attractive to investors whose tax brackets are quite high, therefore garnering them a greater after-tax return from tax-free interest than they would realize from taxable interest.

Let's consider a hypothetical example of the Smiths. Currently, they are in the 35-percent tax bracket. They are considering investing $100,000, but are unsure of whether they would benefit from municipal bonds. The bonds they are thinking about pay an interest rate of 6 percent. They are also looking at a bank CD for this money, which pays 8.2 percent. Which investment could earn them a higher after-tax return? The Smiths would earn 6 percent after tax from their muni bond, but they would only earn 5.33 percent after tax from the bank CD. Therefore, the muni bond would earn a greater after tax return for the Smiths. (See Tables 7.2 and 7.3 for comparisons with the updated tax brackets.)

$$(1 - \text{tax bracket}) \times \text{taxable yield} = \text{tax-free yield}$$
$$(1 - .35) \times 8.2\% = 5.33\%$$

When considering the tax implications of purchasing municipal bonds versus other fixed-income investments, also determine whether you will be paying state and local taxes on the interest and capital gains. Usually, the muni bonds will be exempt from state and local taxation. These are sometimes referred to as "triple-tax-free municipal bonds" because of the income tax exemptions on the interest and sometimes on the capital gains.

For example, the Smiths have a state income tax rate of 4.4 percent, no local income tax rate, and they itemize their deductions. Their effective state rate is 4.4 x (1 - .35) = 2.86 percent. Their total tax rate is 37.86 percent. In this case, the municipal bond they are considering would be free from state income tax, as well as federal income tax.

However, the bank CD yield of 8.2 percent isn't exempt from any taxes. Therefore, their after-tax rate on the muni bond remains 6 percent, whereas the after-tax rate of the bank CD is 5.095 percent.

$$(1 - .3786) \times 8.2\% = 5.095\%$$
Amounts are hypothetical.

However, if the Smiths don't itemize, or if the deductions are mostly phased out on their federal income tax return, and the state

Table 7.2 After-tax rates of return comparison – years 2004 and 2005[1]

(1) Federal tax bracket	(2) After-tax return from a muni bond paying a tax-free yield of 6%	(3) After-tax return from a bank paying 6% taxable	(4) After-tax return from a corporate bond paying 7.5% taxable	(5) Necessary rate of return for the investor to realize 6% after tax
15	6%	5.10%	6.38%	7.06%
27	6%	4.38%	5.48%	8.22%
30	6%	4.20%	5.25%	8.57%
35	6%	3.90%	4.88%	9.23%
38.6	6%	3.68%	4.61%	9.77%

[1]These figures are based upon the new tax rates for the year 2002 and 2003. They also do not account for possible state and local income taxes that may affect the after-tax returns.

Table 7.3 After-tax rates of return comparison – years 2004 and 2005[2]

(1)	(2)	(3)	(4)	(5)
Federal tax bracket	After-tax return from a muni bond paying a tax-free yield of 6%	After-tax return from a bank paying 6% taxable	After-tax return from a corporate bond paying 7.5% taxable	Necessary rate of return for the investor to realize 6% after tax
15	6%	5.10%	6.38%	7.06%
26	6%	4.40%	5.55%	8.11%
29	6%	4.26%	5.33%	8.45%
34	6%	3.96%	4.95%	9.10%
37.6	6%	3.74%	4.68%	9.62%

[2]These figures represent the tax brackets for the years 2004 and 2005. It's important to remember that, as current tax law stands, the tax rates will continue to decrease until the year 2006. Neither Table 7.2 nor Table 7.3 accounts for the newly implemented 10-percent tax bracket.

income tax they pay isn't deductible or mostly deductible, their combined effective income tax rate is 39.4 percent. Then the after-tax yield on the bank CD would be 4.97 percent. It's important to remember that this analysis doesn't apply to U.S. Treasury securities or other direct government obligations because they are already exempt from state and local income taxes.

$$(1 - .394) \times 8.2\% = 4.97\%$$

Amounts are hypothetical.

There are many kinds of municipal bonds, in terms of how the bonds are backed financially. They include general-obligation bonds, special tax bonds, revenue bonds, insured municipal bonds and more.

GENERAL-OBLIGATION BONDS.   Municipal bonds are usually not secured by physical property; instead, they are debts payable from the state or local governments' general tax revenues. G-O bonds are normally considered to be high-quality and highly secure investments, in line with the creditworthiness of the issuer.

HOUSING AUTHORITY BONDS.   Housing authority bonds are issued to pay for low-rent housing projects and are backed by the promise of unconditional, annual contributions by the Housing Assistance Administration, a government agency. These bonds are considered among the highest in quality.

INDUSTRIAL DEVELOPMENT BONDS.   These bonds are issued either by a municipality or a municipal authority to finance and promote areas like industrial parks. They are backed by the lease payments made by the industrial companies that use or fill the facilities that are paid for by the bond issue.

Municipal bonds are also rated, just like corporate bonds are. The quality ratings for munis are second only to U.S. government and government agency securities. Moody's and Standard & Poor's, again, are the companies that rate these bonds.

INSURED MUNICIPAL BONDS.   Although state and local municipalities who issue bonds are generally thought to have good credit, and thus, have highly rated bond issues, many muni bonds carry insurance to protect the investors from the default risk. Any insurance carried on the bonds strengthens their credit rating, usually up to the highest level.

REVENUE BONDS. The principal and interest on revenue bonds is paid from the income received from specific projects or entities. Examples of revenue bonds are water, sewer, gas, and electrical facilities; bridges, turnpikes, tunnels and highways; and hospitals and power plants.

SPECIAL TAX BONDS. These bonds are usually backed and payable through a single tax, or series of special taxes. They may also be payable through another specific income source.

Municipal bonds can be prerefunded, and are also subject to high credit ratings. Prerefunding a bond issue means that the issuing municipality has purchased U.S. government securities that have the same maturity term as the municipal bond. These securities are then held in a special account, where they are the collateral for the muni bond, therefore reducing the risk of default.

Similar to corporate bonds, muni bonds also have an interest rate risk and call provisions. However, you must determine whether the tax-free interest outweighs the possibilities of having your bond redeemed prior to maturity or having the interest rate increase. Usually, though, investors in higher tax brackets enjoy having some municipal bonds in their portfolios to help increase their overall, after-tax return on their investments.

U.S. Government Obligations

There are a number of different kinds of marketable U.S. government securities, including Treasury bills, notes, and bonds.

TREASURY BILLS. Treasury bills are sold at a discount (less than the face value) and mature at face value. They mature at different periods, usually 13, 26, and 52 weeks. Bills are considered highly liquid, secure, short-term investments.

TREASURY NOTES. Treasury notes have maturities ranging from 1 year to 10 years. They are sold at or near their face value and pay their interest on a semiannual basis.

TREASURY BONDS. Treasury bonds also pay their interest on a semiannual basis and are sold at or near their par values. However, T-bonds have maturities that are greater than 10 years, going all the way up to 30 years. Generally, analysts use the 10-year and 30-year yields as benchmarks when discussing the economy and interest rates. Like T-bills and T-notes, Treasury bonds are highly secure investments.

Treasury bills aren't callable, due to their short-term maturities. Treasury notes are also not callable. However, Treasury bonds may be. Some longer-term bonds may be callable at par five years before they mature. Otherwise, they aren't callable. The fact that generally these securities aren't callable, coupled with their high credit rating, makes Treasury bills, notes, and bonds an important part of some investors' portfolios.

Generally, the interest and capital gains on Treasury notes and bonds is fully taxable for federal income tax purposes, but exempt from state and local income taxes. This somewhat increases the after-tax yield when compared with equivalent yields from corporate bonds or other interest-yielding accounts. If Treasury notes or bonds are purchased at a premium, the premium amount may be amortized over the remaining life of the bond, just as it can in the case of corporate bonds. The sale of Treasury notes and bonds also brings about the same result as corporate bonds when it comes to paying federal income tax.

INFLATION-INDEXED TREASURY NOTES AND BONDS. The U.S. Treasury has introduced Treasury Inflation-Protection securities. These are T-notes and bonds that have a fixed interest rate, which is applied to the principal amount that is adjusted for inflation or deflation periodically. The inflation or deflation amount is based on the adjusted consumer price index. These securities pay interest semiannually, just like regular T-notes and bonds, and the principal is paid upon maturity. This principal includes any inflation or deflation adjustments that have been made over the life of the security. At maturity, the greater amount of either the original par value or the inflation-adjusted principal will be paid. Therefore, if serious deflation occurs and at maturity your note or bond is not worth the original par value, you will receive the greater amount, in this case, the original par value. These notes and bonds are designed to protect investors from any inflation risk.

Because the principal amount and the interest paid on these are subject to adjustments, there are tax consequences. Each year, the investor will have gross income from not only the interest amount paid, but also the amount that the principal has been adjusted by, if the principal is increased for inflation. If the principal were decreased for inflation, the taxable amount would decrease. Even though the principal isn't paid until the bond or note matures, current tax law stipulates that the adjustments be taxable for the year in which they occur. Because of this, many advisors believe that these inflation-adjusted securities may be best for tax-qualified plans, such as IRAs, since the annual income isn't taxed until distributions begin.

For example, the Smiths decide to purchase a 10-year inflation-indexed Treasury note with the face value of $10,000. Its current coupon rate is four percent. Let's assume that for the year following the Smith's purchase, inflation is 3.5 percent. At the end of that year, the note's principal amount would be adjusted to $10,350; the interest paid to the Smiths would be based on this new amount, or $414 per year. The principal amount will continue to be adjusted like this for the lifetime of the note. Thus, the corresponding interest rate will also adjust to the new principal amount each year.

$$\text{Face value} = \$10,000 \times \text{Interest} = 4\% \times \text{Inflation} = 3.5\%$$
$$\text{New face value} = \$10,000 + 3.5\% = \$10,350$$
$$\text{New interest rate} = \$10,350 \times 4\% = \$414 \text{ (paid annually)}$$

All amounts are hypothetical.

U.S. Savings Bonds

There are two types of savings bonds that are currently being issued: the Series EE and Series HH. U.S. savings bonds are registered, nontransferable, and noncallable securities. Because they are nontransferable, they aren't marketable—you can't sell them to another party, you can only redeem them. They are also unable to be accepted as collateral for a loan because of this provision.

Series EE bonds are sold in par value amounts of $50 to $10,000, but the purchase price is 50 percent of the face value (i.e., you purchase a Series EE bond with a face value of $5000; your cost is $2500). Any single investor can purchase up to $15,000 in *face value* of EE bonds in a single calendar year. The other limitation on EE bonds is a maximum purchase of up to $15,000 par value each for bonds that are registered in co-ownership form. Series EE bonds do not pay current interest the way Treasury notes and bonds do; rather, they are issued at a discount and then pay face value upon maturity.

EE bonds do earn an interest rate that is 90 percent of the average return on marketable Treasury securities, which is called a market-based rate. This is set by the Treasury every six months. EE bonds may be redeemed at any time, provided the owner has held them for more than six months. Redemption within the first five years of the bond's life, though, will decrease the effective yield on the bond.

Upon redemption of EE bonds, the investor is taxed on the difference between the purchase price of the bond and the redemption price, but the interest on EE bonds may be tax-exempt in certain cases. If the principal from the bond is to be used for education, whether it is for your child, grandchild, or yourself, the interest is tax-free, provided your income meets certain limits. Any interest earned on a savings bond is also exempt from state and local income taxes.

Series EE bonds can be exchanged for Series HH bonds at par value. Like the EE bonds, the denominations for HH bonds range from $50 to $10,000. Unlike the EEs, HH bonds pay interest semi-annually. They can also be redeemed at any time, as long as they have been held for at least six months. However, they can be held for up to 20 years to accrue interest. By exchanging EE bonds for HH bonds, an investor can be privy to a long period of tax deferral. As long as the EE bonds are exchanged for HH bonds not more than one year after the EE bonds mature, the tax due on all the interest earned on the EE bonds is deferred until the HH bonds are redeemed.

U.S. Government Agency Securities

While these types of securities are not issued directly from the U.S. government, they do carry some federal guarantees. Some of the agencies that issue these securities are the Federal National Mortgage Association (commonly referred to as Fannie Mae), the Government National Mortgage Association (Ginnie Mae), Federal Farm

Credit Bank, Federal Home Loan Mortgage Corporation (Freddie Mac), and the International Bank for Reconstruction and Development (World Bank). Typically, the yields on these securities are greater than regular U.S. government securities.

PASS-THROUGH SECURITIES. These securities, also known as participation securities, are characterized by participation in a pool of assets from which investors receive certificates documenting their claims in the underlying assets. The most common of these are the Ginnie Mae pass-throughs. These certificates entitle investors to acquire high mortgage yields with both the principal and interest payments guaranteed by the federal government.

An important characteristic of these securities is that, unlike corporate or muni bonds, T-notes, and T-bonds, a portion of the principal is repaid with every interest payment as the underlying mortgages in the asset pool are amortized by the borrowers. This way, the investor is receiving a higher level of secure income. However, pass-through securities are highly susceptible to interest rate risk. As the interest rate drops, borrowers are more likely to refinance their debt, thus paying off the mortgages and returning the principal to the participation investors. The investors would then have to reinvest this money at a lower interest rate.

There is a number of different types of pass-through securities. Participation in pools of mortgages is called mortgage-based securities and participation in pools of consumer loans is called asset-backed securities. Collateralized mortgage obligations are a type of mortgage-based securities, but they may have some different investment characteristics.

Zero-Coupon Bonds

Zero-coupon bonds (zeros) are bonds in which there is no stated coupon rate, and so there is no current interest paid on them. Zeros are also sold at a discount, which is usually quite substantial. Their return to the investor is measured by their yield to maturity.

For example, you wish to purchase a zero with a face value of $10,000 and a maturity date of 2018. You buy it for $2000. Because it is a zero-coupon bond, you will receive no interest payments. However, when the bond matures in 2018, you will receive the $10,000. However, if you were to sell the bond before it matures, you would realize a gain (or loss) if the sale price is more (or less) than your adjusted tax basis in the bond.

Any type of bond can be a zero-coupon bond. They don't just have to be municipals or corporate bonds. The primary benefit of zeros to investors is that they can lock in current interest rates for the duration of the bond. Investors are attracted to zeros because they allow an investor to accumulate a fixed amount of money by a specified date, lock in the current interest rate until maturity, and there is no call risk in most circumstances. But if you need current income before the bonds mature, you should consider purchasing bonds that pay current interest. Zeros may also be used for the long-term end of a bond portfolio since there is generally no call risk.

U.S. government zero-coupon bonds and corporate zero-coupon bonds (issued after July 1, 1982) are currently taxable as ordinary income to the investor even though the investor receives no current interest income from the bonds. The amount that is taxable is the annual amount of accrued original-issue discount. This is calculated by applying the bond's yield to maturity to an adjusted issue price. Because taxable zeros cause the investor to pay taxes, they are generally held in tax-qualified plans such as IRAs and qualified retirement plans. Holding zeros in these types of plans is beneficial to the investor because no tax is due on these until distributions begin.

Municipal zero-coupon bonds are, like other muni bonds, tax-exempt. For these bonds, accrued original-issue discount is not included in the investor's gross income; it is tax-exempt. Therefore, municipal zeros are more frequently held in direct ownership by investors.

Discount Bonds

Sometimes bonds sell on the open market at a price substantially less than their par value. These bonds aren't to be confused with original-issue discount bonds, which are sold at a price that is less than their face value at the time of issue. This is usually the result of rising interest rates, which cause bond prices to fall. These bonds are referred to as "market discount bonds." Investors like these bonds for many reasons. One, market discount bonds grant the investor an automatic call protection since their coupon rates are relatively low when compared with current market interest rates. Two, the bond issuers must generally pay at least face value when the bond is redeemed, which would increase the issuer's cost of the call. All types of bonds, including Treasury bonds and municipals, may be sold at deep discount. The accessibility to market discount bonds depends on the current interest rate. The more the interest rate rises, the more discount bonds you will be able to find; the reverse is also true.

For tax purposes, any gain between the market discount and the resulting value from the sale, redemption, or maturity of the bond will be taxed as ordinary interest income, instead of capital gains, as long as the taxable bonds were issued after July 18, 1984 *or* the bonds were issued on or before July 18, 1984 and purchased on the open market after April 30, 1993. If there is a gain greater than this amount, it will be taxed at capital gains tax rates. Likewise, any loss will be treated as a capital loss. For other taxable bonds, any gain from the sale, redemption or maturity of the bonds will be taxed at capital gains rates.

For those cash-basis bondholders, an election may be made to include the accrued market discount each year in their gross income, and have it taxed annually. However, this usually doesn't happen. If the investor has any unused interest expenses that may only be deducted against interest income, this choice would be helpful.

Any tax-exempt market discount bonds (munis) that were purchased after April 30, 1993 and that had a gain between the market discount and the resulting value from the sale, redemption, or maturity of the bond will be taxed as ordinary interest income, instead of a capital gain.

INFORMATION ABOUT BONDS

You can find information about bonds in the same places you would find information about stocks and mutual funds. Below are examples of how to read the quotes for different types of bonds as they may appear in a publication such as the *Wall Street Journal*.

In the example below, there are three bond quotes. For the first quote, we see that a corporate bond for ABC company is being

Bond quotes

	Cur. Yield	Vol.	Close	Net Change
ABC 8½05	7.8	30	108	+¼—corporate
RST 4s06	cv	11	62	−¼—convertible
XYZ zr04	--	20	64½	+½—zero-coupon

traded. The row of numbers immediately following the symbol signifies what the coupon rate is, as well as when the bond matures. So for this example, the coupon is 8.5 percent, and the bond matures sometime in the year 2005. This information is vital because it helps investors distinguish between the different bonds. This company may have issued several different bonds. Thus, for investors to identify properly which bond they hold, the yield and year of maturity is needed. The second set of numbers, in this case 7.8, provides the bond's current yield. This is found by dividing the bond's annual interest amount by its current price (8.5 ÷ 108). The "Vol." column specifies how many bonds were traded on that day. Here, we see that 30 bonds were traded. The last two columns contain price information. Note that there is a difference between the bond quotes and stock quotes. Instead of showing a high, low, and closing price for the bonds (as is done with stocks), there is just a closing price and the change in price from the previous trading day. Bond prices are quoted as a percent of par value. Par value is $1000. Therefore, in the ABC quote, we see that the closing price for the bond was 108 percent of par, or $1080 (108% × 1000).

For the next example, we have a convertible bond. Convertibles are listed along with the rest of corporate bonds and zeros. They are easily identified because they are listed along with the letters "cv" under the "current yield" column. All the rest of the information about the bond is identical to the ABC corporate bond. The final example is for a zero-coupon bond from the XYZ corporation. Instead of listing a coupon rate along with the maturity year, there are the letters "zr," indicating that the bond is a zero-coupon. In this case, the bond will mature sometime during the year 2004. Also, look at its closing price of $64^1/_2$. This means the bond was trading at $645. If investors hold this bond until maturity, they will receive 33 percent more than if they were to sell the bond on the open market.

Treasury bond quotes

Rate	Maturity (mo/yr)	Bid	Asked	Change	Ask Yld.
8 ½	Feb 08	122:21	122:29	−15	5.87
12 ¾	Mar 06-11	117:13	117:31	−12	5.96

In the preceding box, there are two quotes for Treasury bonds. The first quote is for a bond that matures in February of 2008. The rate column is the same as the coupon rate shown in the corporate bond example. Treasury bonds are quoted in 30-seconds of a point. Therefore, the bid price for the first bond is 122 21/32 (122.656 percent of par) and the asked price is 122 29/32 (122.906 percent of par). If you wanted to purchase 10 of these bonds (with a par value of $10,000), you would pay $12,265.60 ($10,000 × 1.22656). However, if you wanted to buy $10,000 worth of these bonds, you would only buy eight bonds (10,000 ÷ 1226.56) because each bond is trading at $1,225.65.

The second quote is for a callable bond. This is indicated by the notation under the "maturity" column, where it lists the bond as "Mar 06-11." The first date, in this case the year 2006, is when the bond first becomes freely callable. However, the bond is due to mature in March of 2011. Thus, if there is only one date under the maturity column, the bond isn't callable.

CASH INVESTMENTS

Most of us think of the money we carry in our wallets as cash, and that's it. Cash, though, has a broader definition than just the coins and bills we use to pay for goods. It is also the type of investment characterized by a high level of liquidity and little to no risk to your original investment.

Generally, cash investments are short-term, interest-bearing securities that offer investors the opportunity to collect a specified interest rate, keep a high level of security and maintain liquidity with their money. The most commonly used cash investments are bank savings accounts, certificates of deposits (CDs), and money market funds. Some employer-sponsored retirement plans may offer guaranteed investment contracts, which are another form of cash investments.

Cash investments are best used for emergency funds. This is money you want to have some return on, but if you needed it, you could have it in hand very quickly. This may also be money that you would like to invest in the near future, but haven't quite decided which investments are right for you. Because these investments are highly liquid, they tend to offer lower returns than other investments might. Most of these investments also don't have any surrender charges for withdrawing the money.

The Federal Deposit Insurance Corporation insures passbook accounts, money market deposit accounts, and CDs that are issued by its member banks and savings and loan institutions up to a maximum of $100,000. For cash investments offered by credit unions, there is a federal deposit insurance agency that differs from the FDIC.

Any interest earned on savings accounts or money market deposit accounts is fully taxable for federal income tax purposes.

Savings Accounts

Savings accounts, or passbook accounts, are found at any bank, credit union, or savings and loan institution. Because they are extremely liquid, they are characterized as having extremely low interest rates. Passbook accounts also tend not to have check-writing privileges. Most banks also offer interest-bearing checking accounts. However, the interest on these accounts tends to be less than that on savings accounts and there may be quite high minimum balances required in order to qualify to receive interest. Any interest received on either a savings account or a checking account is taxed as ordinary income.

Money Market Deposit Accounts

Money market deposit accounts, which differ from money market mutual funds, typically offer a higher rate of interest than a savings account would. However, there is usually a minimum deposit, and the institution may charge a fee if your balance falls below the required minimum. Money market deposit accounts are federally insured, while money market mutual funds are not. The interest rates for these accounts tend to be less than they would be on other, longer-term, less liquid accounts, such as CDs. There is typically no surrender charge for withdrawing your money. Interest received on these accounts is taxed as ordinary income.

Money Market Mutual Funds

These are among the most popular types of investments today. Money market funds invest in Treasury bills, jumbo CDs (CDs that have a certain minimum amount, such as $100,000), commercial paper, and other short-term, interest-bearing securities. The securities held by money market funds tend to have a maturity between 30 and 90 days. Generally, the interest earned on money market funds is greater than that earned on savings and money market deposit accounts.

Some money market funds hold short-term municipal securities, which would entitle the money market fund investor to tax-exempt interest. Both taxable and tax-exempt funds usually offer check writing and telephone-transfer (to another fund within the same fund family) privileges.

Money market funds may be offered through stock brokerage firms and mutual fund companies. Neither the Federal Deposit Insurance Corporation nor any other government agency guarantees an investment in a money market fund.

Certificates of Deposit

CDs are deposits made to a bank or savings and loan institution for a specific period of time, usually a minimum of three to six months all the way up to 10 years. They are insured by the FDIC and offer a fixed rate of return and fixed principal value. While these are cash investments, they aren't as liquid as a savings account or a money market fund. Because of that, they are known to pay a higher interest rate. Typically, CDs offer tiered interest rates: the more money you put in, the higher the interest rate will be. This also works for however long you invest your money. Generally, the longer your money is in a CD, the better an interest rate you will receive. You may also be able to purchase CDs that have variable interest rates. Since your money will be tied up for a specified time period, there may be a surrender charge for redeeming the CD early.

Banks, credit unions, and savings and loan institutions aren't the only place to purchase CDs. This will help if you decide you want to invest in one because you can shop around for the best interest rate. Many stock brokerage houses sell CDs that were issued by banks or credit unions. Through brokered CDs, you may have access to a secondary market for your CD, which could negate the possible surrender charge. They may also offer slightly higher interest rates.

Because you lock in your interest rate when you initially invest your money in a CD, you may be subject to interest rate risk. When the interest rate begins to rise, the corresponding rates on CDs will also rise. By locking in your rate earlier, you will be earning less than if you were earning the current rate. Plus, you wouldn't be able to pull your money out to reinvest at a higher rate without incurring some type of early withdrawal penalty. Interest paid on CDs is fully taxable for federal and state income taxes. However, the surrender penalty may be deductible from your gross income for tax purposes.

There are also market-linked CDs, which are tied to an equity index, like the S&P 500 stock index. These CDs have an FDIC-guaranteed principal, but their return is based on the market's actions, provided that the investor has held the CD until maturity. For example, if you purchased a market-linked CD (MLD) for $5000 and the applicable market index increased, at maturity you would receive your principal of $5000 plus a return based on the index's appreciation. However, should the market go down, you wouldn't receive any return on your money. You would simply receive your original investment of $5000 back. If you were to redeem or sell the MLD prior to maturity, chances are you wouldn't receive 100 percent of your principal.

For tax purposes, the gain on the investment is taxed annually as ordinary income even though the investor sees no current interest income from the MLD. This is why MLDs are usually held in tax-qualified plans.

Commercial Paper

Commercial paper securities are short-term promissory notes issued time to time by major corporations. They typically have maturities from 30 to 270 days, and fairly high minimum amounts like $10,000. The only asset securing these investments is the financial strength of the issuing company. Historically, this has been quite good. Commercial paper may be purchased through broker/dealers and commercial banks. These are considered money market investments because they are shorter-term, high quality securities. Most often, commercial paper is purchased by money market mutual funds and other lenders that are interested in short-term, liquid investments. The interest and any gain on commercial paper are fully taxable.

Guaranteed Investment Contracts

Within many employer-sponsored retirement accounts, such as 401(k)s, guaranteed investment contracts (GICs) are an option. GICs are fixed-interest-bearing contracts generally issued by insurance companies. Since they are purchased through retirement plans, they are, in essence, a contract between the employer and the issuing company. The issuing company accepts funds for investment for a specific period of time during which the money will earn a guaranteed interest rate or rates, and guarantees both the GIC's principal and interest for the specified time period. The participating employee may then elect to invest all or some of their money in the plan's fixed-interest account, to the extent that the plan allows. It's through the GIC that the plan provides for the fixed-interest account. The employee's money may stay in this account for as long as the employee wishes, or for as long as the GIC lasts. Typically, GICs have maturation periods of three to five years. At maturity, the employer and issuing company may enter into a new GIC. This new GIC may have a different interest rate, given the current interest rates and market conditions. Representative current GIC interest rates for certain amounts and time periods may be found in the financial pages of some publications.

GICs are backed by the issuing company. Therefore, when considering investing your money through a GIC, you should take a look at the financial soundness of the issuer. There are state guaranty funds that cover insurance companies, but there is no federal government insurance covering GICs that would be comparable to the FDIC's insuring bank deposits. While they aren't as safe as federal insurance protection, your principal will remain safe even when interest rates rise, barring default by the issuing company.

REAL ESTATE INVESTMENT TRUSTS

Real estate investment trusts, or REITs, are corporations or business trusts that meet federal tax law requirements to be a REIT. They function like closed-end mutual funds, which we discuss in Chapter 5. REITs generally invest in real estate and offer their investors marketability, centralized management, limited liability, and continuity of interests. Plus, REITs can avoid corporate income tax because they pass their earnings along to their shareholders. The distributions are taxed as ordinary income to the shareholder. However, they cannot pass along their losses.

The type of real estate behind a REIT can vary considerably between the different issuing companies. For instance, one REIT may hold the property of hotels, while another may hold restaurants. REITs may also differ in size and origin. While some REITs may be a mix of different types of real estate, some specialize in particular kinds.

Many REITs are traded on organized stock exchanges, and therefore, will be followed and evaluated by independent researchers and firms. There are some that aren't publicly traded, and aren't independently evaluated. When you purchase shares of a REIT that isn't publicly traded, there is almost no secondary market for the shares, which may result in you selling your shares at a possibly reduced rate, sometimes dramatically reduced, depending upon the buyer.

While last year proved to be a poor year for stocks and mutual funds, it was a good year for REITs. Many mutual funds were struggling just to break even, but depending on which index you looked at, REITs were pulling in a total return in the mid-20-percent range. Plus, the dividend yield for many REITs last year was around 11 percent. That's a far cry from the stocks and mutual funds that most people were invested in. Rather than lose money last year on their investments, my clients who were invested in REITs saw that segment of their portfolios make money.

Three different types of REITs exist: equity, mortgage, and hybrid. Equity REITs get their income from rents and capital gains from the property they own. Mortgage REITs derive their income primarily from the interest income from mortgage loans they enter into. Hybrid REITs are combinations of the equity and mortgage REITs.

There are other ways to invest in real estate, including buying and developing land, purchasing rental properties, limited partnerships, etc. However, I usually advise my clients to invest in REITs, when it is appropriate. I feel that the centralized management and the pass-through of income, which has been as high as 11 percent, outweigh the possible advantages of direct ownership.

It's important to note that although the income that is distributed by the REIT to its shareholders is taxable to the shareholders, it's not when the REIT is held in a qualified retirement plan (like an IRA) and reinvested. This is because the interest can flow into a separate account. However, if the qualified plan owner decides to take the interest payments as income, they will be taxed.

WHY BONDS, CASH, AND REITS ARE IMPORTANT

Bonds play an important role in asset allocation because they can provide a level of stability to an investor's portfolio. No wealthy person has become rich, and stayed rich, without some type of bond in his or her portfolio. Bonds, cash investments, and real estate are the cement in a portfolio. They weather the down markets, when all your equity investments are giving you heartache, all the while generating interest income for you, which you can either reinvest, or use currently. For people who are naturally timid about investing, holding REITs, bonds, and cash is essential. However, remember that the price of the bonds and REITs will vary, as do equity investments. The cash positions held by investors will continue to increase, albeit at a slower pace due to the low nature of interest rates for cash securities. Although they tend to look bad when the market is booming and your equity investments keep rising, bonds and REITs provide current income that you may need if you have a large tax bill due to the capital gains and dividends provided by your equity investments. Plus, tax-exempt bonds give you tax-free income now.

One major advantage to REITs is that they offer some protection from inflation. Inflation has a negative effect on equities. As inflation increases, the buying power of our dollar decreases; thus, the buying power of the value of our equity accounts is also less. However, as prices rise, real estate prices also tend to rise. This inflation effect provides a benefit to the REIT investor because it is reflected in the REIT price, and possibly, the corresponding dividends.

Bonds, cash, and REITs may not be as exciting or glamorous as stocks or mutual funds, but they play an essential part in a smart investor's portfolio. Without them, your portfolio may not be adequately diversified.

8

WHEN GOOD INVESTING GOES BAD

In Chapter 3, we discussed how to begin investing. Although that is a very important part to building wealth, it's just as important to figure out how and when you will begin investing. Throughout subsequent chapters, we discuss the different investment vehicles and types of securities that exist, so that you can educate yourself and make better decisions about how you want to establish your portfolio. Now that we've distinguished between the different investment types, we talk about different things that can knock you and your portfolio off course, as well as how to get back on track. These pitfalls include trying to "time" the market, day trading, and buying on margin. Here, we also discuss dollar-cost averaging and the buy-and-hold strategy. Finally, we look at the strategy of selling stocks short, which can be both beneficial and detrimental to your investment portfolio and long-term goals.

TIMING THE MARKET

The concept of market timing is very seductive. After all, who wouldn't want to be in the market during the good times and out of the market during the down times? Market timing is just like a crapshoot. Sure, you may get lucky and wind up gaining more than you anticipated. Or, perhaps, you happened to buy into a stock just before it skyrocketed. But how often does that happen? More importantly, what happens when you don't time the market well?

The key to successful investing isn't timing the market; it's time in the market. Investing and staying invested is a long-term way to build your future. Even when the market is down, or going through some turbulent times, it's better to stay invested than to sell and try to buy later. Especially when faced with short-term market corrections, getting out of the market may prove to be more devastating than sticking it out.

During a bear market, my clients will call and ask my opinion about when I think the market will start to come back. Unfortunately, the fact remains that no one is able to predict what the market is going to do. This leads many people to try and time the market. I also get calls from clients asking me to sell all their equities and put them into a cash position. They say that they will then reinvest when the market starts to come back. What they don't realize is that by the time they think the market is "on its way back up," they have already missed out on 10–20 percent in growth. By selling during a down market, you turn paper losses into actual losses.

Recently, when the market started to go down dramatically, I had a client call and want to liquidate his entire portfolio. He was upset that the market had continued to slide and that he was losing money. He was also concerned because he was taking monthly income out of his investments, which impacted the account values, as well. His overall portfolio was valued at more than one million dollars when we had this conversation. Although he didn't come out and say it, he was scared about losing his money, and wanted to protect himself against any further losses. He wanted to me to sell everything and put it into a cash account. At that time, the money market funds were offering interest rates of about four percent.

I talked with my client, trying to reassure him and convince him that liquidating the entire position was a very unwise idea. Even with all the reasons I presented to him, he was still very upset and firm that he wanted everything in a cash account. One thing that helped me convince him not to cash everything in was his wife. Although she was terrified, as he was, that they were going to lose their money, she knew that by selling everything they would turn their paper losses into actual losses. Together, she and I convinced my client not to liquidate everything. We agreed to move a portion of the money into a money market fund, and that he would draw his monthly income from there, rather than from another account. Even though this wasn't what he truly felt he wanted, he was comfortable with this. And I was glad that he agreed not to sell everything.

I was able to talk him down from moving all his money to moving about 10 percent. Later, as the market continued to decline, he and his wife came in for an appointment. We discussed being invested in the market versus keeping the money in a money market fund. When we initially moved the money, the money market account was earning about 4 percent; when we met for our appointment, it was closer to 3.25 percent. Since my client was taking out nearly 7 percent annually, we knew we had to change something. At that rate he was guaranteed to lose almost 4 percent per year.

We discussed moving his money back into the market. At first, he was a little resistant, but he knew that he had better reinvest, rather than try to time the market. I explained that by holding out until he felt the market was coming back, he was really doing himself a disservice because he was putting himself in the position of missing out on potential growth. During that meeting, we reinvested his money in the stock market.

I know that it sounds like that really isn't the case; that by taking his money out and then reinvesting it he was doing better, but we discuss that in the buy-and-hold section of this chapter.

When it comes to timing the market, history has proven that it doesn't work. (See Table 8.1.) Investors willing to stick out the short-term declines have been rewarded with large gains over the long run. In fact, missing just a few days, even during booming markets, can drastically impact the return on your portfolio. Unfortunately, many

Table 8.1: Should I Get Out of the Market?[1]

Period of Investment	Average Annual Total Return
Fully invested	18.33%
Missed the 10 best days	9.24%
Missed the 20 best days	2.98%
Missed the 30 best days	−2.07%
Missed the 40 best days	−6.38%
Missed the 60 best days	−13.07%

[1]This is based upon the S&P 500 returns from January 1, 1996–December 31, 2000. By jumping in and out of the market, the investor dramatically reduces the returns over time. Note that by just missing the 10 best days, the total return is reduced by nearly 50%. Missing the 60 best days would have reduced the overall return nearly 200%.

Source: American Express Funds.

investors have been sucked in by this type of get-rich-quick form of investing. Because of their actions, there have been some wild days on the market, as prices go up and down.

DAY TRADING

Day trading is just another form of trying to time the market. However, the turnaround time between buying and selling the equities is much shorter than for people who are engaging in market timing. As with market timing, people who day trade may find that their portfolios are in a far worse condition than if they had just left well enough alone.

Essentially, day trading involves purchasing stock at a, hopefully, very low price. Then, over the course of a short period of time, the trader watches the price of the stock very closely. Should the stock increase in price to where the trader would make a profit, the trader then sells the stock and purchases a different stock. Sometimes this means selling the stock when it is just a few cents higher than the purchasing price. Usually, the trader doesn't hold the stock for more than a few days. Sometimes it is just hours, even minutes that the trader holds the stock.

Notice that I am referring to day "traders" as "traders" and not investors. The distinction lies in the process. Investors seek to make money through a variety of securities and equities over a long period of time, while traders strive to make a quick profit in the least amount of time possible. Although we would all like to see our account values increase more quickly than slowly, history has shown that investment results become more and more positive, and larger, over longer periods of time.

Day traders will find that the more they buy and sell looking for that quick profit, they will wind up not only not making the profits they expect and hope for, but also they will wind up causing themselves more harm than good. The first ill of day trading is the enormous cost of commissions paid to brokerage houses. Traders usually don't use advisors or regular brokers to execute their trades for them. Rather, they sit in front of a computer and watch the stock market ticker line go by, as well as watching the prices of the individual stocks they own. Day trading really became popular with the advent of online brokerage firms, such as Datek and E*Trade. With these, the traders could put in a relatively small amount of money and then do all the trading themselves. (Brokerage firms generally require a higher minimum opening balance than on-line firms.)

Even though these traders are handling all their own trading, the on-line brokerage firms continue to charge them commissions or execution fees. There is one on-line brokerage that advertises trades for $8 apiece. Many people don't realize that a buy and a sell are two separate trades, not one. For day traders who are buying and selling many different stocks a day, or even over a period of a few weeks, that cost adds up significantly. For example, John Q. Client opens up an account over the Internet because he wants to "take advantage" of day trading. This on-line firm charges $8 per trade. He initially purchases three different stocks, XYZ Corporation, DEF Conglomerate, and RST, Inc. All of these stocks are trading at relatively low prices, and John thinks that they will go up. He is right; each of the three stocks go up within a few hours. John sells each of the stocks and purchases four more different stocks. He thinks day trading is fabulous because in a matter of hours, he has already made a profit. But what he hasn't thought about is his trading costs, which total $80.

John's trading costs—day 1:

>3 initial purchases at $8/trade   = $24
>3 sells at $8/trade   = $24
>4 subsequent purchases at $8/trade = $32
>**Total trading costs   = $80**

Let's assume that John continues to day trade for two weeks. The second day he begins with the four companies he purchased on day one. He then sells them during the course of the day and purchases four more. This pattern continues for a total trading time of two weeks (10 trading days, with no extended-hours trading). John's trading costs skyrocket to $656.

John's total trading costs:

>4 sells per day at $8/trade   = $32/day
>4 purchases per day at $8/trade = $32/day
>9 trading days at $64/day   = $576
>Day 1 trading costs   = $80

Perhaps during this time, John has been able to make at least $656 in profits from his trading activities. However, if he hasn't, then he will find out that he has actually been costing himself money by engaging in day trading.

Currently, I have a handful of clients who prefer to do some of their trading on their own. They have separate brokerage accounts through my firm, but they handle all their own trading over the Internet. Through these accounts, they buy and sell whatever individual stocks they want, at whatever volumes they want. However, none of these people qualifies as a day trader because they aren't actively trading all the time.

Trading costs are the immediate effect of day trading, but what about the long-term effects? At the end of the year, brokerage firms prepare 1099-DIV and 1099-B forms for all of their clients. These forms report to the IRS the capital gains, dividends, and sale proceeds for all trades and investments the clients hold or did hold at some point throughout the year. For day traders, like other investors, any gains that were made during the year must be claimed on their federal income tax forms. However, because these gains were made on trades where the trader held the stocks for days or other short periods of time, these gains are taxed at the less-favorable short-term capital gains rate, which is the trader's income tax bracket. So, reverting to our previous example, if John shows an overall capital gain of $5000, he will have to claim that as a short-term capital gain, which will be taxed at his ordinary income tax rate. This means that under the new tax law, this gain could be subject to a maximum tax rate of 38.6 percent. Had he held these stocks longer than one year before he sold them, the gain would be taxed as a long-term capital gain, which is a maximum of 20 percent.

And what happens if the market starts to go down, as it has over the past year? Well, then day traders are pretty much stuck. Their goal is to make money as quickly as possible, not to research companies, then buy and hold those stocks. For the most part, if the market goes down, day traders will sell their stocks for a loss, which could be substantial depending on which stocks they hold.

BUYING ON MARGIN

As a rule, I generally try to dissuade my clients, or anyone, from buying securities on margin (credit). The reason is that it's just too risky, especially with the way the market has been behaving over the past two years. While I am not going into too much detail about buying on margin, I am saying this. When the market is gaining, buying on margin can be great. However, when the market starts to head south, buying on margin can kill you financially.

This is how margin works. Let's say you have $200,000 that you want to invest. You would like to invest more money than that, but you only have the $200,000 available right now. You open an account with a brokerage firm, who then approves you for margin trading. (Not everyone can trade on margin—you really do have to be approved.) By law, the brokerage house can loan you up to 50 percent of the total purchase price for stocks. So, let's assume that you would like to purchase a total of $300,000 of XYZ common stock. You invest your $200,000 and you purchase the remaining $100,000 on margin. The maximum margin amount for this example would be $200,000, making the total investment amount $400,000.) You now owe the brokerage house $100,000. They can, and will, charge you some form of interest on that balance. Make sure that if you do trade on margin, you know what kind of interest rates and payments are applicable.

After the initial purchase, you own $300,000 worth of XYZ common. Now, assuming the market goes up, your share increases, not the part you bought on margin. If the price doubles, your shares would be worth $600,000. Of that $600,000, your portion is worth $500,000. You still owe the house $100,000. At this point, you could sell $100,000 worth of stock, plus whatever amount was needed to satisfy the interest owed on the loan, and pay back your loan to the brokerage house to clear up your debt. Then, your portion would continue to go up and down with the market.

Your share	= $200,000
Margin purchase (loan)	= $100,000
Total investment	= $300,000
Market price doubles; account value	= $600,000
Your share	**= $500,000**

Sounds great, right? Now let's assume that the market goes down instead of up. Rather than your investment doubling in price, it's now worth only 40 percent of what you paid, or $120,000. How much is your share worth now? A tidy $20,000. You still owe the house the whole $100,000. And if the price of the stock drops much more, the brokerage house will give you a call and ask you for its money. If the price drops substantially, they will sell off your position to satisfy as much of the loan as possible.

Your share	= $200,000
Margin purchase (loan)	= $100,000
Total investment	= $300,000
Market drops by 60%; investment worth	= $120,000
Your share	= $20,000
Loan balance	**= $100,000**

This is the risk of investing on margin. There are specific rules that govern margin accounts that spell out when the brokerage house can sell your securities and when they can ask for their money back because the market price for the security has dropped. If you have the cash to satisfy these margin calls and can pay off your debt with interest to the brokerage house, then you are in the clear. However, if you don't, then you have to look at liquidating some of your other assets to cover the payment. Like I said, investing on margin is great when the market goes up. You purchase more securities with the money you borrow from the brokerage house, your investment goes up faster because you own more shares, the brokerage firm is making money off of you in the form of interest, and everyone is happy. However, it's not so great when the market goes down. Unfortunately, no one knows what the market is going to do, which poses another risk to investing on margin.

BUY-AND-HOLD STRATEGY

There are ways to make money in the stock market, as long as you are patient. The stock market is the best place to try and make money, because it offers many diverse companies (varying in size and sector) in which to invest. And while there will always be stories of those people who made their money in the market very quickly, the majority of successful investors are those patient people who employ a buy-and-hold tactic.

This approach is used most widely by mutual fund investors. They research the funds they are interested in, buy them, and then hold onto them throughout the good times and the bad. This is a very good approach to investing, but it does have a downside, too. Buy-and-hold should be applied to those investments and equities that make up the core of your portfolio. Use this approach to building your core and to help provide some stability. Those funds or equities that are a part of this core are rarely traded and should be held for at least a couple of years.

If you chose to employ this strategy for your investments, be sure to research not only the mutual fund you will be using it for, but the manager as well. Although I do tend to look at past performance of a mutual fund as part of my research, I also pay close attention to the fund manager. Often times there are new, or newer, funds that don't have any type of track record to go by. These same funds may have the same fund manager as another, successful fund. While this doesn't guarantee that the new mutual fund will enjoy the same success that the other fund did, it will help calm those fears of investing in an unproven mutual fund. Chances are, the new fund will be subject to the same rigorous standards and practices that the other fund is.

You also want to take a look at what the manager is doing with his or her funds. If the market is overpriced, as it was during the last few years of the 1990s, then you want to see that the mutual fund manager is taking steps to make sure that a market correction is not going to hurt the fund. However, knowing if that's the case is not as easy as it sounds, since mutual funds are protected by the Securities and Exchange Commission and aren't required to disclose what their positions are in their underlying equities at all times. The most recent information will either be in the fund's annual report and prospectus or on the fund family's Web site.

Whatever the market conditions are, though, you want to feel confident that your mutual fund manager will be able to react appropriately to help protect the mutual fund and its shareholders. Sometimes, funds will have a limit on what the managers can do. These limits will be listed in the fund's prospectus. The more limits, the less action the manager can take and vice versa. Ideally, you want to see that there are few limits placed upon the fund manager. If there are few limits, the fund manager needs to have a lot of experience to deal with whatever the market throws at investors.

The buy-and-hold strategy should be used the most during bear markets simply because it's not a smart idea to be trading a lot when the market is down. Try not to be too worried about what happens during a down market. It's just a time when investors aren't buying a lot of equities. However, for many people it is the perfect time to jump in, which is why the market will go back up.

You should hold onto your securities because no one can predict the market, and thus, you won't know when the market will begin to rebound. You don't want to miss out on any potential growth just because you couldn't wait for the markets to go back up. My advice for surviving bear markets? Don't look. Don't look at your state-ments, don't look at how the markets are doing on a daily basis, and try to concentrate on other things. I know that is tough. I have many clients who are guilty of watching and charting their investments on a daily basis. These same people want to get out of their investments when the market goes down and then reinvest when the market begins to go back up. As I've said before, you don't know when this will happen and by pulling out of the market, you may miss out on potential growth before you reenter it. (Again, please refer to Table 8.1 for a comparison of what happens when you miss some of the market's best-performing days.)

Special note: Don't be afraid to sell a mutual fund, stock, or other investment that is not performing very well and hasn't been performing very well. Sometimes investments don't come back from their poor performance, and sometimes they will. However, there are occasions when you need to evaluate your portfolio and cut your losses.

DOLLAR-COST AVERAGING

Another strategy designed to combat the unknown elements of the stock market is called "dollar-cost averaging," or DCA. When we discussed systematically investing over a period of time, we touched on DCA. Although we didn't mention it specifically, DCA can pro-vide a good means of getting your feet wet in the market without the potential headache of jumping in headfirst. The tenet of DCA is sim-ple: By investing systematically over a long period of time, you will normally see that you have a lower average cost per share, which can help increase your overall return.

Because no one knows from one day to the next what the market is going to do, investing over several months rather than in one lump sum amount may be a better idea for those investors who are a little more squeamish about investing, or who have a lower risk tolerance. Employing DCA also means that you may wind up purchasing shares at their 52-week high, but you may also buy shares at their all-time low. Over time, the cost of the shares averages out, so that you are neither paying top dollar, nor are you paying bargain basement prices. But employing the DCA method doesn't guarantee a profit, nor will it insure you against a loss.

Dollar-cost averaging is generally used for mutual funds, but may also be used within the subaccounts of annuities, which we discussed in Chapter 6. Let's assume that you want to invest a total of $50,000 in the XYZ Growth Fund, but you don't want to do it all at one time. Rather, you wish to spread out your investment because you don't know what the market is going to do. Therefore, you decide you want to invest $5000 per month for the next 10 months to make up your entire investment. By doing this, you will be purchasing shares at, presumably, 10 different prices, which could lower your average price per share, and thus, increase your potential for making a profit from this fund. (See Figure 8.1.)

Looking at Figure 8.1, which demonstrates a hypothetical situa-tion, as the price per share fluctuates over time, the investor is able to purchase shares at a variety of different prices, which then equal his average price per share. Notice that the hypothetical purchase prices run the gamut over the time frame. This strategy helps decrease the volatility of investing in a single security by investing over time, instead of in a lump sum. Figure 8.2 provides some more examples on dollar-cost averaging.

For investors who wish to invest in a lump sum, they need to be aware that they may wind up putting their money in at the height of the market, or they may be lucky enough to get in when the market is at a bottom point. This is not to say that one way is better than the other. That choice is up to individual investors and their levels of risk tolerance. If you, the investor, believe that the market will be going back up at the time you are ready to invest, then a lump sum invest-ment may be best. However, if you are unsure about which way the market will go, then perhaps using DCA is the best idea. Essentially, DCA is best for investors who have the cash flow to invest a set amount at regular intervals and aren't prone to try and decide whether the market is going to go up or go down. This strategy also works the best for those who like to invest and hold a position for a

Dollar-Cost Averaging

Date	Amount Invested	Market Price Paid	Number of Shares Purchased
4th Quarter 2000	$1000	$23.25/share	43.01
1st Quarter 2001	$1000	$22.75/share	43.95
2nd Quarter 2001	$1000	$28.75/share	34.78
3rd Quarter 2001	$1000	$30/share	33.33
4th Quarter 2001	$1000	$26.50/share	37.74
1st Quarter 2002	$1000	$22.50/share	44.44
2nd Quarter 2002	$1000	$16/share	62.5
	$7000		**299.75 shares**

Total amount invested over the seven quarters	= $7000
Total number of shares purchased	= 299.75
Average market price of shares	= $24.25
Average cost ($7000 ÷ 299.75)	= **$23.35 per share**

Figure 8.1: The above illustrates the advantage of dollar-cost averaging. By investing the same amount of money over a period of time, the investor will realize a different number of shares purchased each time at a different price. However, over time the investor's average cost per share decreases. There is also a difference between the average cost per share and the average market price, which adds to the investor's benefit. These figures are for illustration purposes only and aren't meant to indicate any type of investment performance. Dollar-cost averaging doesn't assure a profit against losses in a declining market. Investors should consider their ability to continue investing through periods of low market prices.

longer amount of time. Either way, the worst situation is to not be invested at all.

SELLING SHORT

When you purchase stocks, mutual funds, bonds, or another investment equity, you are making a long transaction. That is, you pay for securities that you anticipate, or hope, will increase in value, thus increasing your portfolio value. However, selling short is the opposite and is done in anticipation that the security will decline in value, which in return would earn you a profit. There are a number of risks associated with selling stocks short, just as there are with purchasing securities on margin. The difference in risk, though, between the two concepts could be described like this. If the market declines and you

**Dollar-cost averaging lets you participate
in the stock market, without having to time the market**

Jan Feb Mar Apr May Jun	Accumulated shares	Average market price per share	Your average cost per share
(1) $15 $10 $5 $10 $12 $14 $16 $18 $20	42.25	$15	$14.20
(2) $15 $10 $5 $10 $8 $5 $5 $8 $10	85.0	$7.66	$7.05
(3) $15 $10 $5 $10 $8 $5 $1 $1 $4	267.5	$4.83	$2.24

$100 invested per month. Total invested: $600.

Figure 8.2: This is a hypothetical illustration; it does not represent any particular investment. Dollar-cost averaging does not ensure a profit or avoid a loss if the market declines. Investors should consider their ability to continue investing during periods of low market prices.

Source: American Express Funds.

have purchased equities on margin, you become a liability to the brokerage house and yourself. If the market increases when you sell short, you become a liability to yourself.

Investors who practice short sales are generally more sophisticated and have a higher tolerance for risk. Short sales shouldn't be entered into lightly. If you are considering selling some securities short, make sure you have done adequate research and will be able to cover your position.

Selling a security short involves selling the equity that you don't already own. Rather, the brokerage house borrows the security for you to sell, and then later, you receive the proceeds from the sale. Of course, the borrowed shares must be replaced at some point in the future. This is why you hope the market price declines. If it does, then you purchase the stock at the lower price, and make a profit. This is the reverse order of the basic contrarian position (buy low, sell high) since you are selling high and then, hopefully, buying lower.

Selling short is a perfectly legal way to work with the market and make some money. There are a number of rules and regulations that protect the actual owner of the borrowed securities. For instance, you can only short a sale after the price of the stock has moved upward. Therefore, if the price of XYZ common stock goes from $25 per share to $25.50/share, then you can sell it short. However, if the price declines from $25.50 per share to $25 per share, you have to wait. Another rule is that the investor has to have a certain amount of money on hand with the brokerage firm prior to executing the sale. Even short sales require some sort of deposit of capital. You just can't walk into a firm and start selling stocks short! Finally, brokerage firms will hold the proceeds of the short sale until the borrowed stock has been replaced.

As an example, we assume that you want to short XYZ common stock. You sell 500 shares short at $28 per share. Your gross sale proceed is $14,000. (Trading costs and possibly commission will be deducted.) When you go to replace the borrowed stock, the price has dropped to $25 per share, meaning you purchase the shares for $12,500. You gain $1500 on the sale of stock you never owned.

Shares sold short	= 500
Selling price	= $28/share
Proceed from sale	= $14,000
Purchase price for 500 shares	= $25/share
Total purchase price	= $12,500
Gain (loss)	**= $1500**

However, what happens when the market goes up instead of down? Well, then you purchase the shares at a higher price, which will give you a loss. Let's say you sell short 500 shares of XYZ common stock. The execution price for the sale is $28 per share, giving you a gross proceed of $14,000. Then you need to replace the stock. Unfortunately for you, the price has now risen to $30 per share. You purchase the stock for $15,000. Your loss is $1000.

Shares sold short	= 500
Selling price	= $28/share
Proceed from sale	= $14,000
Purchase price for 500 shares	= $30/share
Total purchase price	= $15,000
Gain (loss)	**= ($1000)**

While selling stock short can look like a surefire way to make money, it can also cause you to lose more than you may be willing to. Whether you engage in short selling or not really depends upon what kind of risk you are comfortable with. If you think you can handle the possibility of losing money because a stock goes up in value, then the prospective advantages of this strategy may outweigh the potential costs. However, if the idea of losing money because a stock goes up in value makes you squeamish, then perhaps it would be best if you stayed away from this idea.

PUTTING THEORIES INTO ACTION

Now that we've discussed portfolio killers and some strategies for wise investing, take a look at your accounts. Do you find that you seem to be dumping lump sums into the market only to see the market go down? Are you investing little by little? Or are you trying to time the market?

I have a client who came to see me for the first time during the summer of 2000. He joked that he was bad luck because, he said, every time he and his wife invested more money in the market, immediately it would go down. He even said that maybe we should call our other clients and warn them! Even though his outlook was that the market would go down after his money was invested (and, for the record, the market *did* go down), he continued to invest his money. He knew, as all wise investors do, that to not be invested is a far greater mistake than to invest at the "wrong" time. I've said it before, but it's worth repeating. No one knows what the market will do for sure. The experts can speculate all they want based on prior performance, but that doesn't mean that the market is going to follow its past trends. If you are afraid that once you invest your money the market will go down, try using the DCA method. And if the market does go down, hold your position.

PAPER LOSS VERSUS ACTUAL LOSS

There is a difference between your account value going down and losing money. Many people don't understand this concept. Basically, when the market goes down, equity investment values go down. To most investors, this is troubling. To others, it's not. This is why: The loss is only on paper. I have clients who will call during a down market and tell me that they are losing money and that they don't want to lose any more. What they fail to understand is that there is no real loss until they sell, or liquidate, their position in the security.

A few months after taxes for the year 2000 were due, I met with a married couple who are clients of mine. They, like others, were concerned about the stock market's performance. They told me that they had lost money on their funds and wondered why they couldn't claim the loss for their taxes. I took a look at their account statements and saw that they hadn't taken any money out of their nonqualified (regular) accounts; they had only taken money out of their IRA accounts. I explained to them that because the loss for their nonqualified accounts was only on paper, they couldn't claim it. Plus, the loss they showed for their IRA accounts couldn't be considered because the money was put in there on a pretax basis. I told them that if they had sold some of their nonqualified mutual funds during the year, they would have been able to take the loss.

For example, you purchase $40,000 of the XYZ Value Fund. After a few quarters of positive growth, you receive your statement and see that your investment is now worth $45,000. However, then the market begins to decline. Your next statement shows your investment value at $42,500. This is still a net paper gain of $2500 from your original investment. But then the next quarter shows a drop of $4000, bringing your investment value down to $38,500. You have a paper loss of $1500. This isn't an actual loss until you sell your fund. If you were to cash out of your position at that point (thus, receiving $38,500 for your fund), you would have an actual loss of $1500. But if you don't, and you hold your position in the XYZ Value Fund, you have only a paper loss.

Initial investment = $40,000
Market goes up; account value = $45,000—**paper gain of $5000**
Market goes down; account value = $42,500—**paper gain of $2500**
Market goes down; account value = $38,500—**paper loss of $1500**
Sell the fund for $38,500—**actual loss of $1,500**

This is what many people don't understand, and is one of the reasons why money is such an emotional thing. For this reason, I recommend that during a bear market, clients don't look at their accounts on a regular basis. Many clients of mine like to check out the markets on CNBC, as well as their accounts, every day. Even during a bull market, when account values are consistently going up, this isn't a healthy practice.

HOW MUCH HAVE I LOST? HOW MUCH HAVE I GAINED?

During bear markets, clients will come in and say they have lost X amount of money. By looking at their account statements, I know exactly how much their portfolio has declined. However, when I speak with the client, their number is always more than what the actual decline is. Why is that? The tendency is that when calculating the loss, people use the highest figure to the present.

For instance, one of my clients came in and told me that she had lost a substantial amount of money, when in fact she had only lost $5000. When she calculated her loss, she used the account value from March of 2000, which was the peak of the NASDAQ and Dow Jones indices. She didn't account for what her original investment was. She took her peak account value and subtracted the current value from it.

Unfortunately, she's not the only person who does this. When assessing your account positions, it's vital that you remember where you started. Just because your accounts reached $1.2 million and then dipped to $800,000 doesn't mean you lost $400,000. If your initial investment was worth $750,000, then you still have a net paper gain of $50,000.

Notice that I said "net paper gain." This is just like the paper losses. The gain isn't really your money until you cash out of your position. It's merely a rise in your account value. If you put $750,000 into the market and then sold off all your positions for a total of $925,000, then you have made $175,000. If you don't, and you hold your position, then the increase in the account value isn't an actual gain; it's just a paper gain.

So, the next time you look at your account statement and see a loss, don't overreact. It's only on paper until you do something about it. Likewise, if you see an increase, don't go out and buy things based on your statement. You have to liquidate your position before you can actually realize a loss or a gain.

9

HARVARD, YALE, OR YOUR LOCAL COMMUNITY COLLEGE: WHAT CAN YOU AFFORD?

F or many people, paying for higher education, whether it is for themselves, their children, or grandchildren, is very important. There are a few different investment vehicles that are specifically geared toward education. However, until recently, there weren't very many that were terribly attractive. Until the recent introduction of the Section 529 plans, people striving to save for college were pretty much stuck with three options: Invest money in a fully taxable account under their own name, invest in a fully taxable account under their child's (or other minor, such as a grandchild) name, or invest in an Education IRA. All four of these plans have their own advantages and disadvantages. We discuss these three options in this chapter, but focus the majority of our discussion on the new Section 529 Plan.

INVESTING UNDER THE INVESTOR'S NAME

Let's assume you are a parent who wants to save money for your child's education. You have started early; so early, in fact, that your child has yet to be born! Your only option for this money is to invest it under your name. In this case, we assume you have invested $5000 in an equity mutual fund. There are advantages and disadvantages to this. First, any income distributed by your investment will be fully taxable to you. Therefore, any capital gains and dividends from the fund will be taxed. However, because the money is in your name, you have complete control over it. So, you can redeem your fund shares and use the money for whatever you want, not just education.

Continuing with the example, let's say your child grows up and decides he or she doesn't want to attend college. Your initial $5000 investment has grown to more than $50,000. Had your child decided to attend college, you would have used this money to help pay for

---

Investing under the investor's name

Initial investment = $5000
$5000   = $50,000
Son   = Backpacking in the Himalayas
$50,000   = Car

The money can be used for whatever the investor wants. It does not revert to the minor.

tuition and books, right? But now, your child has decided that he or she would rather backpack across the Himalayas so you would rather use your $50,000 to buy a new car. The money is in your name, you've paid the taxes on it over the years, so therefore, you can buy a car or do whatever you want with that money.

INVESTING UNDER THE MINOR'S NAME

Now let's assume that you want to put aside that $5000 for your son, who was just born. You decide that you are going to put that money under his name, so you don't have to pay the taxes on it. There are two ways to do this. You can open a joint account with your son as the co-owner, but then you would be responsible for the taxes due for all distributions. You want to avoid this, so you open a Uniform Transfers (Gifts) to Minors account, or an UTMA/UGMA. This type of account says the minor, in this case your son, is the owner of the account, but you are the custodian. All income taxes on the mutual fund are your son's responsibility, which for most minors means that there will be no taxes paid because they usually don't make enough to pay taxes.

As custodian, you have the right to make any changes to the investment (i.e., which mutual fund the money is invested, etc.). However, the money is considered, by law, to be a gift. Therefore, when your son turns 18 years old, the account becomes his. So, let's say that the original $5000 has become $50,000 again. This time, when your son tells you that he is going to the Himalayas instead of college, he has a legal right to use that money as he wants. It is under his control, by law, not yours. One way partially around that is to make the account a joint account with you and your son upon his reaching the age of majority. While he would still be the taxpayer on the account, you would also be considered the legal owner of the assets. If the UTMA (or UGMA) account becomes his sole account when he turns 18 (age of majority varies by state), you have no legal right to that money, even though it was your money that has grown over the years.

You, as the parent and money donor, don't have to be the custodian of the account, though. You may designate any adult to be the custodian of the account. However, the same rules apply; the money

---

Investing under the minor's name—UGMA/UTMA

Initial investment   = $5000
$5000   = $50,000
Son   =   Backpacking in the Himalayas
$50,000   =   Son's money at age 18

Because the account is UGMA or UTMA, it becomes the son's at the age of majority, normally 18. However, this will vary by state.

---

is a gift and will revert to the minor when he or she reaches the age of majority. The gift, also, doesn't have to be just cash. The minor may be given bonds, stock, etc., in lieu of cash. The gift tax laws apply to these types of accounts. That is, an individual may give up to $11,000 per year, per individual before triggering any gift tax. Any more money given to a minor by one individual would be taxed. The value of a UGMA/UTMA may also reduce your child's eligibility for financial aid.

EDUCATION IRAS

With the recent changes in the federal tax law, education IRAs have become a more attractive choice to help fund education than they used to be. Education IRAs are essentially a tax-deferred way of growing money to help pay for a child's higher education. The main attraction to these accounts is that as long as the money is used for qualifying expenses, which we discuss, the distributions are tax-free.

Under the old tax law, contributions were limited to $500 per year. Considering the fact that this money was going to be used for college education, that $500 limit was pretty paltry. However, with the change in the law, the new limit is $2000 per year, which is more reasonable. Unlike traditional and Roth IRAs, the person benefiting from the education IRA doesn't need to have any earnings. This works especially well if the education IRA is for a child whose parents have been phased out from being able to contribute.

There are limitations to the amount of income the *donor* can earn and still make contributions. For those who file as single on their taxes, they can have a maximum adjusted gross income of between $95,000 and $110,000 until the ability to contribute is completely phased out. For those filing as married, the maximum adjusted gross income is now between $190,000 and $220,000 (double the limitations for single filers) before the contribution is phased out. Therefore, for families who want to make contributions to education IRAs but fall outside the AGI limits and are ineligible to make contributions, it makes sense to encourage the children to make contributions. Also, any contribution to an education IRA is not counted with any traditional or Roth IRA contributions. They are considered to be completely separate.

Contributions to education IRAs are done on an after-tax basis and cannot be deducted on your federal income tax return. The money will grow tax-deferred and then all qualified distributions will be tax-free. In the past, the only distributions that qualified to be tax-free were any postsecondary tuition costs, fees, books, supplies, and equipment. In addition to those, this year, the government has added many other types of qualifying expenses. Now, the definition includes expenses from elementary or secondary schools, certain types of room and board costs, uniforms, computers, and extended day programs costs.

There are some cases where the amount of money that can be distributed tax-free is reduced by any nontaxable scholarships, fellowship grants, and educational assistance allowances. The change in the tax law has now allowed for the coordination of the benefits from the education IRA and the HOPE and Lifetime Learning credits for education expenses, so that there is no dual tax benefit for the same expenses.

As with traditional IRAs, there is a required distribution age for any unused portion of the education IRA. Additionally, unused money may be rolled over into another education IRA for another family member. A rollover may be made as long as the original owner of the education IRA is under the age of 30. However, if the rollover isn't done and the beneficiary reaches 30 years of age, the remaining portion of the IRA must be distributed to the beneficiary. This money will then be taxed at the individual's ordinary income rate, including a 10-percent early withdrawal penalty. This, of course, seems unfair. After all, the government is requiring you to take out the money that hasn't been used; yet they are penalizing you because it is technically a premature distribution. This is why it's important either to use the entire amount, or roll over any unused portion.

Because the limit on annual contributions to an education IRA is $2000, there is no worry about triggering any gift tax to the recipient. But, when rolling over an unused education IRA, there is potential for gift tax consequences. If the rollover is made to a family member of the same generation (i.e., brother to sister, etc.), there is no taxable gift. However, if the rollover is made from one generation to the next, the gift tax could apply. As long as the education IRA rollover is $11,000 or less, there would be no gift tax. Rollovers that exceed $11,000 would be subject to the tax.

SAVINGS BONDS

An easy strategy to preparing for your child's education is to invest in bonds. There are bonds that are specially designed for education purposes, like the Series EE bonds, which we discussed in Chapter 7. For that reason, we don't go into too much depth here. However, by purchasing a bond and matching up the maturity date to coincide with when your child will start school, you will have created a source of money that can be used for tuition, books, room and board, or whatever school costs you want to use that money for. Specifically, you would want to purchase a bond that matures the July or August before your child is due to start school.

When considering bonds, you will also want to invest in bonds that reinvest the interest that accrues, rather than in bonds that distribute their interest on a regular basis. Savings bonds and zero-coupon bonds are popular choices because they don't have any interest to distribute before the bonds mature. Another advantage to the savings bonds is the fact that they are specifically designed to be used for education. Therefore, any gain that would normally be taxed in another investment is tax-exempt as long as the money is used for education purposes. Your child could use this money for books, or you could use it to pay tuition costs. As long as the money is used for a credible school cost, then the interest earned on the bond won't be taxed. It's important to note that there are some limitations to the interest being tax-exempt. If you plan on using a savings bond for education costs and are worried that you will be taxed on the interest, consult with your CPA, as they will be able to help you based upon your individual situation.

SECTION 529 PLANS

Qualified tuition programs, or Section 529 plans, have been in existence in many states and in various forms since 1986. The programs were named after Section 529 of the Internal Revenue Code, which was enacted in 1996. Essentially, these are programs that are operated at the state level and gave the participant a number of benefits that include tax-deferred earnings. In this way, they were akin to a traditional IRA or a 401(k) retirement plan.

The accounts are opened by one person for the benefit of another (i.e., a mother can open one for her son). The custodian doesn't have to be related to the beneficiary (the person who will be attending college) of the account. The beneficiary can be changed at any time. For instance, you open a 529 plan for your daughter, who decides not to go to college. You can change the beneficiary on the account to another family member of the original beneficiary. The new tax law permitted the term family member to include any first cousins, which is a change from the old tax law that prohibited first cousins as a part of the definition. Or, if your child dies, the beneficiary can be changed. Changes in beneficiary are done without any penalty.

As with education IRAs, or investing under the donor's name, the custodian of the 529 account retains complete control of the money until the time it is distributed. This gives the custodian greater peace of mind knowing that the money that was set aside for college won't go to fund something else. Plus, with the advantage of being able to change the beneficiary, you ensure that the college money will be used for college. It may just be that the original intended recipient is not the one who winds up using it!

529s also benefited from the government's recent tax law change. As of January of 2002, any qualified withdrawal will now be completely tax-free for federal income tax purposes.* The withdrawals have been tax-free from state income taxes in some cases. All contributions are made on an after-tax basis; thus, they cannot be deducted. As with the education IRA, the new tax law again coordinates the benefits of the 529 tax-free withdrawals with the HOPE and Lifelong Learning credits so that the distribution from the 529 cannot be used for the same expenses for which the credits are being claimed. Plus, you can now make contributions to both an education IRA and a 529 plan for the same person in the same year. Under the old tax law, this was prohibited.

Section 529 plans now exist in all states. Any resident of any state may invest in a 529 plan from any other state. There are also no limitations on the type of university the funds can be used for. There are state-assisted tuition programs that parents can invest in, which we won't be discussing, that specify that the funds may only be used for in-state colleges and universities. With the 529s, there are no such limitations. Therefore, a child in California whose parents have used the 529 plan to save for college may use the money when the child attends college in Texas, and so on.

529s also allow greater flexibility in the amount of money that can be saved. The limit for education IRAs is $2000 per year. 529 plans don't have a limit on the amount that can be contributed per year. In fact, the tax laws allow for an individual to give up to $55,000 in one year to the beneficiary of a 529 plan without triggering any gift tax. The catch to this, though, is that the gifting individual cannot give any more money to that beneficiary for the next five years. Essentially, the $55,000 is the gift of $11,000 for five years made all at one time. For married couples, the maximum gift would be $110,000.

---

*The Economic Growth and Tax Relief Reconciliation Act of 2001 is scheduled to "sunset" effective 12/31/2010. Following 12/31/2010, qualified distributions from 529 plans may be taxable. Individuals contributing on behalf of someone who will be attending a higher education institution after 2010 should consider this potential impact.

Some programs may have a limit on the amount of money that can go into a 529 over the lifetime of the account, which is usually around $250,000. But that shouldn't be a deterrent to utilizing a 529 plan.

EXAMPLE:

Billy will be attending college in seven years. His parents establish a 529 plan for him, to which his grandparents wish to contribute. They invest $110,000 in Billy's 529 plan without having to pay any gift tax. How?

$$\$110,000 \div 2 = \$55,000$$

Each grandparent gifts $55,000 to Billy's 529 plan.

$$\$55,000 \div 5 = \$11,000$$

Since the maximum gift without triggering gift tax is $11,000, the $55,000 from each grandparent becomes a five-year gift. They will not be able to give any more money to Billy until the five-year time period has elapsed. At that time, they can give Billy more money if they want.

Besides the tax-deferred growth and tax-free distributions, another case for investing in a 529 is that it doesn't discriminate against the wealthy. This is particularly important because children of wealthy parents are less likely to receive financial aid and grants for college. Unlike the education IRA, which has limits on the adjusted gross income of the donor, the 529s have no preset income limits. Any person with any amount of income can give money to a 529 plan for education purposes.

There are times when colleges and universities fail to account for the fact that parents may not be helping their child currently pay for college. Let's assume that Jim is 18 years old and will be attending his state university in the fall. Even though he will receive in-state tuition rates, the school is still very expensive. His parents have set aside money for Jim in a 529 plan, but have told him that they will not be contributing any other money. Jim is on his own to pay for whatever the money in the 529 plan won't cover. Jim decides that he is going to apply for financial aid because he doesn't want to deplete his 529 account. Because Jim is from a wealthy family, the university turns him down. Had Jim's parents just used the education IRA, Jim would have a very limited amount of money to help him pay for tuition, books, room and board, etc. But by investing in the 529 plan, there is a great potential that Jim's parents contributed more money to the 529 than they could have to the education IRA.

Fortunately, for those who get turned down for financial aid, there is an appeals process. On the average, 10 percent of those turned down for aid appeal. Out of that 10 percent, half receive an increase in financial aid.

There are some downsides to the 529 plan, though. When compared with education IRAs, there is decreased flexibility in the types of securities you can invest in. While some plans offer age-based portfolios, others offer just fixed portfolios. An age-based portfolio is a method of investing which the younger the child is, the riskier the investments are. As the child grows up and approaches college age, the portfolio changes to a different mix of investments that provide less fluctuation. The goal of age-based portfolios is to achieve a high rate of growth while the child is young and has plenty of years before heading off to college, while reducing the amount of value fluctuation as the child gets older. Plus, as the child gets older, you want to be sure that you can access the money and convert it to cash to pay the tuition bills.

A good rule of thumb is to keep about 80 percent of the portfolio in equities, with the rest in bonds and cash, from the time the child is born until age 12. After age 12, gradually reduce the amount of equity back into bonds and cash to help reduce volatility. By doing this, you also help decrease any impact a market downturn would have on the account.

The ability to move from one account to another requires that you change plan sponsors. As with IRAs, if you do change plan sponsors, you have 60 days to put the money back into a 529, plan without incurring any taxes. However, the government does allow for rollovers of 529s, as long as it done no more than once a year. It used to be that if you were rolling over a 529 you had to change the beneficiary of the account. That is no longer the case. Now, when you roll over the account, you can retain the same beneficiary each time.

WHICH IS THE BEST OPTION?

Certainly, the case for any type of savings can be made. While there isn't one perfect plan for everyone, the 529 comes closer than any other type of account. Since each individual state has its own program and money managers, it's vital to check out the different types of plans to make sure that you are investing in the one that best suits your needs. The easiest way to do this is to ask your advisor, rather than trying to investigate all the different plans.

A college education continues to be one of the most expensive things to pay for. The rising costs are outpacing both cost of living and inflation. In fact, according to the College Board, a nonprofit educational organization, the average cost of college for the 2000–2001 school year was $9229. This was for a student who attended a public college and includes tuition, room and board, fees, and books. (See Figure 9.1 for a breakdown of the percentages for each category.) For a student attending a private university, these same costs jumped to $24,946. For a four-year stay at a private school, at those amounts and with no inflation, the total amount is a whopping $99,784!

Put simply, 529 plans offer the tax-deferred growth and tax-free distributions that benefit any student. Anyone, at any income, can contribute to them; and they have flexible contribution limits so that the beneficiary may receive up to 25 times the amount he or she would with an educational IRA, and 5 times as much as he could with a regular or UTMA/UGMA account.

However, for those investors who are in the lower tax brackets, the education IRA is also a fine means of complementing the 529 plan. You would retain more control over the money and the securities it's invested in, plus the ability to switch between investments

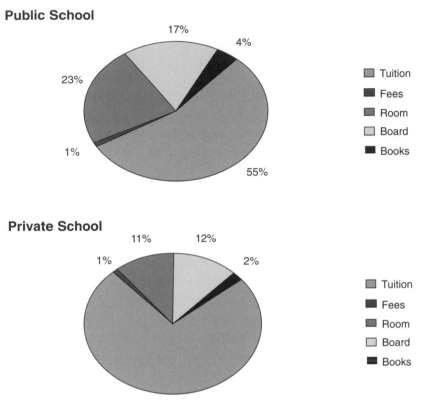

Figure 9.1. Using the amounts from Chapter 8 ($9229 for public schools), these are the percentages for each expense category. Note the difference between tuition for a public school and tuition for a private university (55 percent and 74 percent, respectively). *Source: http://www.ed.gov.*

more freely. The education IRA can also be used for elementary and secondary education costs, while the 529 may only be used for college. Don't forget to include savings bonds in your investment choices. Although not typically suited for large education costs, such as tuition, they would work very well for smaller charges, like books.

Plus, there is possible financial aid to consider. If you think your child would be able to qualify for financial aid, it may be best to invest your money in an account under your name, rather than the child's. When considering if a student is eligible for aid, colleges employ a formula to see how much aid the student may receive. Most formulas require that students contribute up to 35 percent of their savings, while parents are only required to supply 5.6 percent of theirs.

Overall, there really is no easy answer. (See Table 9.1 for a comparison of education plans.) Again, as with diversification, you may find that a little mix of everything is the best option for you. On the other hand, you may discover that the 529 has all the perks you want. Or, you may want to have as much control over the money as possible, in which case either investing under your own name or in an education IRA would be the best answer.

Table 9.1   How the Different Education Plans Compare

	Section 529 Plans	Series EE Savings Bonds	Education IRA	Traditional and Roth IRAs	UGMA/UTMA Accounts	Mutual Funds
Tax benefits	Federally tax-free withdrawals for higher education; tax-deferred earnings.	Earnings are tax-exempt for state and local taxes; Tax-deferred for federal taxes.	Earnings are exempt from federal taxes as used for qualifying education expenses.	Traditional IRA may be tax deductible; withdrawals taxed at owner's rate. Roth earnings are tax-exempt if taken after age 59 ½.	If child is under age 14, first $750 of earnings is tax-exempt, next $750 taxed at child's rate and any remaining at parent's rate. After age 14, all earnings tax at child's rate.	All earnings and gains are taxed at owner's rate. No special tax benefits apply.
Investment limits	Varies by state. May be as high as $250,000 per beneficiary.	$15,000/year.	$2000/year for each beneficiary.	$3000/year. Will increase to $5,000/year by 2008.	None.	None.
Qualified expenses	Tuition, fees, books, supplies, room and board, and equipment.	Tuition, fees, and other "credible" education costs.	Same as for the Section 529 plan.	Same as for the Section 529 plan.	Any expense pertains.	Any expense pertains.

Table 9.1 How the Different Education Plans Compare (Continued)

Affect on financial aid	Savings plans are part of the parents' assets. Prepaid plans are considered part of the student's assets.	Considered part of the parents' assets if for a child. But are student's assets if education is for oneself.	Considered part of the student's assets.	Not considered for financial aid.	Considered part of the student's assets.	Considered part of the parents' assets unless specifically in student's name.
Investment decisions?	State sponsor and program manager.	Bonds have guaranteed returns.	Owner.	Owner.	Owner.	Owner.
Income limits?	No.	No.	Yes.	Yes.	No.	No.
Affects tax credits?	Yes.	Yes.	Yes.	No.	No.	No.
Flexibility	Earnings taxed at owner's rate plus a 10% penalty when funds aren't used for qualified costs.	May be redeemed as soon as six months after issue. There is a penalty if redeemed in first five years.	Earnings on non-qualified withdrawals taxed at owner's rate plus 10% penalty.	There are no penalties for early withdrawal when used for higher education.	Money can be withdrawn at any time as long as it's for the minor's benefit.	Money can be withdrawn at any time for any purpose.

10

MAKING APRIL 15TH YOUR FAVORITE DAY

There's an old saying that death and taxes are the only guaranteed things in life, and that you can't get away from either one of them. While you may not be able to cheat death, you may be able to get away with paying less, maybe even much less, in taxes. Remember that I ask you in Chapter 1 to write down what your goals and fears are? Did you list "paying less in taxes" as a goal? Chances are, you didn't write down "pay more in taxes," because let's face it, no one wants to pay taxes. People certainly don't enjoy it. But, unfortunately, taxes are an essential way for our government to raise money, and so, they need to be paid. There are ways, though, for you to minimize your tax burden and keep more of the returns that you work so hard to achieve.

When you were younger, your parents probably told you that you needed to study hard, find a good job, and work hard to make money. What they didn't tell you is that the more money you make at your job, the more money you give to the government in the form of taxes. And, it's not only the federal government that gets you; it's the state and sometimes even the local governments that tax you as well. But you do work hard for your money, and I'm sure that you feel it's unfair to pay as much in taxes as you do.

I've never heard any of my clients or friends say that they were so happy with the way things were going that they were going to pay the government extra in taxes this year. That would be a ludicrous statement, right? Yet every year, thousands of people pay more in taxes than necessary. Why is this? There could be a number of reasons why. Some people believe that it's their accountant's job to help them save money in taxes, but most tax professionals simply prepare returns. In fact, if you want to save money in taxes, you need to see your accountant before the end of the calendar year, not just when you drop off your tax forms.

Plus, many people fail to take advantage of the itemized deductions, believing that the standard deduction is better. For many people, itemizing would be an ideal way to save money on taxes. However, the more money you make, the quicker the government phases out this option. Then there are different types of investments that help reduce taxes.

Throughout this chapter, we discuss the different ways to help save on federal and state taxes. We also touch upon the different investment vehicles you can use to divert interest and gains from your tax reporting. These days, there aren't very many good tax shelters left for you to use, but we take a look at how the remaining tax shelters will benefit you. Estate taxes, however, are saved for a later chapter.

Another mistake people make is to consider the tax implications of everything they invest in or purchase, such as a home. Using this mindset can often hurt you rather than help you. An important guide to this is that the tax write-offs are an added benefit, not the ultimate benefit. That is, do what's best for you and your goal to become wealthy, not just what's good for this year's taxes.

ADVANTAGED PLANS

It used to be that limited partnerships were the best tax shelter. Thousands of investors sunk billions of dollars into these equities, seeking tax breaks. However, they sacrificed their rate of return for tax savings. Now, there are fewer tax shelters that exist, and fewer people using them to their advantage! Hopefully, after reading this, you won't be one of them.

IRAs

These accounts are most commonly used to accumulate wealth for many reasons. First, they allow you to grow your money at a tax-deferred rate. Second, you don't have to begin taking money out of the account until you reach $70^{1}/_{2}$ years of age. Third, you can deposit up to $3000 per year before tax. (You deduct the amount you contribute from your taxes.) Although $3000 doesn't sound like a great deal of money, over time it does accumulate. Plus, the more money you contribute each year, the faster it will grow.

Roth IRAs

The main difference between IRAs and Roth IRAs is that the Roth contribution isn't tax-deductible. However, it's a great way to shelter your money and let it grow tax-deferred. The Roth is also subject to the same maximum contribution limits as the traditional IRA, but when you begin to take the money out, it will be distributed tax free. So, while contributing to a Roth won't save you money on your tax bill currently, it could save you, potentially, a large amount of money during your retirement.

401(k), 403(b), and 457 Accounts

Most people are familiar with these types of retirement accounts that are offered by employers, typically large companies, and tax-exempt organizations, such as most nonprofit organizations, hospitals, and schools. The beauty to these accounts is that they help lower your current taxable income. When you invest in a 401(k), 403(b), or 457, the money comes out of your paycheck before the tax is taken out.

Then when the tax is calculated, it is done so on the remaining amount of the paycheck. Therefore, if your paycheck is for $1000 per week, and you divert $100 each pay period to your retirement account, you are only taxed on the remaining $900, thus lowering your taxable income and tax due.

This year, the federal government has increased the amount of money you can invest in a 401(k), 403(b), and 457 to $11,000 per year. This number will continue to increase until the year 2006, when it reaches $15,000 per year. Therefore, you could potentially reduce your taxable income by up to $11,000 this year!

SEPs

SEPs, or simplified employee pension plans, are retirement plans that use IRAs or IRA Annuities as the receptacle for contributions. SEPs are often attractive to small business owners because of the reduced administrative tasks and expenses. Documentation, reporting, and disclosure requirements are simpler for SEPs than for qualified plans. However, in exchange for simplicity is the loss of flexibility. For example, under an SEP, all employees must be covered as long as they meet specified requirements, and the benefits must be fully vested at all times. SEPs allow employers to make contributions to an employee's retirement without utilizing a more complicated retirement plan, like a 401(k). You can use SEPs if you are incorporated or if you have self-employment income, so check with your CPA to see if you qualify to establish a SEP.

From a design perspective, the SEP is quite similar to the profit-sharing plan. The plan may also allow employees to make pretax salary deferrals, like in a 401(k) plan. The maximum employer contribution to the SEP is 25 percent of the compensation of all employees eligible to participate in the plan. If an employer sponsors several profit-sharing plans and SEPs, all plans are aggregated under this rule. The maximum amount that can be allocated to each participant from employer and employee contributions is the lesser of 100% compensation or $40,000 (indexed for 2002). The cap for the compensation that applies to SEP is 200,000 (indexed for 2002).

Annual income	= $75,000
25% of $75,000	= $18,750
SEP contribution	**= $18,750**

Annual income	= $325,000
25% of $325,000	= $81,250
SEP contribution	**= $40,000 (Maximum Limit)**

Keogh plans

The term Keogh Plan refers to an employer-sponsored plan that covers a self-employed individual such as a partner in a partnership, an individual member of limited liability company, or a sole proprietor. The plans are named after a congressman that first introduced legislation allowing self-employed individuals to sponsor these types of plans. For many years these plans were subject to more stringent rules and limits on contributions than plans sponsored by corporations. Today, all types of business choose from among the same group of quilified plans. A sole proprietor, instead of establishing a Keogh Plan, establishes a profit-sharing plan, defined-benefit plan, or other plan from the array of tax-advantaged retirement plans. The only distinction that still exists is the manner in which self-employed individuals detrmine their income for purpose of applying the limitations. The self-employed indviduals' contributions or benefit is based on net earnings instead of salary. Note that net earnings can be determined only after taking into account all qualified business deductions, including the deduction for the retirement contribution. Therefore, the amount of net earnings and the amount of deduction are dependent on each other.

Profit-Sharing Plans

The maximum employer contribution to the profit-sharing plan is the same as for an SEP, that is 25 percent of the compensation of all eligible employees. For these plans, though, you need to establish a vesting schedule, which will allow you to phase your employees into the plan over time.

For example, you participate in your company's profit-sharing plan. After two years there, you decide that it would be best if you were to find another job. Because of your company's vesting schedule, you may only be able to take a portion of your profit-sharing plan with you; typically after two years it would be 40 percent. You are always able to take 100 percent of your contribution. The 40 percent only refers to the employer's contribution. Generally, after five years of participation, an employee is 100-percent vested and would be able to take all of the proceeds from the plan and roll it over into another plan. Vesting schedules often work as a deterrent for employees who may be prone to frequent job switching.

Money-Purchase Plans

These plans are also part of the Keogh plans and can be set up separately. The difference between the profit-sharing and money-purchase plans is that employers need to establish a set percentage of the payroll that will be deposited into this account. These plans are rigid and don't allow for any flexibility. While your employer may be able to deposit up to 25 percent of payroll, whatever he chooses he needs to stick with. Therefore, if he decides that he will contribute 20 percent of payroll, then he will continue contributing 20 percent. The maximum annual contribution that an employee can receive is the lesser of 100 percent of salary or $40,000.

Annuities

Annuities are a great tax shelter because there is no limit to the amount of money you can invest in an annuity during a given year. However, there is no tax write-off for this investment. The money simply grows on a tax-deferred basis until you annuitize the account. Plus, within variable annuities you can switch between the different annuity sub-accounts at no cost and without triggering any type of taxes.

I regularly recommend annuities to clients who would benefit from tax-deferred growth of their money. I once read an investment book where the author cautioned against investing in annuities because of the surrender charges (which we discussed in depth in Chapter 7). However, I disagree with those who believe that annuities are a poor investment choice. There are many good reasons for investing in annuities and I'm not against recommending annuities if I believe that they are good for the client.

Life Insurance Policies

There may come a time when either a financial advisor or an insurance agent tries to sell you on the idea of using a life insurance policy as a means to accumulate the cash value on a tax-deferred basis that can then be used for retirement. This isn't a good idea because the policy is insurance and it's an expensive idea. When you pay the premium on the policy, a part of it pays the cost of insurance. The rest then goes into a separate account where it grows tax-deferred. Therefore, just because you are paying in $200 per month doesn't mean that the whole amount is going to be invested. Your cost of insurance could be $100 out of that $200, leaving just $100 per month being invested. It's far better to direct that $200 into a different account where the whole amount can grow.

There are many financial advisors and insurance agents who would like you to believe that life insurance is an investment vehicle. Yes, life insurance does allow your money to grow tax-deferred. However, these are insurance policies first and foremost. If you are considering purchasing a life insurance policy make sure that you need the insurance. Do not purchase one because you have been told that they are great investment tools. Life insurance policies are good for estate planning, and I have recommended them for that purpose, but never for an investment choice.

These investment choices, however, aren't totally fail-safe. Rather, they are only as good as the underlying equities are. While you should definitely remember to try and save as much on your tax bill as possible, don't sacrifice investment results and rates of return only because you are saving on your tax bill. If you decide that another security offers a better track record and potential return, but is currently taxable to you, it may be a better idea to invest in that security rather than the tax-deferred accounts.

Another important factor to tax shelters is that the government tries to not let you take advantage of them if your income is substantial. Contributions to Roth IRAs are phased out at certain income levels, as well as the tax-deductibility of traditional IRA contributions. Before you jump in and decide that one of these investments is a good idea for you, you need to know if it will be beneficial to you in the long run. Plus, you need to see if you will even benefit from the tax deduction, or if your adjusted gross income is above the required maximum.

TAX-FREE INVESTMENTS

We discussed the different types of tax-free investments in the bonds chapter but it bears repeating here. There are a number of different types of bonds that you can invest in that will give you tax-free returns and interest. The first type is government securities, such as Treasury bills, notes, and bonds. These equities are fully taxable for federal tax purposes, but are tax-free from state and local taxes. If you live in an area of the United States that has high state and local tax rates, these would be a good way to help save on those taxes. Now if you live in a state like Wyoming that has no state income tax, there is no reason from a tax point of view to invest in U.S. government securities.

Municipal bonds that are offered by state and local municipalities are free from federal taxes. Plus, if you live in the area from which the bond is issued, they will be free from state and local taxes as well. Therefore, if you live in Albany, New York and purchase a New York State general obligation bond, you would receive tax-free income from the bond. However, if you purchased the same bond, but lived in Michigan, you, generally wouldn't receive the state income tax-free, although it would still be tax-free on the federal level.

Beware that you don't undermine your tax-free investment income by purchasing the equity within a qualified plan. By holding tax-free muni bonds and muni bond funds within an IRA, 401(k), or other tax-qualified plan, you negate the benefit derived from the bond or bond fund. This is because when you begin to take distributions from your qualified plan, you will be taxed on the amount coming out, regardless of what the money was invested in. For this reason, it's best to hold taxable income-producing equities, such as income-geared mutual funds or stocks with historically high dividends, inside a qualified account. To own a tax-free investment inside a qualified account is to needlessly tax yourself on tax-free income. Who would want to do that?

Another potential mistake is when people in the lowest tax bracket purchase municipal bonds and bond funds. Because their tax bracket is already as low as it can go, the advantage of owning muni bonds is lost on them. Muni bonds and bond funds are the most advantageous for investors who are in the higher tax brackets. If you are considering investing in either individual muni bonds, or in muni bond funds, figure out what your tax bracket is, and then decide if the tax-free interest is worth it. It may not be.

TAKING A LOSS

Some mutual funds have a history of producing very high capital gains distributions for their shareholders. That's great, and most people don't have much of a problem paying taxes on those gains as long as their funds are performing well. But what about when there is a bear market and mutual funds aren't performing very well? These same funds will still produce relatively high, or higher, capital gains at the end of the year. Then their shareholders are going to have to pay taxes on these gains when their funds may have even declined in value over the year.

A simple strategy that I occasionally employ is to produce a capital loss for a client. All you do is sell an equity that is currently selling at a price less than what the client paid for it, thus producing a capital loss. For example, you purchase the XYZ Value Fund at $22 per share. You've held the fund for a couple of years and it has done relatively well. After all the capital gains and dividends have been reinvested, your average cost per share is $20.50 per share. However, this fund is prone to distributing high amounts of capital gains, and given the performance of the fund this year, you decide you don't want to have to pay taxes on a fund that isn't doing very well. Currently, the mutual fund is trading at $18 per share so you sell your 1000 shares. That's $1.50 per share less than your average cost per share, resulting in a capital loss of about $1500. That loss can be used to offset any capital gain you have to claim on your taxes, thus reducing your tax burden.

Now, if you hadn't had your dividends and capital gains reinvested, and you had been taking them as cash distributions since you had purchased the fund, assuming that everything else remained the same, your resulting capital loss would be $4000.

Shares owned	= 1,000
Purchase price paid	= $22/share
Average cost per share	= $20.50/share
Price shares sold for	= $18/share
Capital loss (approx.)	**= $1500**

Shares owned	= 1,000
Purchase price paid	= $22/share
Price shares sold for	= $18/share
Capital loss	**= $4,000**

After producing a capital loss, the money is then reinvested into another fund. Generally, I try to pick another fund that has a similar feel to it (i.e., growth to growth and value to value). However, you need to be careful about what the money is reinvested in. If the IRS feels that the second fund is too similar to the first fund, and you reinvested the money in the second fund within 30 days of selling the first, they will disallow the capital loss. Therefore, you need to pick another equity that is different than the one that was sold. This law is to prohibit investors from selling equities low and then repurchasing the same equities just so they can claim a loss on their taxes. The law, though, is written so that there is a broader interpretation of what the similar equities are, so be careful. If you manage your money yourself and wish to claim a loss in this manner, it would be a good idea to consult a professional so that you don't inadvertently disallow your loss.

One of my clients has found that by producing a capital loss, we greatly benefit his tax situation. What I have done for him is sell one or two of his nonqualified mutual funds to produce a capital loss. Then, within his IRA, we sell the same number of funds. With the proceeds inside the IRA, we purchase funds that were similar to the nonqualified funds. With the proceeds of the sale of the nonqualified funds, we purchase funds that are similar to the IRA funds we sold. This way, he can claim a loss on his taxes without sacrificing his long-term investment results.

When carrying a loss and claiming it on your tax forms, there is one important rule to remember. You can use your entire loss to offset a capital gain, but if the loss exceeds the gain, you can only use up to $3000 of that remaining loss to offset other income. For instance, using our previous example, and assuming you received dividends and capital gains in cash, you create a $4000 capital loss. On your income taxes, you report that you had a total capital gain of $2750 for the year, but you had a $4000 capital loss. That loss will offset the gain, resulting in your not having to pay capital gains tax on your $2750. The remaining $1250 can be used to offset part of your ordinary income for tax purposes.

However, let's assume that you report that you only had a capital gain of $850, but that you still had the $4000 loss. You offset the $850 and are left with $3150. You may use up to $3000 to offset your ordinary income on your taxes. You won't be able to use the remaining $150 *this year*. You can carry over whatever loss remains to the next year's taxes to use against capital gains and other income. These losses can be carried over indefinitely, meaning that if your loss is $9000, and you use $1000 to offset capital gains, and then use $3000 to offset ordinary income, you'll be left with $5000. If you don't use that whole $5000 on the next year's taxes, whatever is left over can be applied to the following year's taxes, and so on.

TO ITEMIZE OR NOT TO ITEMIZE?

Many people make the simple mistake of taking the wrong deduction on their tax forms. While for some, taking the standard deduction is the best way, for others, itemizing the deductions is the best alternative. Plus, the most beneficial method for you may change from year to year. That's why it's best to calculate your taxes using both the standard deduction and itemizing to see which way suits your situation the best.

There is often some confusion about what can be written off and what can't. Here's a list of some of the more common items that can be written off:

- medical and dental expenses (in excess of 7.5 percent of adjusted gross income)
- state, local, and foreign income and property taxes
- state and local personal property taxes
- residential mortgage interest and investment interest (limited amounts)
- charitable contributions (limited to 50, 30, or 20 percent of AGI depending on certain aspects)
- casualty and theft losses (reduced by $100 per loss and in excess of 10 percent of AGI)
- job and other expenses (in excess of 2 percent of AGI)
- moving expenses (subject to some limitations)

There are also many other potential deductions that are often overlooked:

- fees for tax preparation services and IRS audits
- financial planner fees
- cellular telephones and charges if certain requirements are met
- contact lenses
- amortization of taxable bond premiums
- appreciation on property donated to charities
- commissions on property sales
- depreciation of home computers if certain requirements are met
- fees for safe-deposit boxes

As I mentioned previously, the IRS phases out and limits otherwise available deductions for personal and dependency exemptions, as well as certain itemized deductions for people in higher tax brackets. Those individuals whose AGI exceeds a certain amount ($137,300 for 2002) will begin to have their itemized deductions limited, or phased out. That income threshold is the same whether you

AGI	= $237,300
Threshold*	= $137,350
Difference	= $100,000
3% of $100,000	= $3,000
Total deductions	= $6,200
$6,200 x 80%	= $4,960

Your deductions will be reduced by $3,000. In order for the 80 percent rule to come into play, your AGI would exceed $302,633.

*Based on 2002 tax figures.

are single, head of household, widowed, or married filing jointly. These amounts are annually indexed for inflation, so that each year they increase a little bit.

When the deductions are reduced, they are done so according to the smaller of two limitations. The first limitation is that the deduction will be reduced by 3 percent of the amount that the taxpayer's AGI exceeds the threshold amount. The second says that the deduction cannot be reduced by more than 80 percent of the allowable itemized deductions. So, for example, in 2002 you file your taxes and itemize your deductions. Your filing status is married filing jointly, and your AGI is $237,300. The amount by which your deductions will be reduced is $3000, just so long as that number ($3000) isn't more than 80 percent of your total itemized deductions.

Medical expenses, investment interest, casualty losses, and wagering losses to the extent of wagering gains are not counted in the phaseout process. So, let's say that you carry a portfolio on margin (borrowing money from the brokerage house to buy securities), have incurred debt, and are paying interest on that debt. This is categorized as investment interest and would remain fully deductible regardless of what your AGI is. Of course, this is still limited to the extent of your investment income. The important deductions, such as charitable contributions, are the ones that the government phases out.

The idea of limiting itemized deductions brings us to the very important question of whether or not to pay off your mortgage. Truly, being able to deduct the interest you pay on your mortgage is a very appealing concept that many homeowners take advantage of. However, this deduction is one of the ones subject to the IRS's phaseout restrictions. Many times, people will continue to pay on their mortgage, with the misunderstanding that the interest is fully deductible. They aren't aware that the government restricts the amount you can deduct once your income reaches a certain level. For that reason, there are people who are needlessly paying mortgage interest, when they could be paying off their homes and using the money they would have been using to pay interest to invest.

Take a look at what your AGI was on last year's tax forms. Was it more than the $128,950 threshold? Are you anticipating that this year's income will be the same, if not more than last year's? If you answered yes to these questions, see if you have been deducting your mortgage interest on your taxes. If you have been, then you know that the amount you are deducting is also subject to being reduced because of your elevated income level. However, if your income falls below the threshold amount mark, then you will be able to continue to utilize the mortgage interest deduction to its fullest extent.

There are people who continue to take the standard deduction when itemizing would be the best option. Are you one of them? When preparing this year's taxes, check to see if you would be better off to itemize rather than to take the standard deduction. After all, it's your money; wouldn't you rather keep it instead of letting the government have it?

INCOME SHIFTING

Another strategy to consider if you own your own business and have children is to employ them. By having your children on your payroll, you pass the company's earnings down to them, thus ensuring that their income will be taxed at the lowest possible rate, the newly imposed rate of 10 percent. You may even find that your children make so little in income that they don't even have to pay taxes. Either way, the income will flow away from you and your higher tax rate to them.

There are other ways to shift income from you to family members either by creating trusts or custodial accounts, or by making outright gifts to relatives. Let's consider that you are married and have a combined income of $125,000, putting you in the 30-percent marginal tax bracket. In addition to your income, you have $25,000 worth of corporate bonds that pay interest of $3,500 annually. That interest amount is fully taxable to you and your spouse. But why should you pay taxes on it? Why not give those bonds to your 16-year-old child who currently doesn't make enough income even to pay taxes? You could agree that the interest generated by the bonds, as well as the principal (if they are due to mature soon) will help pay for your child's college. Assuming your child will then have to pay taxes, his or her tax liability caused by the interest will be $275.

Interest	= $3500
Child's tax rate	= 10%
Minimum standard deduction	= $750*
Tax liability	= 10% × ($3500 − $750)
	= **$275.00**

*Assume the child has no earned income. Standard deduction amount based on 2002 tax figures.

By passing the income to your child, you not only reduce your income by the $3500 that you receive in interest annually, but you reduce your tax liability by $1050. However, this strategy is not as easy as it seems. If your child is younger than 14 years old, the investment income is taxed at the same rate as the parent's income, to the extent that the investment income exceeds $1400. This means that if you were to give your corporate bonds and their applicable $3500 annual interest to your 8-year-old daughter, she would be taxed as follows: the first $1400 (minus the $750 deduction) would be taxed at her rate (10 percent); the remaining $2100 would be taxed at your higher tax rate, in this case 30 percent.

The federal government allows income shifting to take place because they assume that it isn't done solely to reduce, or avoid, taxes. Rather, they assume that the main purpose for shifting the income is to produce a pool of savings that will be used for some specific purpose at a later point in time, such as higher education. They also allow it because the person shifting the income isn't allowed to move just the income; they need to move the income-producing investment. This means that you just can't give the interest away from your corporate bonds and keep the bonds under this strategy. You have to give away the corporate bonds (income-producing investment in this case), as well. This isn't to say that you can't just give away money. If you were to give away the $3500, it would be considered a gift and would fall under the IRS's codes of gifting. The interest from the corporate bonds would still be considered part of your gross income. In order to get that income off of your tax forms, you would need to give the bonds away, too.

OTHER WAYS TO SAVE ON TAXES

When you see a mistake, are you likely to correct it, or do you just glance over it? If we're talking about your taxes, hopefully you would correct it. Chances are that the mistake you are catching would have cost you money. There are a number of simple mistakes that people make on their taxes that, if corrected, could help them save money on taxes. Some of these mistakes are just silly errors that are easily eliminated.

Withholding Too Much
Most people I know get refunds at the end of the tax year. However, many of these people are receiving too much. I'm not saying that the government is paying them more than they are entitled to, I'm saying that these people have been withholding too much money from their paychecks. Tax refunds are good, but the smaller they are the better. Why is that? Because the more money you pay into the government during the year from your paycheck, the less money you have to help achieve your goals.

By lowering your withholding from your checks, you will increase the amount of money that goes into your pocket. This is money that can be used to help increase your investments or used as cash to buy something that you might otherwise put on a charge card and pay interest on later. Plus, when was the last time you received your refund from the government plus interest on that amount? Probably never. When you withhold too much from your paycheck you are essentially giving the government an interest-free loan for the year. Think about what you can be doing with that money, and then think about what the government is probably doing with your money. I'm sure you have better plans for it.

Compromising Wealth for Taxes

When trying to build wealth, most people focus on saving money in taxes as their number-one priority, but is that really the way to go? It's important to do proper research before deciding that an investment that will save you in taxes is more important than a taxable investment that may perform better. Saving money in taxes is important, but it's not your ultimate goal. Make sure that you are making decisions that are in the best interests of your long-term goals, not just so you can save on taxes. Realistically, strategies that are employed solely to save on taxes shouldn't work for investment purposes because that wasn't why they were undertaken in the first place. When deciding which road is the best to take for your investments, consider why you are choosing to do anything. Is it because you want to save on taxes? Or is it the best decision based upon your risk tolerance and financial objectives?

Real Estate Trade-Ups

Did you know that you don't have to pay taxes on the gain of your home if you purchase another, more expensive house? Section 1031 of the Internal Revenue Code says that you can delay paying tax on the gain of the sale of your home as long as you roll that money into the purchase of a new, more expensive house. The only stipulation to this is that you have to live in the house, or keep it as your primary residence, for at least two years. The allowable appreciation for a taxpayer filing as single is $250,000. For those who are married, the allowable

> **Special note:** I have quite a few clients who came to me from other firms. When they first come to see me, they have many different statements from multiple companies. I have found that many people truly don't know what their assets are because they simply have too many accounts at too many firms. It's very easy to get swept up in the latest advertisement from a bank or mutual fund company; then, before you know it, you have a torrent of paper coming to your mailbox every month from way too many investment companies. In order to combat this, try to find a company that will allow you to hold your existing mutual funds and other assets in one consolidated account, like a brokerage account. There are many firms that will allow this, and it will make keeping track of your investments much easier. You don't want to compromise your investment strategy or results by limiting yourself to one or two investment companies; however, you also don't want to lose track of your portfolio because you have too many accounts at different firms.

appreciation is $500,000. Therefore, as long as you continue to trade up in value, you won't have to pay any taxes on the appreciation. However, once you liquidate (sell off your property and don't purchase another home), you will have to pay the tax on the gain.

Statements? What Statements?

Poor record keeping is a killer for many people. Make sure that you keep track of all your investment statements, check registers, charitable contributions, and all other pertinent financial data. Not having these papers may result in paying your CPA and the IRS more money than necessary because you may wind up missing deductions that will help lower your taxes.

But there is also such a thing as too much record keeping. I have a client whose father recently passed away. His father was a meticulous record-keeper. However, he also kept things that were of no importance. Therefore, upon his father's death, my client had to wade through the quagmire of paper that his father had kept for years and years. It's very important to keep good records of your investments and transactions, but that prospectus that's eight years old? It's all right to throw that away.

Mathematical Errors

These are probably the easiest to fix, but the most difficult to find. Many times the only mistake in a client's taxes is that two numbers are added incorrectly or aren't entered correctly. The most common mistake that I see happens when people use spreadsheets they have formulated themselves to help them. If there is an error in the spreadsheet, it will continue into perpetuity as long as you don't know the error is there. This is why it's important to have someone else double-check your work. If they find an error that you missed, they may have just saved you some money. However, that's not to say that all errors result in your paying more taxes. There are times when the errors that are made result in the government's paying more back to you. But, when the IRS goes over your return and finds an error, if it's in their favor they'll let you know. If it's not, they'll let it go.

Doing Your Own Taxes

If you are a trained tax specialist or a CPA, then doing your own taxes makes sense. Even if your taxes are simple you don't itemize, and you use the 1040EZ form, then doing your taxes is alright. However, if that's not the case, then perhaps you should consider hiring a professional. The advantages of hiring a professional outweigh the potential cost of paying someone to prepare your taxes.

First, whomever you hire will be more objective about your tax situation than you will be. Second, tax professionals are trained in up-to-date tax codes. They know what they're doing and what the best way to do it is. They also know the best way to save you money on your taxes and whether you should itemize or not. Third, hiring someone will help stem the tendency to procrastinate. Are you one of those people who stand in line at the post office at 11:30 p.m. on

April 15 to send in your taxes? Or perhaps, you've been so busy that you had to file for an extension? If so, then hiring a CPA is probably a good idea.

Plus, you know that little box on the bottom of the second page of the tax forms, the one that says preparer's signature? By hiring someone to prepare your taxes for you, if there is a problem, it becomes their problem, too. If you make a mistake, the IRS hunts you down, right? But if your CPA makes a mistake, it's his or her problem, too, because it's the CPA's job to make sure that things are done correctly. Therefore, the onus of doing the job right falls directly onto the CPA, not you. This may result in fewer sleepless nights for you!

Not Using Qualified Plans
We talked about this earlier. Qualified plans are one of the best ways to help lower your taxable income and shelter your money from current taxes. Not utilizing these types of accounts is one of the surest ways to cost you money, both currently and over time.

Investing in Bonds Needlessly
The tax advantages of muni bonds are for those with higher incomes. While I'm not advocating that those in the lower tax brackets stay away from municipal bonds, I am saying that there may be other investments better suited to those investors. Evaluate your tax situation and make your decision based on that. If you want to add some stability to your portfolio by using bonds, there are different types of bonds that exist that may give you higher returns. And, those after-tax returns may be higher than those returns offered by nontaxable muni bonds.

BE YOUR OWN BOSS

For many people who own their own businesses, they have found that working for themselves is far more rewarding than working for others. But, they'll also probably tell you that it's a lot more work. There are a number of ways that individuals can own their own business: sole proprietorship, partnership, corporation, LLC, etc. The way your businesses is established could mean a lot on tax day. Some forms of ownership, like partnerships and S-corporations, have their business year end at the same time as individuals do: December 31, or the end of the calendar year. However, C-corporations can choose when their year ends. This could amount to a large difference as far as taxes are concerned. "Incorporation" doesn't mean a huge building with hundreds of employees, with you at the helm of a multinational enterprise. A corporation is an entity without a soul, a few legal documents that reside in a file folder at your attorney's office. But should you incorporate your business? Can you even consider this as an option?

The answer to the second question is almost always yes. Although there are associated costs with incorporating, incorporating your business may be the best option from a tax standpoint. (Though you may find that your business is better suited to another form of ownership.) You just have to follow the rules that go along with it. But what if you work for someone else? Can you still incorporate? The answer is still yes, as long as you have income other than your employment income. For example, if you own some rental property and derive an income from that property that is separate from your work income, then it may be in your best interests to incorporate your side business of owning and running the rental property.

Business owners are allowed to pay their expenses before they pay their taxes. This is something that employees aren't allowed to do. Look at your most current paycheck stub. What is the first thing that comes out of your pay? If you invest in your company's retirement plan, that does. Otherwise, taxes come out first. And by taxes, I'm including federal, state, local, and Social Security taxes (FICA). Then the rest of the money goes to you, and you try to use it in the wisest way possible. With business entities, it earns as much as it can, spends as much as it can, and then is taxed on the rest. In this manner, business entities, such as corporations, are probably the biggest tax loophole left! By owning your own corporation, or being self-employed, even everyday things, such as car payments and gas for your vehicles can become business expenses. You just have to use your pretax dollars from your business for these things.

An important advantage to incorporating is to protect your personal assets. What if one of your tenants from your rental properties sued you? If you incorporated your rental property business, then the tenant would be suing the corporation, not you as the individual. But if you hadn't incorporated, you, the individual, would be sued. How accepting are you of losing your personal property in a lawsuit?

Sole Proprietorships

All the business's assets, liabilities, and operations are a part of the owner's personal financial situation. As the name indicates, there can only be one owner of the business, and no separate business entity exists. Because of that, for tax purposes, everything from the business (profits, losses, etc.) is passed through to the owner. The business doesn't file its own taxes, and there are no papers to file to set up the business. The owner is also personally liable for his or her business and any legal action that may be taken against it. The best bet for a sole proprietor to help protect against any type of legal claim is to purchase commercial liability insurance.

Although there is the advantage of being the only person in control of your business (i.e., no shareholders or partners to answer to), it also becomes a potentially huge liability when you consider that you are solely responsible both on the business front and personally.

General Partnership

Partnerships are associations between two or more persons to carry on a business. The definition of "person" here is very broad and can be an individual or an entity, such as a U.S. citizen, nonresident alien, resident alien, corporation, limited liability company, trust, or other type of partnership. However, there are no registrations to file, and a written partnership agreement is not required, although it is usually a good idea.

The partners of a general partnership are jointly liable for the debts, claims, or other obligations arising from the partnership. There is an unlimited personal liability for claims against the business, even those resulting from another partner who is acting for the business.

From a tax perspective, general partnerships are like sole proprietorships. That is, they are pass-through entities and pay no tax on their own. All partnership gains, losses, credits, and deductions are taxable to the partners individually. While the partnership pays no taxes, it does report the taxes because it is required to determine each partner's share.

Thus, as with a sole proprietorship, the partners derive no preferable tax treatment (aside from being able to divide the tax liability between two or more entities) by holding the business as a partnership.

C Corporations

These are corporations that are established under the state law in which they are formed. C corporations may have as many shareholders as they want, whether that be one or more. They are also not limited to the type of stock they issue. Therefore, they could have several different classes each of common stock and preferred stock, one class each of common and preferred, or a variation. The shareholders of the C corporation are limited in their liability to the amount of their investment, but they can still participate in the management of the business without jeopardizing this limited liability. Generally, many shareholders of C corporations are also employees.

As far as income tax goes, C corporations are responsible for their own taxes under the IRS's code Subchapter C. They may also be responsible for the corporate alternative minimum tax,[1] as well. C corporations are not pass-through entities, but they may be subject to the corporate double-tax. That occurs when the corporation is taxed, as well as the shareholders. However, the shareholders are only taxed on the dividends that are declared and distributed by the corporation. Usually in closely held C corporations, the business elects not to declare dividends (to the extent that it is possible), so as to avoid any double taxation. The tax strategy is to take out the profits in other, legal, ways so that there are deductions that may be taken against the business's profits.

A C corporation's taxable income is its gross income subject to tax, minus any allowable deductions. Corporations normally deduct their ordinary and necessary business expenses, although there are some exceptions. They may also have what is known as a net operating loss. This is when the corporation's deductions exceed its gross income. Corporations generally may carry this NOL, first back 2 years, then forward over the next 20 years.

As mentioned earlier, C corporations can determine when their business year ends. This allows you to split up when you pay your personal taxes and when the corporation pays its taxes. Also, if you

---

[1] In the case that the C corporation is a small business corporation (usually those whose gross receipts are less than $5 million), they are exempt from the corporate AMT.

discover that your company will be making more than anticipated, the business can give bonuses or move income to you before the end of its year, but after you need to pay your taxes.

S Corporations

S corporations are those that are incorporated under the state laws in which they were formed. It also elects to not be taxed as a corporation. Otherwise, S corporations are similar to C corporations. Shareholders continue to have a limited liability in the corporation, but can participate in the management without risking their liability. Again, many shareholders may also be employees of the firm.

Similar to general partnerships, S corporations don't pay any taxes. However, they do compute taxes and report them to the IRS. All gains, losses, credits, and deductions are passed down to the shareholders. They are taxed even if the corporation doesn't declare any dividends. However, if the corporation did declare and distribute dividends to its shareholders, these dividends would generally not be taxable since the shareholders are the ones who pay taxes on the corporation's gains and income.

Only small business corporations may qualify to become S corporations, and then they are subject to certain requirements:

- The corporation must be domestic.
- There may be no more than 75 shareholders. (A husband and wife count as one shareholder.)
- The corporation may only have certain classes of eligible shareholders.
- S corporations may only have one class of stock.

Limited Liability Corporations

An LLC may be a sole proprietorship, corporation, or partnership. Keep in mind, though, that a minimum of two members is required for federal tax purposes to operate an LLC as a partnership. Consequently, all tax benefits depend upon how the LLC operates.

An LLC is an entity formed under state law by filing articles of organization as an LLC. An LLC with two or more members is classified as a partnership for federal income tax purposes unless it elects to be taxed as a corporation or was formed before 1997 and was taxed as a corporation. An LLC with one member is not treated as a separate entity for income tax purposes unless it elects to be taxed as a corporation.

So, what's the best way to hold your company? There is no easy answer for that. It's something that you should discuss with your CPA. These previous sections are not designed to be all-inclusive about each of the types of businesses you can own. We've left out limited liability companies, limited partnerships, and a few others that may be more suited to your situation. But, this is just a way of showing the positive tax implications of incorporating your business and comparing the tax consequences of corporations to those involved with owning a sole proprietorship or general partnership.

TAX REDUCTION, NOT TAX EVASION

While we're discussing possible ways to reduce the amount of money you pay out to the government in the form of taxes, it's important to specify that tax reduction is legal, but tax evasion is not. Unfortunately, there are many people in the world who will try and convince you to follow their advice to help eliminate the need for you to pay taxes.

Recently, criminal investigations into fraudulent types of trusts from around the country have begun to receive national attention. The federal government has even issued a warning to taxpayers to avoid scams that promise to "untax" you from the income tax system. These scams include using both domestic and foreign trusts to divert income from individuals so that they don't have to pay income tax. However, these schemes are not only illegal, they will wind up costing the participant quite a lot of money. If you find yourself in the middle of one of these schemes, you'll also find yourself out of a lot of money. First, there will be a fee for the service that is provided by the scam promoters. This could be as little as $1000, but there have been cases where the service fee is as high as $70,000. Of course, the promoters will charge whatever they think they can get out of the individual; they generally target those whose income is greater than $100,000 per year. Second, once the IRS finds out (and they will) the participating individual will face fines, interest, possible jail time, and the payment of all back taxes. Does that sound like a good idea to you?

While the IRS does recognize a number of legal trust arrangements, they are usually formed for estate-planning purposes, charitable giving, and for holding assets for beneficiaries. There is an independent trustee who manages the trust, holds legal title to trust assets, and exercises independent control. Then, any income received by the trust is taxable to the trust, beneficiary, or taxpayer, unless the Internal Revenue Code specially exempts the trust.

These are some of the types of trusts that you should stay away from because they are being used to promote fraudulent trust scams:

- Asset Management Company: Here the promoter encourages the participant to form an AMC, where one of the promoter's staff is the recorded trustee. However, after the trust is formed, the participant replaces the staff member as trustee. The goal is to make it look like the participant isn't managing his or her own business and to start the layering process.

- Business Trust: A business owner transfers the business into the trust. The trust then distributes payments to "unit holders" or other trusts so that it looks like there is limited taxable income.

- Equipment and/or Service Trust: This trust holds equipment that is "rented or leased" and may provide services to the business trust, usually at much higher rates. The business trust, in turn, reduces its income by claiming deductions for the payment of services to the equipment and/or service trust.

- Family Residence Trust: In this trust, the family residence and all furnishings are transferred to the trust. The trust, claiming to be a rental business, then "rents" the residence to the owner, who becomes the caretaker of the property.

- Charitable Trust: This trust claims to be a charitable organization that has had income and assets transferred to it. This "charitable organization" then pays for personal, educational, and recreational expenses. The payments are then claimed as charitable deductions.

- Final Trust: Named because it is usually the last trust the assets flow through to after going through several other trusts; the final trust is usually established in a foreign country that will impose little to no tax on trusts. A final trust has many arrangements that allow money to come from other trusts. The money then is available or distributed to the original owner.

A good rule of thumb when it comes to protecting yourself against fraudulent schemes is that if it sounds too good to be true, it probably is. Another thing to look out for are books that propose that you don't have to pay taxes. They base their claims on outrageous statements like the IRS has no jurisdiction outside Washington D.C. and Puerto Rico. Or they will say that we don't have to pay taxes because we are sovereign citizens. No matter what they claim, it's all false. But more importantly, people have used these claims to defend themselves against paying taxes in court, and have lost. They then are subject to the back payment of tax, as well as fines and interest. P.T. Barnum once said, "There's a sucker born every minute." Don't let that be you.

There are many different ways to save on your taxes. After all, no one wants to pay taxes. We've really only touched the tip of the iceberg. There are more, complex strategies that can help you save on your taxes that your CPA can help you implement if they are right for you. But what's also important is that you don't find yourself doing things solely to save on your taxes. Reduced taxes are an added bonus, not your ultimate goal. It's vital to look at your tax situation and bracket to determine what your best course of action is. Everyday life changes all the time, right? So does your tax situation, especially now that the federal government has decided to revise the tax laws and lower everyone's bracket each year until the year 2006. (See Table 10.1 for the new tax brackets.) Therefore, what was the right strategy for you last year may not be the right thing to do this year. Make sure that what you are doing is the right move for you, not just for your taxes. If you are unsure how to proceed, check with your CPA.

The more money you make and the wealthier you become, the more important your CPA becomes. The more your CPA knows about your situation now, the more he or she will be able to help you in the future. Don't be afraid to ask questions, either. No one wants to pay more than their fair share, and you may find that by asking questions, you uncover a new way to save yourself some money!

Table 10.1   New Federal Tax Rates

Old law	28%	31%	36%	39.6%
2001	27.5%	30.5%	35.5%	39.1%
2002–2003	27%	30%	35%	38.6%
2004–2005	26%	29%	34%	37.6%
2006 and after	25%	28%	33%	35%

These new tax rates were instituted during the year 2001, and were accompanied by tax refund checks for the majority of tax payers in anticipation for the year 2001's taxes (those due by April 15, 2002). While the law has been changed to reflect these new tax rates and their steady, albeit gradual, decline over the next few years, it's important to note that this new law has what is known as a sunset provision. That is, unless Congress passes new tax laws prior to 2011, both these tax brackets and the law that enacted them are due to expire in 2010. Higher-income taxpayers will also see that they will no longer lose their personal exemptions or have their itemized deductions reduced beginning in 2006. That law will also be repealed in 2010 barring any further action from Congress. The above table doesn't take into account the existing 15-percent tax bracket, or the newly instated 10-percent tax bracket.

GUARDING AGAINST THE FINANCIAL PITFALLS OF DEATH

How much is your life worth? How much money would your loved ones need to carry on with day-to-day life if your income were suddenly gone? Do you know, or would you rather not even think about it? Many people are very outspoken on the topic of insurance—they dislike it, but it's easy to see why. First, many people believe that insurance salespeople are not exactly forthright and honest in their dealings. And while that certainly may be the case, that's not an honest assessment of the insurance profession as a whole. Second, insurance brings up uncomfortable feelings that many people don't want to deal with, which is also completely understandable. Finally, as anyone can tell you, insurance is expensive. I can't tell you how many times I've sat across the table from a client who told me that he didn't want insurance, and didn't want to have to pay for it, because it was something he would never use.

True, many people buy insurance and then never use it. But, do you drive your car without insurance? Or have you canceled your homeowner's insurance policy? I'm willing to bet you haven't canceled them, nor would you even think about it. But, when was the last time you used either of those policies? If the answer to that question is "not very recently" or "never," would you consider dropping your coverage because of that? Again, I'm going to say that you wouldn't.

Insurance involves a transfer of risk. By purchasing life insurance, for example, you are acknowledging that you have a financial interest in your life, and therefore you face a risk if something were to happen. With risk you have the option to do one of the following: Avoid it, prevent or control it, assume it, or transfer it. By avoiding risk, you simply don't engage in an activity that you think could cause harm. For instance, if you are afraid that you could get into an automobile accident and be sued, you could avoid driving. That sounds a bit extreme, and certainly avoiding certain risks could cause a bigger inconvenience than not avoiding that risk. However, if the cost of avoidance is less than handling the risk in another way, then that may be the most attractive way to go.

Preventing or controlling the risk is another, simpler way to minimize the risk and associated potential loss. Taking our previous example, preventing the risk of getting into an automobile accident would be to take a defensive driving course and being a cautious driver. Controlling the risk, or minimizing the effects of a loss, would be to have a car with air bags and wear your seatbelt.

When you assume the risk, you are signifying that should anything happen, you are fully ready and financially capable of handling any such loss. Therefore, you bear the responsibility of whatever may happen, no matter what the cost. So, you get into an accident and are sued. Since you have decided to assume the risk and have no insurance, you carry all the obligations that go along with the accident and lawsuit process. Not many people can afford to assume the risk, nor is the wisest idea. This is generally called self-insuring because you are responsible for your actions, not a third party.

Transferring the risk, however, means that you have decided that if you get into an accident, you don't want to be totally responsible. You would rather pay someone else to handle the burden. This is where insurance comes in. By transferring the risk, you pay an insurance company to take the risk off your hands. That transfer comes in the form of an insurance policy, whether that be a homeowner's policy, car insurance, life insurance, or another form. You pay the insurer a premium, and in return, if something happens, the insurer either pays you or, possibly, in the case of a car accident, another party.

Insuring your life means different things at the different stages of your life. Not only do we talk about what types of insurance are out there, we talk about the times in your life when insurance isn't appropriate. Throughout this chapter, we discuss four different types of life insurance: term, whole life, universal life, and variable life. Life insurance is very important from an estate-planning point of view, and we talk about that in a subsequent chapter. For now, we deal with life insurance strictly from a protection-planning angle. The case for and against each of these four types of insurance can be made. Hopefully, though, this chapter will better educate you and make you feel more comfortable about facing some situations that you may not have wanted to talk about in the past.

LIFE INSURANCE

It used to be that there were three different, traditional types of life insurance: term, whole life, and endowment. However, as time goes by, more and more types of insurance contracts become available to the public. Some types of insurance, like second-to-die policies, serve more as an estate planning tool, rather than a purely protection-oriented asset. When faced with purchasing life insurance, there are two main categories to chose from, with each of the categories having their own subcategories. The main types of insurance are term, and cash-value or permanent insurance.

TERM INSURANCE

As its name implies, term life insurance provides protection for a specified amount of time. Should the insured (the person whose life it covers) die while the policy is in force, the insurance company will pay out the face amount of the policy. The general standard for a term policy is 10 years. However, you can purchase 1-year term, or in some cases, 5 or more years. Term policies are also available in whatever face value amounts you deem necessary to cover your needs.

Term is the purest form of insurance in that it provides that the insured's beneficiary will receive the face value of the policy should the insured die within the specified time frame. There are no extra benefits or investment choices with term, as there are with other types of insurance. What you see is what you get.

Because term is a no-frills insurance policy, it is also the most inexpensive way to insure your life. You know those commercials on television that tout insurance protection for just dollars a month? They usually say, "Tom, a 40-year-old, nonsmoking male can get a policy for just $18 a month." Those types of policies are term insurance. The reason they are so inexpensive is because there is limited risk to the insurance company to actually have to pay out the face value, or death benefit, since the insurance company is only assuming the risk for a specified amount of time. In fact, the younger the person, the less expensive protection becomes. However, as a person ages, the cost to insure that person becomes increasingly more expensive. When I refer to term insurance, I am always careful to say that it is "inexpensive" instead of "cheap." Human life is not cheap, and since these policies are designed to provide some financial relief for the insured's beneficiaries, they aren't cheap either, no matter what the premium is.

There are a few types of term policies, but the most common types are level and decreasing term. Term policies are also convertible and renewable, which we will cover, too.

Annually Renewable Term

This type of policy, also called yearly renewable term, acts just as the name implies. As the insured gets older, the amount of the premium increases. Therefore, the policy may be relatively inexpensive when the insured is younger, but as the person ages, the cost of the premium will increase dramatically.

Level Term
Level term policies are also commonly referred to as "straight term" policies because the amount of coverage doesn't change as long as the policy is in force. That is, if you purchase a 10-year level term policy with a $100,000 death benefit, it will remain a $100,000 death benefit from day one to the very last day of the policy. These policies are written for a given number of years, such as 1, 5, 10, or more.

The premium amount for a level term policy remains the same for the life of the initial term. So, by purchasing a 15-year term policy, you will pay the same premium for those 15 years. However, should you decide to renew the policy, you will see an increase in your premium because you are now 15 years older. Thus, as you renew your term policy, the premiums will continue to increase. Some term policies will allow you to renew for the exact same time period as the initial period, while others will allow you to renew on an annual basis once the original time frame has expired. The premium price for level term is more stable than for annually renewable term, but it will also be more expensive.

Decreasing Term
Sometimes a term policy will keep a level premium throughout all periods of coverage, but the death benefit will decrease. These are decreasing term policies. These are used when the amount of coverage needed diminishes over time. For instance, you and your spouse purchase a home with a 30-year mortgage. While you both work, your spouse doesn't earn as much money as you and is concerned that if something were to happen to you, he or she would be unable to continue with the mortgage payments. In this case, you could purchase a decreasing term policy for 30 years. Because the amount owed on the house decreases every year, you wouldn't need a level term policy that would carry the same death benefit throughout the whole 30 years. Rather, your decreasing term policy could coincide with how your mortgage decreases.

Another popular use for decreasing term is with families with young children. The policy would ensure a sufficient level of income while the children are growing up. As the children grow older, the need for as much coverage decreases until the youngest child has moved out and is on his or her own.

Renewability and Convertibility Provisions

When a someone takes out an insurance policy, that person generally has to answer questions about his or her health and hobbies to make sure that the insurance companies see them as a suitable risk. Many times, the prospective insured must even have a physical, but this usually depends on how much coverage that person is requesting. Most term policies are renewable for successive terms without the insured having to show proof of insurability again, although the amount of successive renewable terms may be limited. If you decide to purchase term insurance, be sure your policy has a guaranteed renewable provision, which is usually provided at no cost by the insurer. This will protect your ability to renew your policy should you become uninsurable due to an illness or accident. Never buy a policy that doesn't have a renewability option.

Term policies may also have the ability to be converted into whole life or other types of permanent policies for the same, or lesser, amount of coverage. Again, the insured wouldn't have to prove that he or she is insurable since that person already had a term policy. Insurance companies usually protect themselves by establishing a maximum age, at which time the insured would no longer be able to convert. The biggest advantage to converting your policy is that you would then have protection for the rest of your life as long as you continue to pay your premiums. This option is standard in most term policies.

PROS AND CONS TO TERM INSURANCE

Term insurance offers an inexpensive way to purchase large amounts of coverage for a specified (albeit relatively short) amount of time. When you add in the fact that you can renew the coverage, as well as convert the policy to a form of permanent insurance, you have three very good reasons to purchase term insurance. However, the cost of the premiums continues to go up as you grow older and renew your policy. This cost is what drives people toward whole life, or another form of permanent insurance, and away from term. It's also the reason why many people let their policies lapse and even go without any type of coverage.

Recently, the insurance industry has begun to offer a 30-year term policy, which helps combat the cost problem. By purchasing a 30-year level term policy, you could theoretically have the same coverage into your old age for the same premium amount. It's important to make sure that your policy locks in the premium amount for the life of the policy, if that's the way you decide to go. Remember, though, that no matter what the cost of term insurance, its objective is to provide a large amount of protection for an affordable cost over a specified amount of time.

CASH-VALUE LIFE INSURANCE

This is a vast category that includes whole life, and universal life, as well as variable universal life policies. The aim of this type of policy is to develop a cash value within the insurance contract. The cash value develops because of the level-premium approach to paying for this type of protection, as opposed to having the premiums increase over time, as is the case with term insurance. Cash-value policies may be split into different categories. For our purposes here, we discuss the three basic types of cash-value insurance: whole life, universal life, and variable universal life.

WHOLE LIFE INSURANCE

This type of insurance policy covers the insured's whole life, thus the name "whole life" insurance. Whole life not only offers a death benefit, but it also offers a cash value feature. This cash value is the result of the investment of paid-in insurance premiums. Therefore, the insured also earns a modest return on the premiums paid for the insurance policy. The rate at which the cash value grows is usually fixed, but is generally guaranteed to be more than a set minimum interest rate (i.e. four or five percent). The longer the policy owner pays the premiums and keeps the coverage, the more time the cash value has to appreciate, which results in a larger cash value over time.

But what if you decide that you don't need the insurance coverage? Does that mean that you no longer have access to your cash value? No. If you decide that you want to cancel your whole life policy, you are forfeiting the right to a death benefit when you die. However, because of that forfeiture, the insurance company is obliged to give you the cash value from your policy. Insurance companies put aside assets in anticipation of paying off life insurance claims. As time passes, the amount of money set aside for each insured (the cash value of each policy) increases to reflect the increase in paying off claims. After all, the chance of death increases with the age of the policyholder. As long as the policy is canceled prior to the death of the insured, the insurance company must return the cash value. Since the insurance company is holding and accumulating that money to pay off the insured's future death claim, the company no longer requires that money once the policy is canceled.

There are a wide variety of types of whole life policies, but we only touch on three main types: continuous-premium, single-premium, and limited-payment.

Continuous-Premium Whole Life
This type of policy is the most common because the policyholder pays premiums throughout either the lifetime of the policy or his or her own lifetime. Continuous-premium whole life is also referred to as a "straight life" policy since you pay straight through your life. The premiums remain level as long as the policy is in force. Therefore, the younger you are when you purchase a straight life policy, the lower your premiums will be. However, the younger you are when you purchase a policy, the more you will usually wind up paying as a whole since you will be paying for coverage for a longer period of time. But your annual premium will be less than it would be if you were to wait until you were older to purchase a policy.

A person should buy life insurance because there is some type of need, not just because the premium would be lower if the policy was purchased at age 25, rather than at age 40. Generally, for younger people, permanent life insurance isn't as important as other things may be. I generally recommend that younger people direct their money into retirement accounts rather than insurance, unless there is an actual need for it.

As compared with other types of whole life policies, straight life offers the greatest amount of permanent death protection, but the least amount of savings per dollar of premium paid. For most people, especially families, straight life is the best choice for permanent insurance coverage because the emphasis is on the death benefit, not the savings feature.

Many people may think that once you start paying the premiums for a straight life policy, then you are stuck unless you cancel the policy. That's not necessarily true. Once a policy has accumulated some cash value, if you want, you can "trade in" the policy for another, paid-up policy that has a lower death benefit. As long as your policy has a change-of-premium provision, you can do this at no cost.

Single-Premium Whole Life

As the name implies, a single-premium life policy is paid for at its inception with one premium. The policy is then in force for the rest of the insured's life, unless it is otherwise canceled by the insured. The single-premium policy (SPWL) is, as a rule, not well suited for younger people and young families. Because of its investment attributes, the SPWL is appealing to those people looking for a tax-sheltered investment vehicle.

As with other types of cash-value policies, the earnings and interest of an SPWL accumulate on a tax-deferred basis. While the policy also provides life insurance coverage and will pay a death benefit upon the insured's death, the amount of the coverage is usually the minimum allowed under the IRS's rules. Generally, the death benefit is treated as an added bonus to those who purchase this type of coverage. As with other types of policies, the death benefits will pass through to the beneficiaries on a tax-free basis. Minimum premiums are usually $5000, but most people put in more, thus garnering a larger amount of tax-deferred earnings.

While this type of policy sounds great, it's not without a catch. If you needed to take a loan from your policy, or just make a withdrawal, and you are younger than $59^1/_2$, you will be penalized by the IRS. First of all, the money withdrawn will be treated as a gain, not a return of your original premium. Therefore, it will be taxed as income. Secondly, you will face a 10-percent early withdrawal penalty because you aren't $59^1/_2$ years old yet. These are the main reasons the SPWL isn't suited for younger people and young families. Instead, the SPWL is more appropriate for middle-aged people with higher incomes who may want to supplement their retirement income or cover future, potential estate costs.

Limited-Payment Whole Life

Limited-payment policies also cover the insured throughout his or her entire life. But, they are a split between the single-premium and continuous-payment whole life policies. Limited-payment policies are designed to have the insured stop paying the premium after a certain period of time. Common types of policies are 20-pay life, 30-pay life, paid-up at age 55, and paid-up at age 65. This is the way it works: Under the 20-pay and 30-pay life policies, the policyholder pays the same level premium for the 20 or 30 years, depending on the policy type. After that time period elapses, the policy is paid up and the insured owes no more money in the way of premiums. For the paid-up at age 55 and paid-up at age 65 policies, the policyholder pays the premiums until that person is either 55 or 65. Again, the policy is then fully paid for. Naturally, the older the insured is when he or she takes out the policy, the larger the premiums will be, especially when choosing the paid-up at a specific age policies. Once the policies are paid for, they remain in force for the rest of the insured's life.

Beware of salespeople who try and sell you a limited-payment policy using the following two arguments: a large savings element, and limited payment time. The aim of life insurance is to provide financially for the beneficiaries of a deceased person. They take care of the financial loss that occurs when someone dies. They aren't specifically designed for an accumulation of savings. Plus, as we discussed earlier, those people who elect to purchase a straight life policy only need to pay the premiums for as long as they want to. As long as there is a cash value, those straight life policies may be converted into paid-up policies with a smaller death benefit, thus negating the limited payment argument.

Limited-payment insurance policies are a good deal for certain people. But, when faced with a choice between a limited-payment policy and a straight life policy, chances are the straight life policy will be a better fit. Again, it's always important that you are purchasing insurance because you need it, not just for a tax-deferred investment. There are other types of tax-deferred investments that offer better rates of return that will suit your needs better than an insurance policy.

PROS AND CONS OF WHOLE LIFE INSURANCE

The main advantage of whole life insurance is the ability to accumulate a cash value on a tax-deferred basis. This cash value also contributes to the total value of an estate when the policy is owned by the insured. You can borrow against this cash value, if needed; plus, if you no longer need any type of insurance protection, you can cancel your policy and the cash value will be returned to you.

Another advantage is that the coverage is for the insured's entire life, unless the policy is canceled. As compared with term, the coverage from a whole life policy is designed to last for as long as the insured is either alive, or wants it. Term policies expire after a specific amount of time. Of course, term policies can be renewed, but the cost of the premium will increase. Conversely, the premiums of a whole life policy remain level as long as the policy is in force.

Because of the savings feature, many people have said that they are forced to save because of the premium payments. Additionally, policyholders can budget their premiums over a longer period of time (with the exception of single-payment policies), thus eliminating the potential risks of coverage not being affordable. This also reduces the chance that people who need coverage will be without it.

However, whole life policies aren't without their drawbacks, too. Although term policies need to be renewed, and there is an added cost at every renewal as compared with whole life policies, term policies purchase more coverage for the amount of premium paid. This is because of the very nature of term insurance, but could be a contributing factor to the fact that term policies are popular.

Interestingly, the cash value also poses a disadvantage to the policies. But that is more due to the misuse of the policy than for any other reason. Whole life insurance policies shouldn't be used in place of other investments, especially when the other investments can earn the investor a potentially larger return. As a general rule, the interest rate for the cash values of whole life policies is rather small and not competitive with other types of interest rates. Although it's guaranteed, investing your money in the stock market may mean a great deal when it comes to overall return. Assuming no need for insurance, how would you feel if you made a 6 percent return on your money in a policy's cash value, instead of a 11-percent return in the stock market? Would you be happy? I certainly wouldn't be. This isn't to say that you should invest your money in the stock market instead of purchasing an insurance policy. What I am saying is that if you don't need the insurance, don't buy it. The accumulation of the cash value won't be significant, and you'll be paying for insurance you don't need.

UNIVERSAL LIFE INSURANCE

Universal life policies combine term insurance with a tax-sheltered investment account. The term insurance provides the death benefits, while the investment account pays interest, usually at competitive money market account rates. The difference between whole life and universal life is that the universal life premium is unbundled: The portion of the premium paid for death protection and the portion paid into the investment account are identified separately. This contrasts with whole life, where the premium paid goes toward a policy with a stated face value amount of coverage, as well as a cash value that accumulates according to a specified fixed schedule.

When a premium is paid for a universal life policy, it is split up. Part of the premium goes to pay administrative fees, while the remainder is put into the cash value, or investment account. There the money will grow at a certain rate. This rate is periodically revised due to fluctuations with market yields, but it will be guaranteed to be at least a certain amount (such as three percent). Then, each month, one month's cost of insurance is withdrawn from the investment account, which is then used to purchase the required death protection. As long as there is enough money in the investment account to purchase death protection, the policy will remain in force. However, if this account should grow to an abnormally large amount, the amount of insurance protection will need to be increased. This is so the account can retain its tax-deferred growth status. The IRS requires that the death benefits in a universal life policy must always exceed the cash value by a specified amount.

This raises an important question. Because the premium is split, and the investment account is separate, is this actually whole life? Since the cost of insurance is subtracted from the cash value, the answer is yes. However, the cash value accumulates because of interest credited to the account. According to current tax laws, as long as the total value of the investment account is less than the total amount of premiums paid, the growth of the investment account will be tax-deferred. However, if a policy is canceled and the cash value is returned to the policyholder, and the cash value is greater than the amount of total premiums paid, the gain will be taxed. But, like other types of insurance policies, death benefits are received tax-free and the cash value grows on a tax-deferred basis.

Universal life policies have two types of death protection: Option A and Option B. First, Option A provides level death protection. When the cash value increases, the amount of pure insurance protection decreases. The second choice provides a specified death protection plus the appreciated cash value. With Option B, the death benefit varies with the rate of earnings in the investment account. It will also increase along with the growing cash value.

PROS AND CONS OF UNIVERSAL LIFE INSURANCE

Universal life policies are extremely flexible. Because the insurance protection comes from either the accumulated cash value or the annual premium paid, if you don't want to pay the premium, you don't have to. You just need to be sure that there is sufficient cash value within the policy to cover the cost of insurance. The cost of insurance will then be deducted from the cash value. Certainly, the older you are, the more it will cost to pay for the insurance, so it's important that there is enough in the investment account to cover this.

The amount of coverage can also be easily increased or decreased. Plus, you can change the policy from a level benefit type to the cash value plus a specified death benefit. If you choose to increase the coverage, you will generally be asked to prove insurability again. But you won't need to do anything if you are decreasing the amount of coverage.

This flexibility makes a universal life policy very attractive. The policy can change with you as your needs change. For example, when you get older and aren't in need of as much insurance protection, you can decrease your coverage. Or, if you don't want to pay your premium and want to use it for something else, you don't have to worry about your policy lapsing because the cost of insurance will come from the investment account.

However, the flexibility of the premium payments is also a drawback. If you were to economize on your premiums early on in the life of the policy, you may find that in the later years of the policy, you will be subject to larger-than-anticipated premiums. Plus, if the interest rate declines, the investment account may not grow fast enough to cover the cost of insurance. Also, just because there is flexibility with the payment of premiums, that doesn't mean that at some point the premiums would disappear. Usually, the premiums never disappear. Even if they did, they would probably reappear once the interest rates declined to the point where they wouldn't cover the cost.

Check to see what the guaranteed interest rate is before you purchase your policy. Typically, policies will state that they pay current interest on policies. This could be five or six percent, as compared with the guaranteed minimum of, say, three percent. It's important that you know what the policy's interest rate is tied to. Many times, the interest rate for policies is that of the 90-day Treasury bill.

VARIABLE LIFE INSURANCE

While universal life offers a separate investment account that earns a competitive interest rate, variable life takes this concept one step further by allowing the policyholders to choose how they want their dollars invested in the cash value account. Variable insurance gives the insured the possibility of higher returns than would otherwise be attainable with either whole or universal life. However, there is no minimum guaranteed *return*. Plus, the amount of coverage varies with the results of the investment account. As with the other types of policies, there are multiple forms of variable life insurance: straight variable life and variable universal life.

Straight variable life insurance has a fixed premium, whereas variable universal life has flexible premiums. The policyholder can choose how much of the premium amount goes toward death coverage, just like with universal life. Straight variable life also has a guaranteed minimum death benefit that is established when the contract is originally issued. This aspect doesn't change the fact that the premium is still invested and that the both the cash value and death benefit vary with the performance of whatever the premium is invested in.

Variable universal life offers the most flexibility of all forms of life insurance. It is also the more popular form of the two types of variable life policies. As with straight variable life, the value of the separate account varies with the investment results of the underlying subaccounts. However, the policyholder can choose between two options for the death benefit. Option A provides for a level death benefit, while Option B specifies that the death benefit be the face amount of the policy plus the cash value at the time of death.

Just as with variable annuities, there are various subaccounts within a variable life policy. The policyholder can choose how the premium is allocated between the different subaccounts so that he or she can try to receive the best possible return on the money, all the while receiving beneficial tax treatment. These subaccounts usually represent each type of asset class; thus, an insured person could opt to split his or her premium between a growth fund, fixed fund, and bond fund, for example. The growth of the cash value of a variable life policy is also tax-deferred. And, as with other types of life insurance, the beneficiary of a variable policy receives the death benefit tax-free.

Variable life insurance policies are becoming increasingly popular as the investing public decides that not only do they need insurance coverage, but that they can still potentially generate some type of profit. Another reason is that, in contrast with whole life and universal life, the cash value doesn't just earn a specified interest rate. Because the policyholders can choose what type of investments the premium can be invested in, people generally feel that this type of permanent insurance is more beneficial.

PROS AND CONS OF VARIABLE LIFE INSURANCE

The types of subaccounts vary with the company that is offering the policy, however; you can generally choose from a wide range of asset classes. In fact, the subaccounts are set up like mutual funds. You could choose to have a portion of your premium invested in a junk bond fund, or perhaps a high-growth fund. The possibilities are only limited by the insurance company. You will also be able to switch between funds at no cost, just as you would be able to with an annuity. Plus, since the investment account grows on a tax-deferred basis, you won't be generating any capital gains tax when moving your money between accounts.

With variable policies, the emphasis is more on the separate accounts and the investment aspect of the policy than it is with any other type of policy. Because of that, variable policies have increased expenses that you wouldn't necessarily see with universal or whole life policies. In addition to commissions for the insurance agent that sells you the policy, there are annual fees for servicing the insurance and managing the portfolio. These all help lower your overall return.

As with universal life, variable life policies have been misused. It's very important that you make an informed decision when purchasing this kind of policy. Because the cash value goes up and down with the market, the potential to lose money is great. Of course, there is also a great possibility that you will gain quite a bit, or just break even. Although this is an insurance product, you should enter into a purchase as if you were about to buy a mutual fund. Make sure you do your research before committing to any type of policy.

OTHER TYPES OF LIFE INSURANCE

There are various other kinds of policies through which you could obtain life insurance. Some of them are beneficial and come at little or no expense to you. Others are best left alone because they are just a waste of money for you. One type of policy is most often used at businesses. As part of a benefits package, many employers will offer life insurance for their employees. This type of insurance is group life insurance because there is one master policy that covers many different people. Usually group life, when offered by an employer, is paid for solely by the employer, with the death benefits going to whomever the employee designates. Group life is almost always term insurance because of the lower costs. However, this kind of insurance doesn't just have to come from an employer. Usually, any type of group, like a labor union, alumni organization, etc., can obtain a group life policy for those eligible members. Any type of group life insurance should be considered when you are looking at your life insurance needs.

Two other types of insurance are credit life and mortgage life. Credit life insurance is generally offered by banks, credit card companies, and other lenders. The premium for credit life is typically rather high, and is tacked onto your monthly bill. While the purpose for credit life is to pay off any outstanding debts to that particular lender, it is a waste of money. Any kind of insurance that you have, be it group life through your job, or a regular term or permanent policy you have on your own, should cover your outstanding debts. Mortgage life insurance is another form of term insurance that would pay off your mortgage in the event that you died before the debt was repaid. As with credit life, the premium is usually pretty high and a waste of money. You would be better off shopping around for a regular term or permanent policy.

DO I NEED LIFE INSURANCE?

This is a question I have faced a number of times when meeting with clients. Unfortunately, there is no pat answer for everyone. Whether you need insurance is determined by your individual situation. A good place to start is to look at the cash flow statement you prepared for yourself. How much money do you have coming in every month? How much is going out? If something were to happen to you, would your family, or heirs, have enough money to eradicate your debt and pay off any other types of estate costs? If the answer to the last question was no, then perhaps you should investigate some form of life insurance.

A good rule of thumb as to whether you need insurance focuses on whether or not you are married and/or have children. Generally, those individuals who don't have children have a decreased need for life insurance. That's not to say that just because you don't have kids, you don't need insurance. You might. But, typically, single people with no children are in no need of life insurance. Again, though, this really depends on your particular situation. Life insurance is designed to provide financially for your dependents after you are gone. Therefore, if you have no dependents, you may not need insurance.

Likewise, as you grow older, your insurance needs change. For example, when you have younger children, your need for insurance is greater than after they have grown up and moved out of the house. At that point, they would no longer be your dependents, so you wouldn't need to provide for them financially. Plus, as you build your assets, your need for life insurance should also decrease. This is because you would be more able to self-insure, and your dependents and heirs would be able to pay off any debts or estate costs by using money that is already there. But, if your spouse has already died, you may need more coverage. This will depend on what type of estate you have amassed. As you get older, you will also need to consider what types of retirement benefits you will receive, such as social security or pension benefits from your employer. These will also affect the amount of coverage you need.

HOW MUCH INSURANCE DO YOU NEED?

Now that you have established whether or not you need insurance, deciding how much coverage you actually need becomes your focus. Putting a price on your life may seem like an overwhelming task, but it's important. While pulling a number out of thin air and using that as your coverage amount might seem like an attractive idea, you could wind up with too little coverage, which wouldn't suit your needs. Or, you could wind up paying more than necessary because you have too much coverage.

The three main ways of calculating how much insurance you need are the rule-of-thumb method, human needs approach, and capital preservation approach. The rule-of-thumb method says that your coverage should be about five times your gross income plus your mortgage, debts, funeral expenses, and other funding needs. As long as your situation is pretty normal and you don't have any outlandish expenses, the rule-of-thumb method should work well for you.

The human needs approach focuses on what your family will need after you are gone. It takes into account your final estate and funeral expenses, estate settlement costs, and the amounts of money needed to pay off your mortgage and other debts. It also factors in the fact that your children will need income until they are of legal age and that your spouse may need income for the rest of his or her life. Any special needs and college costs must also be added to the mix. From that total, any social security or veteran's benefits should be subtracted. Finally, it is assumed that if your family takes a lump sum and invests it wisely, the principal and income will be enough to provide for their needs.

The capital preservation approach is similar to the human needs approach because it considers all the financial needs of your family. However, with this method, your family's needs are met with the income earned from your assets. The assets would stay intact for your beneficiaries.

Deciding which method is best for you may be a little time-consuming, but it's worth it. (See Table 11.1 for comparison of premiums.) Plus, if you have hired a financial advisor, that person is more than capable of helping you decide how much coverage is necessary.

Table 11.1 Premium Comparisons[1] (Death Benefit—$450,000)

	Policy type	Premium (paid monthly)	Premium (paid annually)
Male, age 25	10-year Term	$22.08	$247.50
Female, age 25	10-year Term	$19.70	$220.00
Male, age 25	VUL	$178.73	$2,144.75
Female, age 25	VUL	$132.75	$1,593.00

[1]Although there is no age difference between the male and female examples, there are differences in the amount of premiums the two will pay. This is because women have longer life expectancies than men do. The column marked "Premium (paid annually)" is if the insured chooses to pay the premium on an annual basis. For the term policies the annual outlay of money is more if the premium is paid on a monthly basis, but for the VUL policies, the amount stays the same. If paying the premium on a monthly basis, the male would spend $264.96 per year and the woman would pay $236.40 annually. If any of the variables used in the above illustration were to change (i.e., age, death benefit, smoking status), the premium amounts would vary.

12

FINANCIAL SUITS OF ARMOR

In the previous chapter, we discussed the need for and types of life insurance. Insuring your life, to help protect your dependents and family in the case that you die prematurely is very important. But, there are other types of insurance that are equally important that you may use while you are still living.

One of the main cases against life insurance is that, generally, the person who purchases the policy is the one who will never receive its benefit. That is, the person who pays for the contract is, generally, the one whose life is insured, and therefore, the death benefits won't be paid until after the person has died. But there are two main types of insurance that are designed to be used by the insured while they are still living: disability and long-term care insurance.

Disability insurance is designed to help replace a person's income if that person is injured and becomes unable to work and earn a living. There are different factors that go into the various types of policies, all of which we discuss. Long-term care insurance covers the costs associated with nursing homes, in-home care, and other forms of long-term care. Both supplementing an income and paying for long-term care are vitally important aspects to the financial planning process. By planning ahead for each of these events, you cover yourself and help keep on track for your financial goals. Think about it. If you have this goal of accumulating wealth and work very hard to reach this goal, would you want something to happen to derail your plans? One of the reasons we include this type of protection planning is to supplement the investment process. As a financial planner, I hate to see when someone has worked very hard to accumulate money, only to see all that hard work wiped out by an accident or the need for long-term care. Both of these can be extremely expensive, even in the short-term.

Of course, I've heard every excuse in the book for not wanting to purchase either disability or long-term care insurance. But I've also seen what's happened when the person who needed it didn't have it. So, we touch on some these excuses and the reasons why they are just excuses, not actual reasons.

ELIMINATION PERIODS

Both disability and long-term care insurance have elimination, or waiting, periods. These are periods of time that must elapse before any type of benefit is paid. These can range between the different types of policies and insurance companies offering them; however, normal elimination periods are either 30 or 90 days. Some types of plans allow you to choose how long you want your elimination period to be. The longer the waiting time, the lower the premium usually is.

Another important aspect to elimination periods is that, typically, once you have satisfied it once, you won't have to do it again. Therefore, if you become disabled and have a 30-day elimination period before your coverage begins to pay benefits, you will only have to wait that one 30-day period. If you were to go back to work after a few months and then became disabled again, your benefits would begin immediately, and you wouldn't have to wait for those 30 days.

DISABILITY INSURANCE

The Health Insurance Association of America has made some startling discoveries about the need for disability insurance in this country. They estimate that a 35-year-old worker has a 12-percent chance of becoming disabled for a three-month period. By the time a worker reaches the age of 55, this chance has increased more than five times, to a 70-percent chance! Interestingly enough, these odds are the same as the odds for death. However, most people have life insurance, but no disability insurance. Why take the chance that you could perhaps become disabled and not have any protection to help you financially get through that time?

The best way to protect yourself against the adverse effects of being unable to work due to a disability is to purchase disability insurance (DI). This form of insurance will provide income to you and your family on a weekly, biweekly, or monthly basis, as long as the injury or illness is covered by the insurance. There are a few forms of DI that workers can obtain; here we cover the three main types. The first comes from the government in the form of Social Security disability benefits. The second is from a worker's employer, and the third is DI purchased by the worker.

The need for some sort of DI is great, but, it is often overlooked. People are too concerned with insuring their lives, the lives of their children, and preparing for other types of life changes, such as a college education or retirement. Unfortunately, for most people, any missed time at work would be financially devastating. While you are off work and are using whatever savings you have, you could wind up wiping out most, if not all, of the savings you have accumulated for yourself. Many times, workers do receive some type of DI as part of their benefits from their employer, but that may not be enough.

What Is a Disability?

Disability policies will all have a specific definition for what is considered a disability. Some policies will have a very broad interpretation of the word, while others will adhere to a rather strict definition. The most liberal definition is known as the "own occupation" rule. It says that you are considered disabled if you cannot perform at least one primary duty of your own job. Under this rule, a surgeon who has lost his or her motor skills and could no longer operate would receive full benefits even though he or she could still meet with patients and consult with other surgeons and doctors. However, you can opt for a residual benefit feature, which would pay you partial benefits if you could only work for a lower salary or part-time.

Most policies use a stricter definition of disability, known as the "any occupation" interpretation. Under the any occupation definition, a person is considered disabled if he or she is unable to perform any occupation for which that person is reasonably suited or trained for. The basis for this is the individual's education, training, or work experience. This type of policy is considerably less expensive because it gives the insurer the leeway of determining whether benefits should be paid.

Some types of individual policies include a presumptive clause, which allows the insurer to discard the any-occupation and own-occupation rules. This clause states that the insured is presumed to be totally disabled under certain conditions, such as loss of both hands or feet, loss of eyesight in both eyes, or loss of hearing in both ears. Through this clause, the insured would receive full benefits even though they may choose to remain employed.

Social Security DI
There are two main types of social security DI benefits: cash disability income benefits, and the freezing of a disabled worker's wage position in order to determine that person's future retirement or survivorship benefits. A worker is considered eligible to receive benefits when he or she has a medically determined physical or mental impairment that is very severe. The impairment must be so severe that the worker must be deemed unable to engage in *any* substantially gainful work or employment. Any substantially gainful work amounts to what is termed an "all occupations" definition. That is, you can't be able to do anything for pay. Nothing. Not only is that definition difficult to fulfill, the rules about it are very strict.

If you become disabled and have satisfied the unable-to-work provision, you must then wait 5 months before you can collect any type of benefit. And, you must remain disabled for that entire five months if you wish to collect the benefits. After your first 5 months of waiting, the benefits begin to trickle in. However, to continue collecting, your disability must be expected to last at least 12 months from when the impairment started, expected to result in death, or have already lasted 12 months. It's also important to note that the Social Security Administration rejects approximately 40 percent of all disability claims it receives.

The social security program uses your current wage subject to social security taxes to determine what your benefits would be. These benefits are paid to the disabled worker and that person's dependents. Regardless of whatever private insurance a disabled worker has, he or she will receive social security benefits. Let's assume that Joe Client is 35 years old. His wife, Mary is also 35, and they have two children, Tommy (age 5) and Lindsey (age 2). Joe makes $40,000 per year and becomes seriously injured in a train accident. Joe remains impaired for the five-month waiting period and begins to collect his benefits. For this illustration, we'll assume Joe's benefits are $1249 per month.

Joe's monthly benefit = $1249—until recovery, death, or age 65

Mary's monthly benefit = $972—until Lindsey reaches 16 (14 years)

Tommy's monthly benefit = $972—until he is 18 years old (13 years)

Lindsey's monthly benefit = $972—until she is 18 years old (16 years)

However, there is a maximum family benefit, so in Joe's case, he and his family would only receive about $2289 per month ($27,468 per year). As long as Joe remains disabled, his family will continue to receive $2289 per month for the next 16 years (at that point, Mary, Tommy, and Lindsey would no longer be eligible). They would then receive $1249 per month for 14 years, or until Joe is 65 years old. Once Joe turns 65, his social security benefits would begin.[1]

Even though these benefits are coming from the government, that doesn't mean that they are guaranteed to be tax-free. They may be tax-free, but they may not be. For the preceding example, it's likely that Joe's benefits would be tax-free. But assuming that he did have to pay federal income tax, and if Joe falls in the 15-percent tax bracket, the nontaxable (gross) equivalent of his social security benefits would be $2693 per month ($32,316 per year). That falls quite short of his $40,000-per-year gross salary.

How does that sound as a sole form of benefits? Most people I know don't want to wait five months to collect benefits, nor do they wish to tap into their savings to help cover those five months. The benefits don't begin to cover what a worker would normally bring home in pay, plus they may also be taxable. Relying on Social Security benefits in the case of a disability is not a financially responsible, or wise, decision.

DI as Part of a Worker's Benefits

As part of an employee's benefits package, many employers will include some sort of disability insurance, which is paid for entirely by the employer. This is not only a benefit for the employee, but, if used, will also cause the employee to face some tax consequences that may not have been considered. Employer-sponsored DI plans are a benefit for the employer, as well, because they provide the employer with another tax deduction. An employee may receive short-term DI, long-term DI, or both from his or her employer.

The biggest benefit to an employer-sponsored DI plan is that employees don't have to pay for their own insurance. Plus, the amount that the employer pays for the insurance is not included in the employee's gross income. So, not only does the employee not have to pay for the coverage, but he or she is also not taxed on the premium amount. Of course, if the coverage is used, this may come back to

---

[1] The figures used in the example are merely illustrative and aren't meant to convey what actual social security benefits would be. Those are determined on a case-by-case basis by the Social Security Administration. You can also visit their Web site at *www.ssa.gov* to receive an approximation of what your benefits would be.

haunt the employee. However, if the coverage isn't used, then the DI still remains a benefit, since the employee hasn't paid out any money.

Employers are able to take out a group policy for all eligible employees, so, their premium amount is much smaller than if all the employees were to take out separate policies on themselves. This also makes entry into the plan much easier for the employee. Simply by filling out the applicable forms and waiting the required amount of time (usually employers mandate that an employee wait three months before being allowed to participate in any type of benefits program), the employee has disability coverage with no out-of-pocket cost. The coverage will then remain in effect for as long as the employee remains eligible.

Typically, DI plans are split into two categories: short-term and long-term. Short-term benefits usually have a schedule of weekly benefits that are based on earnings categories. However, they have relatively low maximum benefits. That is, the overall payout is rather small when compared with long-term plans because short-term plans only cover a specific amount of time, such as 6, 12, 26, or 52 weeks. These plans are designed to cover a moderate amount of earnings over a short period of time.

Long-term plans typically kick in after a short-term plan has expired, so that there are no overlapping benefits. This type of coverage takes care of more serious, long-term illnesses and disabilities. Long-term coverage is specified by a percentage of earnings, such as 70 percent, and is accompanied by a higher base amount of benefits, which could provide the recipient with monthly benefits of $5000 or more. Generally, the elimination period for long-term DI is longer than it is for short-term since the recipient is generally receiving short-term DI benefits during that time.

A very important consideration about employer-sponsored DI is that the employer pays for it, not the employee. And, since the premiums paid aren't included in the employee's gross income, any benefits received under the plan may be taxable to the employee. Generally, the tax code provides that money received through accident or health insurance due to personal injuries or illness be excluded from the individual's gross income for tax purposes. This rule, though, excludes any benefits received from an employer-sponsored plan where the contributions were made by the employer and not included as part of the employee's gross income. Thus, if you receive $627 per month in disability benefits from your employer's DI plan and you didn't contribute any money toward the cost of the insurance, that $627 would be considered your gross income and you would be liable for taxes on it.

An employee's coverage may be terminated, also. This would occur when the employee quits or retires. The employer may also decide to terminate the coverage, which would result in all covered employees no longer having the insurance. Or, if the employer fails to pay the premium (unless there is an error), the coverage will be canceled. If the employee quits, he or she doesn't have this option to extend the benefits, or roll them over into an individual plan. That person will then have to wait to fulfill his or her new employer's elimination period before having coverage again.

Because employer-sponsored DI coverage is designed for work-related accidents, it shouldn't be taken into account when considering financial planning. Relying on this type of DI to cover you is like planning to die in a car accident. You don't know that you will become disabled on the job, just like you don't know how you will die. Should you become disabled at work, this insurance will help cover your expenses, but, if you aren't hurt at work, then it will be of little use to you.

Individual DI Plans

The best way to make sure that you are covered in the case of a disability or debilitating illness is to purchase your own DI insurance. Although there is a growing importance placed upon group forms of coverage, there are also a number of reasons why an individual would need his or her own coverage. First, the amount of coverage provided by the group plan is insufficient. Second, the duration of benefits may not be long enough. Plus, many people simply do not want to rely on a group plan, especially if the benefits will wind up being taxable to them. Benefits paid under an individual plan would normally be tax-free.

Just like with other forms of DI, there are elimination periods with individual plans. But because you are paying for your own coverage, you may be able to choose the length of your elimination period. Again, the premium amount is tied to the length of the elimination period. While cost is a factor, don't let it be the overriding aspect to picking out your policy. It's more important to be sure that you are fully covered in the case that you need it, rather than saving a few bucks in the immediate future.

Individual policies may cover illness in addition to accident (known as accident and sickness coverage), as opposed to just disabilities resulting from an accident (accident-only coverage). It's important to insure yourself against illness, as well as accidents. If you are unable to work due to an illness and receive benefits from your coverage, you'll find that those will help even if your medical bills are totally covered by your health insurance. Plus, your medical bills may not be covered by your health insurance.

With today's individual DI policies, you can choose from a wide array of coverage periods. You could opt for a short-term type of policy, with coverage ranging from six weeks to a few months. Or, you could choose a policy that would cover you for the rest of your life. Whatever period you select should be based upon your needs, not someone else's desire to sell you a bigger policy.

As far as individuals are concerned, the own occupation is the better of the two disability definitions. When coupled with the longer coverage period, this is the best option for the insured. However, since the coverage is better, the premium will be more expensive. Do your homework and compare the different premium amounts and coverage options from many different insurance companies to find the policy that best suits your needs. Don't be swayed by cost alone.

Do you need disability insurance?

Ask yourself these two questions:

1) Is your salary the main source of income for your family?

2) How would you replace your income if you were unable to work?

If you can answer these questions to your satisfaction (or if you already have some form of DI), then you don't need to worry about thinking about this. However, if you don't like your answers, or if you are unable to answer the second question, it's time to think about some type of disability insurance. Remaining unprotected is one of the surest ways to not reach your goals, and perhaps devastate you and your family financially.

Determining Your Need

The point of disability insurance is to replace all or most of your income should something happen that would render you unable to earn a living. Since most plans would allow you to receive your benefits tax-free, you really only need to concern yourself with replacing your net income (what you bring home after taxes). By looking at what benefits you currently have available to you, you can estimate what your need is and how much coverage you should purchase in an individual plan.

The first thing you should do is look at last year's tax return. Take your gross income and subtract all taxes paid, including social security tax. Don't include any income you receive from dividends or from outside sources, just refer to your job income. Then divide this total by 12 to calculate your monthly net income.

Then, estimate your social security benefits. Not all people are eligible, so don't be surprised if you find out that you won't be able to receive them. If you are eligible, you can receive an estimate of your benefits on the social security Web site (see previous footnote), or by calling your local social security office. It's important not to rely on this, so although you can use these figures to help estimate your need, please keep in mind that 40 percent of all claims are denied. The likelihood of receiving benefits is very small, and it takes five months to begin receiving them. There are other types of benefits that you may be eligible for through both the government and other types of group policies. I'm not going into these here, but just be aware that social security and employer-sponsored plans aren't the only types of DI that you may have as an option.

If you are eligible for any employer disability benefits, you can contact your employer to see what type of benefits you would receive. A good idea is first to ask your employer about any sick leave or wage continuation programs they may have because these would act as a form of short-term coverage. Whatever you wish to include, be sure you are aware of what the tax ramifications would be.

Add up any monthly benefits you are counting on receiving and subtract that number from your net income. This resulting number is the amount of money you would still need to help cover your bills and replace your income. (See Figure 12.1 for a sample worksheet.) Of course, any type of investment income (i.e., dividends or interest) and spousal income (if your spouse works) would still continue, and so, are ignored as part of the beginning gross income amount.

There are some provisions to consider when purchasing DI. First, many policies offer a cost-of-living adjustment (COLA), to help protect you against inflation. If you purchase a policy that will pay you a flat benefit of $3000 per month now, that $3000 won't have the same purchasing power in five years. With a COLA, the benefit is annually adjusted for inflation, is usually in line with the Consumer Price Index and takes effect once the insured is disabled. However, your insurance company may cap its rate to avoid for super-high adjustments.

Many insurers will also offer a waiver of premium option. For those insurers that offer it, it will be automatically included in your policy. This provision is especially beneficial because it says that once you are disabled for a period of time (normally 60 or 90 days), all your future premiums will be waived for the duration of your disability. This also acts somewhat as an increase in your benefit because you will retain the premium amount in your pocket, rather than paying it out to the insurance company.

Then there is the guaranteed insurability option that allows you to purchase additional disability income insurance while you are still healthy. With this provision, you don't have to prove insurability again, which is nice.

What is my need?

1. Gross income excluding dividends, interest or other outside income _____

2. Taxes paid, including Social Security tax _____

3. Subtract line 2 from line 1 _____

4. Divide line 3 by 12 to find net monthly income

5. Estimation of existing monthly benefits

   a. Social Security _____

   b. Other government benefits _____

   c. Company benefits _____

   d. Other group benefits _____

6. Total monthly benefits (add lines 5a through 5d) _____

7. Estimated monthly disability benefits needed (subtract line 6 from line 4) _____

Figure 12.1: This worksheet will help you to estimate what your needs would be if you were to suffer a disability and be unable to earn a living. The figures you come up with on line 7 will be the monthly amount that you need to help cover your entire take-home pay and what you should consider when purchasing and Individual DI plan.

LONG-TERM CARE INSURANCE

With the advancements made in health care and technology today, the world's population is living longer than ever before. Because of that, there is also an increase in the need for nursing home and other forms of long-term care. But long-term care isn't just for elderly people, there are many cases when the people needing some form of long-term care may be in their forties, or younger! From this need arises an unfortunate problem. There are those who are in need of care, but are unable to afford it. This is a needless problem that can be easily remedied, as long as you are open to discussing the possibility, and realities surrounding long-term care.

By the year 2050, nearly five percent of our population will be at least 85 years old, whereas, only one percent of the population was that age in 1990.[2] This will translate into an increased percentage of people who will need long-term care, or will already be in either a nursing home or receiving in-home care. As people age, their ability to do little, everyday things diminishes. Most everyone knows people who have hired special care workers to come into their home, or are living in a nursing home simply because they were unable to care for themselves properly anymore.

The odds of your entering a nursing home increase every year. If you knew that you were going to need some form of care, be it in-home or nursing home care, what would you do? Do you know how you would pay for it? If you answered "yes" to the second question, congratulations. At least you have thought about it. But your answers may not be the best suited to your situation. There are a few ways to help protect yourself, as well as your spouse and dependents, from the costs of long-term care. If you answered "no" to the second question, you are not alone. Most people have not considered what they would do. Perhaps they may be unwilling to entertain the thought of needing some sort of plan. Unfortunately, today's reality dictates that we consider the unpleasant. Simply put, we have to plan in order to make sure that we will be taken care of.

---

[2]*Personal Financial Planning*, Eighth Edition, By Lawrence J. Gitman and Michael D. Joehnk. Harcourt Brace College Publishers, 1999.

Many of my clients are over the age of 50. Therefore, they have already seen age and frailty in their own parents. One of my client's mother is in a nursing facility because she suffers from Alzheimer's Disease. He understands the need for long-term care insurance and has a policy for himself and one for his wife. Many of my other clients understand this. They also recognize that the chances are great for them to enter into a nursing home or need long-term care. However, I also have clients who have never known anyone who was touched by this. They aren't as open to the possibility of needing any type of care, and are simply unwilling to discuss it.

What I've found is that while I can't push clients into talking about it, I can gently persuade them into thinking about it on their own. Usually, they will decide that they do need to talk to me about it. Those people who choose to face their fears and the unpleasantness that generally accompany thoughts of long-term care are better off. Those who continue to ignore these needs are usually the ones who find themselves flailing their arms instead of flying.

Long-term care consists of different types of care. It doesn't necessarily translate to nursing home care, although this is the most common form. Individuals needing long-term care may wish to enter a skilled nursing home, or they may want to receive care in their own homes. Skilled nursing facilities generally have a large staff and the equipment necessary to provide most, if not all, services needed at any time by their patients. They also provide rehabilitative services on a daily basis for those who need them. Intermediate-care facilities provide custodial care on a primary basis, but they also have skilled nursing and rehabilitative services. Custodial care facilities are residential places that are designed to provide primary custodial care. However, they aren't equipped to provide any skilled nursing services. Adult day care, an increasingly popular choice, is offered only on a nonresidential basis. Home health care may provide skilled nursing care, as well as rehabilitative services, from the comfort of the patient's own home.

Once you've made up your mind that long-term care is something you need to consider, the question becomes, "What should I do about it?" Quite simply, take a look at your options. This also involves coming up with some sort of action plan. Typically, the first resource people look to is their family members. A common response I hear when I bring up long-term care is that the client's family will take care of them. The second response I hear is that they will use Medicare or Medicaid. The least popular response I hear is that the client would like to purchase long-term care insurance.

While all three responses are likely scenarios (varying with each individual), the most positive of the three is to purchase insurance. Through insurance, you are transferring the risk to an insurance company, who, in case you need long-term care, will pay part or all of the cost of your care. In exchange for this coverage, you pay a premium for the insurance. Let's take a look at each of these three answers and see why they will or won't be the best general answer.

Family Care

As I said, the most common answer I hear from clients when we talk about long-term care is that their family will take care of them. This is a very admirable sentiment, but it is also very presumptive. The first thing to consider is, while you may want them to take care of you, do *they* want to take care of you? Don't just assume that since you think they will take care of you that they will. What you would be asking, even in the short-term, is very time-consuming, financially and emotionally expensive, and intrusive.

For many people, when they refer to their family, they mean their children. Do your children have children? If so, your children would not only be taking care of their own children, but also their parents. Do your children work? How do you expect them to balance the chores of work with the rigors of taking care of you? Chances are, they would be unable to do both, so they would have to quit their jobs. Taking care of someone who needs long-term care is a full-time job in itself; and one that doesn't pay any money. They would be trading a job that pays them a wage, where they could leave all the job pressures at the office, in exchange for a job where they would be on call 24 hours a day, seven days a week at home. This is a huge trade-off, especially for someone whose heart isn't in it. Not to mention the possible added costs of bringing you into their home. If you use a wheelchair, they may have to add a ramp. The list goes on; this is just one example.

I've met people who have told me that they have promised their parents that they wouldn't put them into a nursing home. But that doesn't mean that the children are then stuck caring for their parents at home. And by stuck, I do mean stuck. Even if the parent doesn't move into the child's home, the child is still responsible for making sure that everything is going smoothly.

Let's consider the example of Bill and Sally Jones. Both Bill and Sally work, earning a combined salary of nearly $150,000 per year. They live a relatively quiet lifestyle, but they do enjoy traveling and taking vacations together. Bill's mother has been quite ill and has been advised by her doctor that she needs full-time care. Many years ago, Bill, an only child, promised his mother that he would never put her in a nursing home, a promise that Bill intends to keep. Since his mother needs full-time care and is unable to do some things on her own, Bill and Sally decide that she will move in with them.

Bill's mother doesn't have a lot of assets, nor does she have any type of long-term care insurance. Bill and Sally sell her home and use the proceeds to help pay for her care. After a couple of months, they decide that Sally should quit her job so that she can take care of Bill's mother. Their combined income drops from $150,000 per year to $90,000 per year. Taking care of Bill's mother has become a full-time job for both Sally and Bill. Not only has their income dropped, they are no longer able to do the things they enjoy, like traveling. Since they are Bill's mother's primary care givers, there is no one else to take care of her if they decide they want to go somewhere. So, they don't go.

Obviously, this is a worst-case scenario against the family care option. But, there are other things to consider, as well. Is your family member able to care for you? I don't mean just financially, but physically. If you were unable to walk, would they be strong enough to lift you into a wheelchair or bathtub? These are very important things to consider. If your family members are unable, or unwilling, to perform physical tasks, then they won't be able to take care of you.

The third thing to think about is the emotional toll it will take on both you and the people taking care of you. Taking care of a loved one, especially a parent, is a very emotionally tough prospect. For so many years, the parent has taken care of the child and now the child is being called upon to take care of the parent as the parent's health increasingly deteriorates. For the parent, the stress is equally harsh.

They've always been the caregiver, not the one needing care. The role reversal may be too much for either party to handle.

Finally, are your family members knowledgeable enough to take care of you? If you require special treatment, they may not be. You may truly need a professional nurse or caregiver to watch over you and make sure that everything is going the way it should. They will also be trained to notice any warning signs of further deterioration, which your child or other family member may not be.

Medicaid and Medicare

We discuss both Medicaid and Medicare in more depth in a later chapter, but many people believe that these forms of government assistance will be there for them in the case that they need some type of long-term care. The realities of these two programs are startlingly different than what people popularly perceive. First, Medicare and Medicaid are two separate entities. Medicare is a federally run program, while Medicaid is run on the state level and is a form of welfare.

In order to use Medicaid to pay for long-term care costs, you must first be eligible and meet certain financial requirements. These financial requirements dictate that your income must not be above a certain level, plus there is a limit on the amount of assets you can have, all of which vary by state. If you don't meet the requirements, then you are ineligible for Medicaid. Therefore, many people do what is commonly referred to as "spend down" their assets in order to qualify. Spending down means liquidating and distributing your assets to the point where you are essentially left with nothing. At that point, you can apply for Medicaid to pay for your care costs.

Generally, although this may vary by state law, those receiving Medicaid benefits are allowed to keep a small portion of their income, a very small portion, which may be as small as $50 per month. If they have more money than that, they are expected to pay, in part, for their own care. While the requirements are strict, the federal definition of "income" is very broad. It says that income is anything you receive in cash or in kind that you can use to meet your needs for food, clothing or shelter. If you are financially destitute, then Medicaid is the only option for you. But if you have sizeable assets, do not consider Medicaid because you will have to divest yourself of everything you have. Is that what you want to do?

It's important to remember that if you are married and your spouse is still living, the rules will vary.

When Medicaid patients need to enter nursing homes and other care facilities, do you think they are able to choose where they want to go? Not really. Nursing homes and other facilities give preference to private-pay patients and those with long-term care insurance. You may find that if you were to pay for your care with Medicaid, you could wind up in a facility very far away from your family, who would then be unable to visit you very often. This is obviously not the preferred choice.

Medicaid benefits cover a broad spectrum of services. They also, with a few exceptions, don't require any type of copayment, deductibles, or coinsurance for those who are eligible. They provide comprehensive coverage for acute care, as well as substantial coverage for long-term care. This includes extended, and unlimited, nursing home stays and some home health care services.

In the case of Medicare, the benefits that apply, coverage of skilled nursing home care and home health care, are limited in the long-term care context. Medicare home health care coverage only applies to either part-time or intermittent care for housebound patients. These patients must be under a physician's care who must certify the need for the care. Medicare nursing home coverage covers skilled nursing care or skilled rehabilitative care occurring after a medically necessary hospitalization for at least 3 consecutive days, admission to the nursing facility within 30 days after the hospitalization, and only if a physician certifies the need for skilled care. Medicare would then pay for the first 100 days in such a facility, while requiring a copayment for days 21 through 100. They will not, however, cover the cost of care for custodial care.

Medicare is better suited to provide benefits for acute medical conditions, rather than long-term care coverage. Should you need any type of long-term care, you should investigate if you would be eligible for any type of Medicare benefits.

Long-Term Care Insurance
The third option for those thinking about long-term care is to purchase long-term care insurance. Like disability insurance, this insurance

provides for the insured in the event that they need some form of long-term care, and it comes in a variety of forms. This allows the purchaser to determine better which coverage would best suit his or her needs.

Long-term care insurance will cover a variety of services. These include skilled nursing home care, intermediate nursing home care, custodial nursing home care, other custodial facility care, in-home health care, in-home care, adult day care, respite care, and hospice care. With all these choices, it's easy for an individual to pick a policy that will be the best suited for his or her anticipated needs. Since most people say that they don't want to go into a nursing home, purchasing a policy that covers in-home care gives you the flexibility of staying in your home.

This kind of insurance can cover different time periods. Generally, you can choose from two, four, or six years' worth of coverage, or you can opt to be covered for your entire lifetime. While at face value, lifetime coverage may seem like the most desirable, it is very expensive and most people never use that much coverage. The amount of time you choose constitutes the maximum coverage period. But, if you don't want to put a time limit on your coverage, you can choose to institute a maximum dollar amount. That sets the amount of money that the insurer will pay in benefits over the lifetime of the insured. Depending on personal preferences, one may be better than the other. However, I have found that the time limit option is the best because the cost of coverage continues to increase, thus diminishing the overall effectiveness of the maximum dollar option.

The insurance benefits can be paid in one of two ways. First, the policy may pay the expenses as they are actually incurred. That is, if your long-term care costs are $137.50 per day, your policy would pay $137.50 per day. These are called expense reimbursement policies. The other way benefits are paid is on a per day basis. These policies, called per diem policies, pay a stipulated daily amount. So, if your cost is $137.50 per day, and your policy had a maximum daily benefit of $125, you would have to pay $12.50 per day out of your pocket.

This daily benefit will also pay for any in-home care, as long as you elect for that option when purchasing the policy. Again, you have choices regarding the amount of in-home care the policy will pay for. These are generally described as a percentage of the daily maximum for skilled nursing home care. In-home care can have 100 percent of the daily maximum, 75 percent, 50 percent, or some other percentage. The higher the percentage, the higher the premium will be.

Policies will also offer some inflation protection. Since $100 will purchase more today than it will in 10 years, you don't want to be stuck with a policy that doesn't account for some type of inflation. Here you have two different choices for your inflation protection. First, you can choose to have no protection. Or, you can choose to have a set percentage added to your daily benefit every year, which is usually set at 5 percent. This is in the hopes that your coverage will then keep pace with the rising costs of nursing home and in-home care costs. Of course, since there is an added benefit, there will be an added premium amount for it. Weigh the pros and cons of purchasing inflation protection because it can add anywhere from 25 to 40 percent onto your premium amount.

While no one wants to use their long-term care insurance, in the event that you do, you will be subject to a waiting period before the benefits begin to kick in. You choose your elimination period, just as you do with disability insurance. It can be as few as 20 days, or you can wait up to 90 days before benefits begin. The longer your elimination period, the less your premium. Most policies allow you to have only one elimination period. Therefore, if you opt for a 90-day elimination period and you need care for 100 days, you will receive benefits for 10 days. But, if you need care again, the entire time will be covered and you won't have to wait the 90 days again. Also, once you begin to use your policy (after the elimination period), your insurance company will waive your premiums. This ensures that you aren't paying for your policy at the same time you are receiving benefits.

Long-term care policies also offer renewability clauses. A guaranteed renewability clause assures you that you will have continued coverage for your entire life, as long as you continue to pay the premiums. This doesn't mean that your premiums will remain at the same level, though. The insurer retains the right to raise premiums for your policyholder peer group if the insurer experiences a high level of claims. When investigating policies, beware of those that have an optional renewability clause. This option provides the insurer the ability to renew the contract, not you.

You also want to make sure that you understand the insurance company's policy of preexisting conditions. While many contracts don't have any language in them regarding preexisting conditions, others do. These clauses allow the insurer to not pay benefits for any physical or mental problems you had at the time you purchased the policy. Some policies have permanent preexisting clauses, while others will only keep them in force for 6 to 12 months.

When Do Benefits Begin?

These days, long-term care policies have several definitions of when the insured person can begin receiving benefits. These are usually referred to as triggering events or definitions of disability. Many policies then follow a triple-trigger policy, which allows the person to be covered as long as they meet one of the following three conditions:

1. The insured is unable to perform a specified number, usually two or three, of daily living activities. These activities come from a list and include walking, getting in and out of bed, eating, dressing, using the bathroom, and bathing. Some policies allow for certain cognitive abilities like short-term memory to be included in the list of daily activities, but many don't.

2. The insured has a cognitive impairment, which typically means the deterioration or loss of the individual's intellectual capacity. This will be measured by clinical evidence and standardized tests. Parkinson's Disease and Alzheimer's Disease are examples.

3. A physician certifies that the insured needs long-term care as a medical necessity. This condition can be very liberally applied since the individual's own doctor is usually the certifying physician.

The use of all three conditions is the most beneficial to the person purchasing long-term care insurance, but most insurance companies only use the first two benefit triggers.

Who needs long-term care insurance?

Not everyone needs long-term care insurance. However, for the majority of people, it's advisable. There are certain things to consider when deciding if long-term care insurance is for you.

■   *Is there a history of debilitating illness in your family?*

If you have many family members who have had some form of cancer, heart disease, or any other type of prolonged illness, the chances that you will also suffer from that are higher than if most of your family members were healthy. This will also increase your chances of needing long-term care.

■   *Are you male or female?*

Unfortunately, it's a fact of life that more women need long-term care than men because women have longer life expectancies than men do, which increases their need for care.

■   *Can you afford the premiums?*

This is a very important factor because long-term care insurance isn't cheap. Plus, with all the different types of add-ons you can choose from, your premium may be more than you can feasibly afford.

■   *Are you healthy?*

If you wait until you have a disease such as Alzheimer's, you become uninsurable and you will have to pay for any long-term care out of your pocket. Purchasing long-term care while you are healthy ensures that the coverage is there when you need it.

What Kind of Coverage Do You Need?

When choosing the type of coverage for your policy, do some research beforehand, so that you know how much local nursing homes are charging, either on a daily or annual basis. Or, if you don't want to stay in the area where you are currently living, check out the nursing homes closer to where you would like to be. It's important that you choose a daily benefit that is in line with, or close to, where you would like to go. Choosing too much coverage will only increase your cost, but choosing too little coverage may not allow you to go to the facility you would normally choose.

You should also pick a policy that allows for more than one type of coverage. By being able to choose from different levels of care, and having that care covered, you will eliminate the possible headaches and heartaches that go along with long-term care. Besides, what good would your policy be if it only covered skilled nursing home care and you only needed intermediate care?

Cognitive Disorders

Most insurance policies will cover nursing home stays for people who suffer from a cognitive impairment. This is defined as the deterioration or loss in intellectual capacity and is measured by clinical evidence and standardized tests that reliably measure the impairment of short-term and long-term memory; orientation as to person, place and time; and deductive or abstract reasoning. An example of a cognitive disorder is Alzheimer's Disease.

However, there are times when a person needs long-term care due to a cognitive impairment that wouldn't be covered. Some insurance policies specifically say that they won't cover any care given if the cause isn't clinically named, while other policies will cover that type of care. For example, let's assume that Mary and Jim Client have been married for 50 years. Mary becomes ill and passes away. Jim begins deteriorating very quickly and his doctor determines that he would be better off if he lived in a nursing home or had some type of full-time home care. However, there is no specific name for what Jim is suffering from. It's not Alzheimer's or Parkinson's disease. Because there is no name for what Jim is suffering from (although some would chalk it up to a broken heart), most long-term care policies wouldn't cover Jim's expenses.

But there are some policies that do cover these types of impairments. The preceding example is just that: an example. There are many other types of afflictions (those which don't have medical names) that could occur causing you to need some sort of long-term care. Your insurance coverage would then be obsolete because your care wouldn't be covered. These are known as "nonorganic" cognitive disorders because they don't have medical names. Organic cognitive disorders have been given names such as Alzheimer's and dementia. Make sure that the policy you decide to purchase does cover these types of situations. Although you may think that the chances of your needing this option are small, and you may pay a higher premium because you have this coverage, it's better to know that you have it and not need it, then to need it and not have it. You may find that you have to read your policy's fine print very carefully to determine whether nonorganic disorders are covered, but in the end it will be worth it.

WHY DI AND LTC ARE IMPORTANT

I've heard many excuses as to why people refuse to purchase either disability or long-term care insurance. But I have to say that for all the excuses I've heard, there are reasons why these types of protection are important and why they need to be a part of a person's life.

The main excuse people offer is that the insurance is too expensive; they just don't want to pay money out of their pocket every month for something they might not need. Expense is definitely a concern for most people, but let's consider the consequences of someone who fails to purchase any disability insurance. Let's assume that my client, Bob, wants to accumulate money for his retirement. Right now he is 48 years old and, so far, has done a very good job of building up a retirement fund. He has approximately $100,000 in his 401(k) at work and about $200,000 in nonqualified accounts. One day, Bob is outside painting his house, falls off the ladder and breaks both his legs. Bob works as a truck driver and needs to be able to drive a car in order to work. Therefore, Bob is unable to work and must take time off.

He sees the human resources department of his company and arranges to take his five remaining sick days, but since the accident happened at home and he has no form of disability insurance at all, that is all the income he will receive. Bob's doctors have told him that he will not be able to work for at least six months. Bob's current salary is $85,000 per year. His wife also works and her salary is

$37,000 per year. Because Bob will be missing six months from work, he will lose out on $42,500. His one week's worth of pay from his sick days will give him a gross paycheck of $1634.62. Where is Bob going to come up with money to help pay for his regular cost of living, not to mention his medical bills?

Bob's salary   = $85,000
Bob's missed salary = $42,500
Bob's sick pay   = $1,634.42
Amount needed   = $40,865.38

(All amounts are in before tax dollars.)

For starters, Bob's health insurance will pay for some, and perhaps most, of his medical bills. Plus, his wife works and her income will not be affected by Bob's accident. But he is the main breadwinner in the family, and his income has been effectively shut down for at least 6 months. This means that Bob is going to have to use some of his nonqualified savings to help pay for his lifestyle. Even if Bob's and his wife's lifestyle isn't that expensive, it's safe to assume that they will deplete a good portion of their savings because they have no form of DI. Bob will not be able to qualify for social security disability benefits because although he will be off work for more than 5 months, he doesn't meet the rule that says he needs to be disabled for at least 12 months. Plus, he has to be unable to work at any job, and, chances are, Bob would be able to find employment somewhere even though his legs are broken.

So, if Bob and his wife take out $50,000 from their nonqualified account to help cover bills and other expenses, they will then be left with $150,000 left in that account. That's still good, but what if they need more money? It will have to come out of the same account, thus continuing to deplete the account. Plus, they will probably have to pay some form of capital gains tax on whatever they pull out, if they haven't done so already. Then, not only will they miss out on the growth of that $50,000 (or more), but they will also want to repay themselves, which may put a strain on their income after Bob returns to work.

Had Bob had some form of DI, he would have been able to retain some of his income while he wasn't able to work. He and his wife wouldn't have had to use their savings, the $50,000 would have grown with the rest of the savings, and most likely, Bob's benefits would have been tax-free.

In the case of long-term care, the results of no insurance can be even more devastating. Right now the average cost of a one-year stay in a nursing home is $45,000. In some parts of the country, like New York or California, it costs more. Not having any long-term care insurance can exhaust whatever money you have saved up.

The other excuse that I hear is that these are types of insurance that people never use. Remember that a 55-year-old worker has a 70-percent chance of becoming disabled for three months and that the odds of needing more than one year of long-term care for a 65-year-old are 1 in 33. Yes, there is a chance that if you purchase DI or LTC you will not use it. However, there is also a chance that you will need it. Which chance are you willing to accept? Don't let the assumption that you will never need disability or long-term care insurance keep you from purchasing it. I haven't met anyone yet who can predict the future, so how can you be sure that you won't need it?

In the case of Bob and no DI, he still has time to go back to work, earn money and save for his retirement. But for many people needing long-term care, there isn't that kind of time. Most of these people have already retired and aren't earning any kind of income, except what may come in from their investments. And, most people aren't earning in excess of $45,000 per year purely off of investment income.

That's why disability and long-term care insurance are so important. They protect you from the "what if" scenarios. Plus, they protect the assets you have already accumulated so that you don't have to use them in an emergency. And really, that's what insurance is all about: protection. When you listed your goals at the beginning of the book, did you list "have enough money?" Ask yourself, if you became disabled or were in need of some sort of long-term care, would you have enough money?

I don't mean to scare you, but I do want you to think. Not protecting yourself and your assets flies directly in the face of trying to accumulate wealth. You may say that by paying money for insurance, you are missing out on investing that money and its growth. That's definitely true. But if you were to need that insurance and you didn't have it, would the growth you enjoyed from that money be enough to cover you for the entire time you were either disabled or in need of long-term care? Accumulating wealth is an admirable goal, but don't sacrifice protection just to help meet that goal. In the long run, you'll thank yourself.

WHY YOU SHOULDN'T COUNT ON THE GOVERNMENT'S HELP FOR YOUR RETIREMENT

A sk someone who is retired today what they rely on for their retirement benefits. Although the answer will vary depending upon their age, chances are they will say that social security provides their main income and Medicare their main health benefits. Plus, there will be a few who say they also rely on Medicaid. But if you were to ask someone significantly younger, say someone who has recently graduated from college, you'd receive a startlingly different answer. Not only don't they see social security as the main source of their retirement income, they don't even believe the program will still exist by the time they would need it!

How do you personally feel about social security and Medicare? Putting these programs into proper perspective will dramatically affect how you look at your retirements and what your needs will be. Because, let's face it, people today are far more concerned with their retirement than their counterparts were 20 or 30 years ago. So, before we look at the best ways to help fund your retirement, we consider how we should view these programs and if you should even count on them to help you during your retirement.

The main questions you should be asking yourself are: what exactly are the social security, Medicare, and Medicaid programs; who qualifies; and how does someone qualify? Throughout this chapter, we look at these three different government programs and discuss how they will affect your life and the lives of those around you, such as spouses and dependents.

SOCIAL SECURITY

Social security was created in 1935 by the Social Security Act of 1935. The act created a basic retirement program for working Americans, no matter what their income was. It also established many other social programs, all of which are administered through the Old Age, Survivor's, Disability, and Health Insurance (OASDHI) program. These other social programs include supplementary social income (SSI), Medicare, public assistance, welfare services, unemployment insurance, and provision for black lung benefits. While all of these programs are essentially dealt with under the same roof, we will only be discussing the old age (retirement), survivor's, and Medicare portions of the act since they have the most relevance on retirement and financial planning. The purpose of social security is to provide a guaranteed income floor for retired workers, so that they may enjoy a more comfortable retirement lifestyle. It was designed to complement the retirement pension plans that workers were offered by their employers. Therefore, Social Security functions mainly as a government-sponsored retirement plan.

In order really to understand how the system works, and then to generate a prediction as to whether the program will be around to

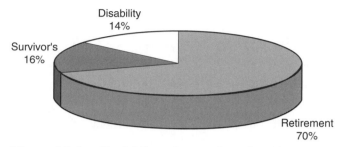

Figure 13.1   Social Security can be referred to as America's Family Protection Plan. We've already discussed how the program provides disability benefits in the previous chapter. And although most people assume that Social Security just sends out retirement checks, nearly 1-in-3 Social Security recipients is not a retiree!

help future generations, we need to discuss how social security is financed, and its solvency.

Social Security's Financing

The benefits paid to Social Security recipients come from the payroll taxes of those people who arc still working today. Many people believe that the social security and Medicare taxes that are taken out of their paycheck (generally listed as FICA taxes, which is roughly 7.65 percent of income) are then set aside for their own use when they retire. This would be like another personal retirement account. However, that's not the case. Today's workforce is the one financing today's retirees. And so, the program is designed to continue throughout perpetuity. Not only do employees pay into the system, so do employers. The employee pays in the 7.65 percent, which the employer matches. That is one reason why self-employed people pay double the amount of social security tax than other "regularly" employed people. The government sees a need to make up for the fact that self-employed people are their own bosses. For those who are self-employed, the FICA tax rate is about 15.3 percent. However, the government then allows them to take one-half of that amount as a tax deduction from their gross income.

When one dollar is paid into social security, it is split into two parts. The first 85 cents goes to a trust fund that pays monthly benefits to retirees and their families, as well as widows, widowers, and children of workers who have died. The remaining 15 cents goes to a trust fund that pays benefits to people with disabilities and their families. Money paid into social security also pays for the program's administration. These fees come from the two trust funds and amount to less than one cent per dollar paid in.[1]

The worker pays in his or her 7.65 percent every year until that person reaches a maximum wage base. This base is increased every year due to inflation. The limit for the year 2002 was $84,900. Therefore, the maximum paid in by a worker whose income was at that maximum level would be $6494.85 ($84,900 × 0.0765). For a self-employed worker, that maximum amount would be $12989.7 ($84,900 × 0.153). In 1991, a new second tax was introduced to help offset the rising costs of Medicare. Now, after the social security maximum wage base is passed, the new, higher Medicare wage base starts. Employees are subject to a tax rate of 1.45 percent on all earnings above $84,900, with the self-employed paying a corresponding 2.9 percent.

So, for those individuals who earn more than the threshold of $84,900, it would appear that they aren't paying the fair share of social security tax. And many people do argue that. However, the program is designed so that there is a link between how much a worker earns during his or her working lifetime and how much that person receives in benefits, and the benefits formula is weighted so that lower-income earning individuals receive a higher percentage of their earnings.

Social Security's Solvency
There is a rampant fear that social security funds will run out eventually. Because of this, many people don't even count on these benefits as part of the income they will receive when they are retired. Politicians try to calm our fears about social security, but the fact remains that by continuing the trend we are on right now, Social Security benefits will be exhausted by the year 2037.

[1]Social Security Administration.

The main reason for the problem is demographics. Quite honestly, people are living longer, more active lives. And while that is a good thing in general, it's not such a good thing when it comes to social security. When the program was created in 1935, an average American had a life expectancy of 77½ years. Now, life expectancies are closer to 83 years, and they're still climbing! (See Figure 13.2.) What this means is that as more Americans retire, there will be a need for a larger pool of workers to be paying into the system in order to support those collecting benefits. However, that's not the way our nation's population is trending.

In 1955, there were approximately seven workers supporting each person receiving Social Security benefits. But in about 30 years, it's estimated that there will be two people paying money in for every one person drawing money out. That estimate includes all the baby boomers who will begin retiring around the year 2010 (approximately 77 million). All these changes in the population and its makeup will strain the social security system.

Congress has been aware of this problem for a very long time. However, they have only recently begun to take action. This is unfor-

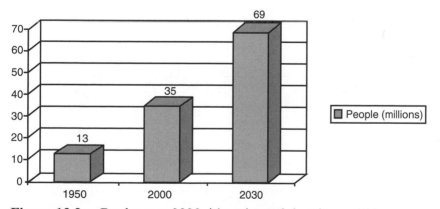

Figure 13.2 By the year 2030, it's estimated that there will be approximately 69 million Americans age 65 and older, or about 20 percent of the population. Compare that with 35 million in the year 2000 (12 percent of the population) and 13 million in 1950 (8 percent of the population), and you can see why Social Security will begin to run out of money.

tunate because as long as Congress continues with the status quo, the more likely it will be that social security will become bankrupt. One of the action steps Congress has taken has been to increase the age at which workers can receive full benefits from 65 years to 67 years. For example, if you were to take early retirement now, retiring at age 62, you would receive about 80 percent of your full retirement benefit (what you would have received if you had waited until you were 65). However, once the age increase fully takes effect, if you were to take early retirement, you would only receive about 70 percent of your full retirement benefit. Other ideas to fix the program that have been discussed include raising the social security tax, raising the maximum wage base for the tax, privatizing the system, and raising the retirement age. Of course, all of this is subject to change.

Currently, social security is taking in more money annually than it is paying out. All the excess funds are put into social security's trust funds, which have about $900 billion right now. Those assets are expected to grow to more than $6 trillion over the next 25 years. However, benefit payments will begin to exceed incoming taxes by the year 2015, and the trust funds will be exhausted by 2037. (See Figure 13.3[2]). If no changes are made to the system, Social Security will only be able to pay out about 72 percent of the benefits owed based on incoming tax money.[3]

Who Benefits from Social Security?
As a blanket generalization, we can say that if you have held a job, you can receive some type of social security benefits. Of course, there are other types of stipulations that apply. But for the most part, any gainfully employed worker can be covered by social security. In order to qualify for benefits, a worker must earn credits. The number of credits needed depends on when the worker was born. If you were born in 1929 or later, you need 40 credits to receive benefits. If you were born before 1929, you need fewer than 40 credits (39 credits if you were born in 1928, 38 credits for those born in 1927, etc.). Generally, you earn 4 credits per year. Therefore, the majority of people

[2]Ibid.
[3]Ibid.

How Social Security Fares over the Next 35 Years

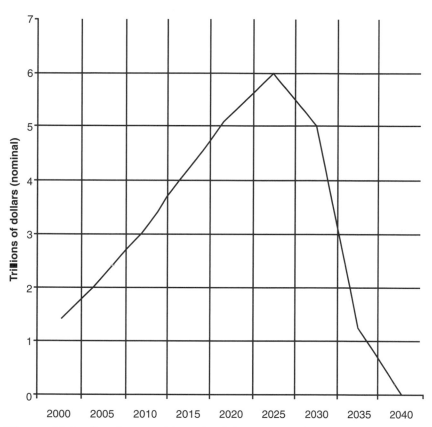

Figure 13.3 By the year 2015, Social Security will be paying out more in benefits than it is receiving in taxes from workers. This trend will cause the program to begin depleting its trust funds to the point where they are exhausted. By the year 2037, Social Security will only be able to meet approximately 72 percent of its benefit obligations. That money will come directly from the Americans who are still working and paying taxes.

working right now need to have worked for 10 years in order to qualify for social security retirement benefits.

If you stopped working before you reach your 40 credits, the amount you have already earned remains on your record. Then, if you go back to work, you will continue to add credits to your record until you qualify. No retirement benefits are paid out until you have reached the required number of credits. However, most people have more than enough credits by the time they retire. All your excess credits do not increase your social security benefit; however the longer you work, the more likely it is that your income will increase, and that will affect how much you receive in benefits.

There are two types of people who are exempt from *mandatory* participation in the program. First, federal *civilian* employees who were hired prior to 1984 and are covered by the Civil Service Retirement System are exempt. The second group is comprised of employees of state and local governments who have chosen to not be covered, although an overwhelming majority of these workers are covered under a voluntary participation in the program. Additionally, certain marginal employment positions, such as newspaper carriers under the age of 18 and full-time college students working in fraternity and sorority houses, are also excluded. The largest segment of exempt workers are those who are state and local government employees because these groups aren't forced to participate since the federal government cannot impose a tax on state and local governments. However, once one of these employees has chosen to be included in the program, they are forced to stay in. They don't have the option of leaving.

What Kind of Benefit Can I Expect?

The amount of money you receive on a monthly basis from the government is determined by how much money you earned while working. The more money you earned during your working life, the more money you will receive in social security benefits. But, your benefit is also affected by your age—specifically, how old you are when you begin to receive your benefits. The government classifies early retirement as retiring at age 62, while full retirement ranges from ages 65 to 67. (See Table 13.1.) The government has instituted a new retirement age to receive full benefits, but they have done so in a staggering fashion. However, this doesn't mean that you can't retire from your job until you are 62 or older. That's just when you can begin receiving social security retirement benefits. As a worker claiming benefits, you must be no younger than 62 years old. There are other exceptions to this, which are discussed shortly.

Table 13.1   When Will You Receive Your Full Benefit?

Birth Year	Full Retirement Age
1937 or earlier	65
1938	65 and 2 months
1939	65 and 4 months
1940	65 and 6 months
1941	65 and 8 months
1942	65 and 10 months
1943-1954	66
1955	66 and 2 months
1956	66 and 4 months
1957	66 and 6 months
1958	66 and 8 months
1959	66 and 10 months
1960 or later	67

If you begin to take your Social Security benefits at age 62, before you hit your full retirement status, your monthly benefits will be less. As mentioned earlier, to take benefits at age 62 when your full retirement age is 65, you will receive approximately 80 percent per month of what you would have received per month if you had waited. If your full retirement age were 67, you would receive about 70 percent of your full benefits by retiring early. This isn't a punishment for workers who wish to receive their benefits early. Rather, it's the government's way of evening things out. To give you full benefits at a younger age would give you more money over your lifetime. The government wants to make sure that no one gets more than their "fair share," so they reduce the amount of benefits you receive when you begin taking benefits before they think you should.

For example, one of my clients retired from her job in one of our local school districts. Although she was taking money from her investments on a monthly basis as an income, she asked me about beginning her Social Security benefits. I told her that since she was 62 she was eligible, but that she wouldn't receive the same amount per month that she would if she were to wait until she was 65. Joyce's monthly benefits at age 65 would be about $1100 per month. But because she begins taking her benefits at age 62, her monthly check will be 20 percent less, or roughly $882 per month.

But not everyone wants to take their benefits early. Some don't even want to start receiving their checks until after they are 65 years old. By not taking your benefits at full retirement age, you increase your benefits in two ways. First, each additional year that you work adds another year of earnings onto your Social Security record. The higher your lifetime earnings, the higher your benefits will be. Second, your benefits will be increased by a certain percentage if you delay your retirement. These increases will be added in automatically starting from when you reach your full retirement age until you begin to take your benefits, or until you reach age 70. The percentages are based on your birth year, just as your retirement age is. (See Table 13.2.) So if you were born in 1952 and didn't want to retire until you were 68 years old, you would have an added increase of 16 percent (8 percent per year increase or two thirds of 1 percent per month).

You also don't have to wait to start claiming your social security benefits until you have actually retired from work. However, there are some limits on how much income you can receive and still have your benefits be 100-percent tax-free. It's important to consult with your CPA to determine whether your benefits would be taxable if you still plan to work or earn some type of income while receiving your benefits. Your earnings in (or after) the month you reach your full retirement age won't affect your benefits. But, your benefits will be reduced if your earnings exceed certain limits in the months preceding your full retirement birthday. If you are younger than full retirement age, one dollar in benefits will be deducted for every two dollars in earnings that are above the annual limit. In the year you reach full retirement age, your benefits will be reduced by one dollar for every three dollars in earnings that fall above the annual limit until the month that you reach full retirement age. After that, you can work without any reduction in benefits and no limit on your earnings. The annual limits are increased every year as the average wage rises.

Table 13.2. Percentage Increases for Delayed Retirement

Year of Birth	Yearly Percentage Increase
1917–1924	3.0%
1925–1926	3.5%
1927–1928	4.0%
1929–1930	4.5%
1931–1932	5.0%
1933–1934	5.5%
1935–1936	6.0%
1937–1938	6.5%
1939–1940	7.0%
1941–1942	7.5%
1943 or later	8.0%

If your family members receive any social security benefits from your record, all the benefits will be affected by your earnings. So, not only will your earnings reduce your monthly benefits, but they will also reduce any other benefits that your family may receive. However, if one of your family members is working, this will only affect his or her benefits, not yours or any others received by your family.

The Social Security Administration has a special rule, though, that they allow you to apply to your earnings and benefits for one year, usually the first year you are retired. Under this rule, you can receive full benefits for any month you are "retired," no matter what your annual earnings will be. However, your monthly earnings must fall below a set limit. If you are self-employed, your work there is also considered.

If you are currently receiving a pension from your former employer, the amount you receive will not affect your social security benefits, as long as you paid social security taxes at that job. However, if you are receiving a pension from an employer that didn't participate in social security, such as the federal civil service, state, and local governments, or work in a foreign country, your pension amount will reduce the amount of social security benefits you will receive.

Also, the month you begin taking your benefits may affect how much you receive. In some cases, the month you choose to retire will result in added benefits for you and your family. Taking your benefits early in the year you are going to retire may benefit you more than waiting, even though you aren't officially retiring until later that year. Under the current law, Social Security recipients receive the most benefits possible with an application that takes effect in January of their retirement year.

Family and Survivor's Benefits

Social security also offers benefits for those who either worked but didn't earn enough credits or fall under different categories other than workers. If you are widowed, married, or even divorced, you can claim social security benefits off of the work record of your spouse (or former spouse). If you are receiving benefits, your family members may also receive benefits if they fall into one of the following categories:

- your spouse age 62 or older
- your spouse under age 62, if that person is caring for your child who is under age 16 or disabled
- your former spouse age 62 or older
- children up to age 18
- children age 18–19, if they are full-time high school students
- children over age 18, if they are disabled

Widows and widowers may begin receiving benefits when they are 60 years old, or 50 years old if they are disabled. This also includes divorced widow(er)s. If you are receiving widows' or widowers' benefits, you may switch to your own benefits when you reach 62 as long as your retirement benefits are more than what you are currently receiving. Often times, a widow(er) may begin receiving one benefit and then switch to the other (unreduced) benefit when he or she reaches full retirement age.

For spouses, they can receive one-half of their retired spouses' benefits unless the spouse begins collecting before he or she turns 65. If that's the case, the benefits are permanently reduced by a certain percentage based on the number of months that are left before the spouse turns 65. For example, if your spouse started collecting benefits at age 62, his or her benefit would be reduced by 12.5 percent, making it 37.5 percent of your benefit, rather than 50 percent. But, if your spouse is taking care of a child who is younger than 16 or is disabled and receiving social security benefits, your spouse will receive full benefits no matter what age.

For those spouses who are eligible for their own benefits, as well as spousal benefits, social security always pays that person's own benefit first. If the spousal benefit is greater than the regular retirement benefits, that person will receive a combination of benefits. First, they would receive their own benefit. Then, they would receive a benefit as a spouse so that the two benefits combined would equal the (greater) spousal benefit.

There are maximum benefit limits that a family is subject to. If you have children who qualify to receive benefits, each will receive

Spousal benefit	= $750
Spouse's own retirement benefit	= $675
Spouse's retirement benefit paid first	= $675
Spousal makeup benefit	+ $75
Total Social Security benefit paid	**= $750**

one-half of your full retirement benefits, but then your family will be subject to the maximum benefit rule. If you find that the total amount of benefits your family is eligible for exceeds the limit, your children's benefits will be reduced accordingly. Your benefit, however, will be left alone.

Divorced spouses may be eligible for Social Security benefits under their former spouse's work record. The couple must have been married for at least 10 years; the divorced spouse can be no younger than 62 years old and may not be remarried. If the couple has been divorced for more than 2 years, the former spouse may claim benefits even if the other person is still working. However, that person must have the required number (40) of credits needed and be at least 62 years old. Whatever benefits the former spouse receives has no bearing on the amount of benefits the working person will receive.

Taxation of Benefits

Approximately 20 percent of people claiming social security benefits must pay taxes on what they receive. Benefit taxation only affects those people with substantial income in addition to their benefits. To help determine if your benefits would be taxable, the social security Administration sends out a benefit statement to every social security recipient. This mailing shows the amount of benefits you have received. Then, when you are (or your CPA) is preparing your taxes, you will be able to determine if you will need to pay taxes on your benefits.

If you find that you will, in fact, have to pay taxes on your benefits, you may realize that you will also have to pay taxes on you benefits in years to come. You can either have taxes taken out of your monthly checks, or you can opt to pay quarterly estimates. Generally, it's easier to have a set percentage taken out of your benefit checks.

MEDICARE

Part of the social security system is a government-sponsored health care program called Medicare. Medicare provides a valuable service for senior citizens, and others who qualify, who may not otherwise be able to afford the health care they need. Medicare, though, should not be confused with Medicaid. Most people believe that these programs are the same thing, but they're not. Medicare is a federally sponsored and funded program, whereas Medicaid is a state-sponsored program. Medicaid is more of a welfare health care system, designed to help those with low income and little to no resources.

Medicare can be a very complex subject, but it's vital that you understand its benefits and drawbacks because by the time you will be eligible for coverage, you may find that paying the normal premiums for other, private health insurance is difficult. Or you may not even be insurable anymore under private health plans. With Americans living longer than they ever have, we've seen an increase in the type and frequency of health care needed. Medicare helps provide seniors with an affordable means of getting the care they need. But by no means does it cover everything.

Eligibility

For the most part, Americans become eligible for Medicare when they turn 65 and are receiving social security benefits. But those individuals who have been receiving social security disability benefits for at least 24 months, and those who have permanent kidney failure are also eligible for Medicare. For those workers who are eligible for social security benefits and don't take them at age 65, and for those who continue to work after age 65, Medicare is still available. Plus, any spouses or former spouses who qualify for Social Security may also enroll in Medicare at age 65.

Medicare is also available to citizens and permanent aliens as long as they have lived in the United States continuously for at least the 5 years preceding entitlement. If they are 65 or older and aren't eligible for social security (or railroad retirement) benefits, they may also enroll in Medicare. But in these cases, they typically must pay the premiums associated with Medicare Part A.

The Two Faces of Medicare: Parts A and B

Medicare has two different parts to it: hospital insurance and medical insurance. These are commonly referred to as Part A (hospital insurance) and Part B (medical insurance). These two parts cover different aspects of health care and work in different ways. For example, most people don't have to pay a premium for Part A, whereas you usually have to pay a premium for Part B, as well as a copayment. (Part A also carries a copayment.) But Medicare doesn't provide any kind of blanket coverage. Your doctor may not even participate in the program. Although this is a federal program, it doesn't mean that physicians are federally mandated to accept Medicare patients. And, as with HMOs and other health plans, doctors can opt out of Medicare.

PART A. As long as you are automatically eligible for Medicare (that is, you satisfy one of the three main qualifying requirements listed above), you don't have to pay a premium for Part A. Part A consists of hospital insurance and helps pay for inpatient care in a hospital or skilled nursing facility following a hospital stay, home health care, and hospice care.

It's important to note that Medicare has instituted benefit periods. A benefit period begins the day you enter a hospital or skilled nursing facility. The period ends when you have been out of the hospital, or other facility, for 60 consecutive days. If you remain in a facility (other than a hospital), the period ends when you have not received any skilled care there for 60 consecutive days. Medicare places no restrictions on the number of benefit periods you can use for hospitals and skilled nursing facilities. There are, however, special limits for hospice care. No such limitations exist for home health care. These periods are used to measure your use of your benefits.

For those people needing some sort of inpatient care, hospital insurance will help pay for up to 90 days in any Medicare-participating hospital during each benefit period. Part A pays for all *covered* services for the first 60 days, except for a deductible amount, which you must pay. Days 61 through 90 are also paid for by Part A for *covered* services. However, there is a daily coinsurance amount you must pay.

Once you have been out of the hospital for 60 days in a row, any subsequent hospitalization would be subject to a new benefit period. Your 90 days of coverage would begin again, and you would again pay your deductible and any daily copayment amounts that were required.

But, what if you needed more than 90 consecutive days of hospitalization? Does that mean that you would have to pay for days 91 through whenever, directly out of your pocket? Not necessarily. Medicare provides for 60 reserve days over the lifetime of the recipient. Therefore, if you needed 95 days of hospitalization, the first 90 days would be covered just like any other benefit period. The last five days would require a daily copayment amount, just like days 61 through 90. Again, Medicare would pay for all *covered* services. Once you use your 60 reserve days, though, that's it. Medicare doesn't issue more reserve days.

When you enter a skilled nursing facility, or if you need inpatient rehabilitation services, after a hospital stay (and you meet other certain conditions) Medicare Part A will help pay for up to 100 days, as long as you receive your care in a participating Medicare facility. As with hospital stays, you have benefit periods, only here they are for 100 days, not 90.

Part A will pay for all covered services for the first 20 days. You don't need to worry about any kind of deductible. For days 21 through 100, all covered services are paid for and you pay a daily coinsurance amount, as you would with hospital stays.

If you find yourself in a skilled nursing facility and you only require custodial care, your stay will not be covered. Medicare will not pay for *custodial care* when it is the only care you are receiving. While custodial care is the most common type of care given in nursing homes and skilled nursing facilities, Medicare won't cover it because they have determined that someone who isn't medically trained could give custodial care, such as help with eating, dressing, etc. So, even if you are in a participating facility, you will have to pay for your own care. (This is one time when long term care insurance comes into play.) Medicare will entertain appeals if your coverage is denied, but not for custodial care appeals.

If you need to stay at home due to health problems, and you meet other certain conditions, Part A can pay the full approved cost of your home health care. It must come in the form of home visits from a Medicare-participating home health agency, but Medicare places no restrictions on the number of visits you may have. Part A will also help pay for any services from home health aides, occupational and physical therapists, and medical social services on a part-time or intermittent basis. Plus, it will also help pay for medical supplies and equipment. You will have to pay a 20-percent copayment for any covered durable medical equipment (i.e., hospital beds and wheelchairs).

When people are diagnosed as terminally ill, many of them turn to hospices for help. A hospice program can help provide pain relief and other programs and support services for terminally ill patients and their families. Because of this, Medicare helps pay for the costs associated with hospice care. The services, as with the other kinds of care, must be provided by a Medicare-certified hospice, and you must meet other certain conditions.

Any patient can receive hospice care benefits as long as his or her doctor certifies that the person is terminally ill and probably has six months or fewer to live. Even if the patient lives longer than six months, he or she can still receive benefits. The doctor must recertify the person is are terminally ill. Hospice care will come in periods. There are two 90-day periods of care, followed by an unlimited number of 60-day periods. As each period begins, the patient's doctor must recertify that the patient is terminally ill. A period begins the first day that care is given and ends when either the 90 or 60 days are up. As long as the physician certifies that the patient is terminally ill, that person can continue to receive care uninterrupted.

I keep saying that Medicare will help pay for covered expense if you meet certain conditions. Medicare has different criteria that patients must meet before they can receive benefits. For example, if you were to enter a skilled nursing facility, in order for your stay to be covered, you must first have been in the hospital for at least 3 days, you must stay in a Medicare-certified facility, and you must enter within 30 days of your hospitalization. For home health care costs to be covered, you must be homebound and have been in the hospital for at least 3 days in the 14 days prior to receiving benefits. There are other requirements, but that's just a taste. (See Table 13.3.[4])

Table 13.3   Medicare Part A

What Medicare covers	What you pay*
Inpatient hospital care	deductible of $792 per benefit period
(up to 90 days per stay plus 60 lifetime	no copayment for days 1–60
reserve days)	$198/day copayment for days 61–90
	$396/day copayment for reserve days
Skilled nursing facility (up to 100 days)	no deductibles
	no copayment for days 1–20
	$99/day copayment for days 21–100
Home health care	no deductibles or copayments
Hospice care	no deductibles small copayment for outpatient drugs and inpatient respite care

*There is no premium in most cases for Part A.

[4]Copayment and deductible amounts are as of 2001.

PART B. Medicare's medical insurance, or Part B, helps pay for doctors, outpatient hospital care, other types of medical services, and supplies that aren't covered under Part A. Each year, Medicare patients must pay a medical insurance deductible before your Medicare benefits begin. Once this deductible is paid, Medicare will generally cover about 80 percent of the cost of the approved charges for the covered services. You will pay the remaining amount as a copayment. (See Table 3.4.)

Part B covers the following services and equipment:

- inpatient medical care
- outpatient medical care
- inpatient and outpatient medical supplies
- ambulance services
- X rays
- laboratory tests
- blood
- yearly mammograms
- pap smears
- pelvic and breast examinations
- bone mass measurements
- diabetes glucose monitoring and education
- colorectal cancer screening
- flu and pneumococcal pneumonia shots
- home attention if you don't have Part A
- partial hospitalization for psychiatric medical attention
- speech therapy
- physical and occupational therapy
- durable medical equipment (i.e., wheelchairs)
- services of certain especially qualified professionals who aren't doctors
- long-term care

Although long-term care is listed as being covered, Part B will also not cover any custodial care. There are even times when the above "covered" services won't be covered. However, you can have Medicare review claims that were denied through its appeal process.

Table 13.4. Medicare Part B*

What Medicare covers	What you pay**
Physician and other medical services (almost any doctor or hospital in the United States	20% coinsurance other charges (up to 15% above Medicare's approved charges)
Outpatient hospital care	20% coinsurance***
Ambulatory surgical services	20% coinsurance***
Home health care	nothing
Clinical diagnostic laboratory services	nothing
Other laboratory tests and X-rays	20% coinsurance
Diabetes self-management (This includes supplies, such as glucose monitors and test strips, and training, all of which are fully covered. No use of insulin is needed.)	20% coinsurance
Durable medical equipment	20% coinsurance***
Physical therapy	20% coinsurance***
Ambulance services	20% coinsurance***
Outpatient mental health services	50% coinsurance
Annual flu and pneumonia shots	nothing****
Mammograms annually (women over age 40 only)	20% coinsurance*** (no Part B deductible)
Pap smears every three years (annually for women at high risk)	nothing
Bone mass measurement	20% coinsurance***
Colorectal cancer screening (annually for men and women over age 50 and those under age 50 but at risk)	nothing for blood test 20% coinsurance for colonoscopy and other tests
Prostate cancer screening (annually for men age 50 and older)	20% coinsurance for digital exam nothing for PSA test

*Copayment and deductible amounts are as of 2001.
**A premium of $50 per month applies to Part B, as does a $100 annual deductible.
***Other charges may apply and will vary depending on the type of service rendered.
****The doctor administering the flu and/or pneumonia shots must accept Medicare assignment for shots to be covered.

(See below.) If you believe, or are told, that Medicare won't cover the care costs you have incurred, have your doctor or the facility bill Medicare first anyway. This will prevent you from paying for any services until Medicare has denied the claim. Plus, Medicare may just pay for the care. After all, it doesn't hurt to try!

WHAT MEDICARE WON'T COVER. Medicare provides for basic health care coverage, but it certainly doesn't pay for everything. The following list isn't all-inclusive, but these are the most common things that Medicare won't pay for:

- custodial care
- most nursing home care
- dental care and checkups
- routine checkups and related tests (some Pap smears, screening, and mammograms are covered)
- most immunization shots (some flu and pneumonia shots are covered)
- most prescription drugs
- routine foot care
- test for, and the cost of, hearing aids and eyeglasses
- private hospital rooms
- phone or TV in your hospital room and other associated comfort items
- services outside the United States
- most chiropractic services
- cosmetic surgery
- experimental procedures
- acupuncture
- private duty nursing

As alluded to before, Medicare provides a review process through which people can appeal their denied claims. If you submit a claim to Medicare and they won't pay it, seek a review. To do this, simply send a copy of the Medicare denial back to your Medicare plan along with a signed letter asking for a review. Medicare very well may pay your claim upon the review, as many people who have asked for a review have received additional coverage and benefits.

Medigap Insurance

Although Medicare provides help for basic medical coverage, it cannot cover everything. Because of these gaps in coverage, people have found that they benefit from supplemental Medicare coverage, which has come to be known as Medigap insurance. Medigap is issued by private insurance companies, not the government as Medicare is. There are 10 standard Medigap policies, all of which extend different types of coverage and may cover the Medicare deductibles, as well as other types of costs that Parts A and B don't cover. Until recently, there were many different, and confusing, types of Medigap insurance. People found that they were either purchasing coverage that wasn't helping them, or purchasing too much insurance. To help rectify this, the Medigap insurance plans were standardized, which has helped many people to understand and select the right Medigap policy for their situation.

The first Medigap plan is called Plan A. This is the basic insurance plan. The others are named Plans B through J. Although private companies offer these plans, they are not allowed to change the names of the policies (they may add to the names, but the letter designation must remain the same), nor are they allowed to alter the types of coverage offered. Insurers are also not bound to offer each of the 10 plans in each state, but if they offer Plans B through J, they must offer Plan A. (See Table 13.5 for a comparison of the 10 plans.)

Plan A offers the core benefits, which all subsequent plans also offer. These benefits consist of:

- coverage for the daily Part A coinsurance amount for days 61–90 of a hospital stay for each Medicare benefit period
- coverage for the daily Part A coinsurance amount for the 60 lifetime reserve days for a hospital stay
- coverage for 100 percent of the Part A eligible hospital expenses after all Medicare benefits are used (limited to 365 days of additional coverage over the lifetime of the insured)
- coverage under Parts A and B for the (reasonable) cost of the first three pints of blood per calendar year—this also covers the equivalent quantity of packed red blood cells in the same time frame
- coverage for the 20-percent coinsurance amount for Part B once the annual deductible is paid

Table 13.5. Medigap Insurance Plan Comparison

Core benefits	Plan A	Plan B	Plan C	Plan D	Plan E	Plan F	Plan G	Plan H	Plan I	Plan J
Part A copayment	X	X	X	X	X	X	X	X	X	X
Reserve days copayment	X	X	X	X	X	X	X	X	X	X
365 lifetime days – 100%	X	X	X	X	X	X	X	X	X	X
Parts A and B blood	X	X	X	X	X	X	X	X	X	X
Part B coinsurance – 20%	X	X	X	X	X	X	X	X	X	X
Additional benefits	A	B	C	D	E	F	G	H	I	J
Skilled nursing facility coinsurance			X	X	X	X	X	X	X	X
Part A deductible		X	X	X	X	X	X	X	X	X
Part B deductible			X			X				X
Part B excess charges						100%	80%		100%	100%
Foreign travel emergency			X	X	X	X	X	X	X	X
In-home recovery				X			X		X	X

Table 13.5. (*Continued*)

Core benefits	Plan A	Plan B	Plan C	Plan D	Plan E	Plan F	Plan G	Plan H	Plan I	Plan J
Prescription drugs								Y*	Y*	Y**
Preventive medical care					X					X

*Plans H and I offer a prescription drug benefit that has a $250 annual deductible, 50% coinsurance and a maximum annual benefit of $1250.
**Plan J offers a prescription drug benefit that has a $250 annual deductible, 50% coinsurance, and a maximum annual benefit of $3000.

Plan B includes the core benefits, plus the following:

• Part A hospital deductible for inpatient care per Medicare benefit period

Plan C includes the core benefits, plus the following:

• coverage for the skilled nursing facility care coinsurance amount for days 21–100 per benefit period
• Part A deductible
• Part B deductible
• coverage for medically necessary emergency care in a foreign country—this benefit is subject to a $250 deductible, minimum 20-percent copayment, and a lifetime maximum benefit of $50,000

Plan D includes the core benefits, plus the following:

• coverage for daily skilled nursing facility care coinsurance
• Part A deductible
• coverage for medically necessary emergency care in a foreign country
• in-home recovery—this benefit covers up to $1600 annually for short-term, in-home assistance with activities of daily living for people who are recovering from injury, surgery, or illness, and is subject to some limitations

Plan E includes the core benefits, plus the following:

• coverage for daily skilled nursing facility care coinsurance
• Part A deductible

- coverage for medically necessary emergency care in a foreign country
- preventive medical care—this benefit pays up to $120 annually for medical care including, but not limited to, flu shots, physical examinations, hearing tests, and diabetes screening

Plan F includes the core benefits, plus the following:

- coverage for daily skilled nursing facility care coinsurance
- Part A deductible
- Part B deductible
- 100 percent of the excess charges for Part B—this benefit provides for the difference between what the physician charges and the Medicare-approved amount for the covered services
- coverage for medically necessary emergency care in a foreign country

Plan G includes the core benefits, plus the following:

- coverage for daily skilled nursing facility care coinsurance
- Part A deductible
- 80 percent of the excess charges for Part B
- coverage for medically necessary emergency care in a foreign country
- coverage for in-home recovery

Plan H includes the core benefits, plus the following:

- coverage for daily skilled nursing facility care coinsurance
- Part A deductible
- coverage for medically necessary emergency care in a foreign country
- 50 percent of the cost of prescription drugs—a $250 annual deductible and maximum annual benefit of $1250 apply

Plan I includes the core benefits, plus the following:

- coverage for daily skilled nursing facility care coinsurance
- Part A deductible
- 100 percent of the excess charges for Part B
- coverage for medically necessary emergency care in a foreign country
- in-home recovery
- 50 percent of the cost of prescription drugs—a $250 annual deductible and maximum annual benefit of $1250 apply

Plan J includes the core benefits, plus the following:

- coverage for daily skilled nursing facility care coinsurance
- Part A deductible
- Part B deductible
- 100 percent of the excess charges for Part B
- coverage for medically necessary emergency care in a foreign country
- in-home recovery
- 50 percent of the cost of prescription drugs—a $250 annual deductible and maximum annual benefit of $3000 apply
- preventive medical care

Each Medigap plan has its advantages and drawbacks. Which plan is right for you is determined by your individual situation. Don't just automatically assume that since Plan J offers the most coverage it's the best one for you. You may wind up paying for much more than you'll ever need. For instance, if you don't do much (or any) traveling in a foreign country, you won't need a plan that covers emergency care while traveling abroad. Although, with the way the standardized plans are set up, the only plans that don't offer emergency care in a foreign country are Plans A and B. As with other forms of insurance, cost is always a consideration, but don't let that dictate which plan you choose. Weigh your needs, expectations, and plans against each Medigap plan to make sure that you are choosing the best one for you.

There are also Medicare SELECT policies, which are Medigap policies that require you to use certain approved hospitals and physicians. These SELECT policies are generally less expensive than other Medigap policies.

Enrollment in Medicare

Enrolling in Medicare is very simple, but determining when the best time is to sign up for you may be more difficult. If you are already receiving social security or railroad benefits, your Medicare enrollment is automatic. The Social Security Administration will contact you a few months prior to your 65th birthday to give you the information you need. Although enrollment is automatic, you have the option of turning down Part B because of the premium. You can determine if you have both Parts A and B, or one or the other by looking at your Medicare card because it will list what coverage you have. If you aren't receiving social security or railroad benefits, you can enroll by contacting your local social security office. Other people who may sign up for Medicare include:

• people between the ages of 50 and 65 who are disabled widow(er)s who haven't applied for social security disability benefits because they are receiving another type of social security benefit

• those who are government employees and became disabled before age 65

• a worker, or his or her spouse or dependent child who has permanent kidney failure

• those who had Medicare medical coverage (Part B) in the past, but dropped the insurance

• those who turned down the medical coverage (Part B) when they became entitled to hospital insurance (Part A)

There are three ways to enroll in Medicare: initial enrollment, general enrollment, and special enrollment.

INITIAL ENROLLMENT. Prior to your 65th birthday, you can submit an enrollment application at your local Social Security office. When you become eligible for Part A, you may sign up for Part B. You have a seven-month window around your 65th birthday in which to apply for Medicare Part B coverage, beginning three months before your birthday. If you apply during the three months before you turn 65, your coverage will begin in your birthday month. (See Table 13.6.) However, if you apply during your birthday month or the three months following your birthday, your coverage will be delayed for up to three months. If you are eligible for Medicare because of a disability or permanent kidney failure, your seven-month period depends on the date that your disability or treatment began.

GENERAL ENROLLMENT. If you choose not to enroll in Part B during the initial enrollment period, you still have another chance each year. A general enrollment period occurs from January 1 to March 31 every year, with your coverage beginning the following July. If you enroll during the general enrollment period, you will face a "penalty" for not signing up sooner. Your premium will be increased by 10 percent for every 12-month period that you were eligible but didn't sign up. For example, you become eligible for Medicare at age 65, but choose not to enroll in Part B until you are 68. Your penalty will be an increase in your premium by 30 percent (3 12-month periods × 10%).

Table 13.6. Coverage Effective Dates

Initial enrollment period month	When Medicare Part B coverage begins
1	The month you become eligible for Medicare
2	The month you become eligible for Medicare
3	The month you become eligible for Medicare
4	One month after enrollment
5	Two months after enrollment
6	Three months after enrollment
7	Three months after enrollment

SPECIAL ENROLLMENT.   A special enrollment period applies only if you are 65 or older and are currently covered by your employer's group health plan, or your spouse's employer's group health plan. If this is the case, you will be able to enroll in Medicare Part B without paying the 10-percent penalty. Right now, the rules allow you the following:

- to enroll in Medicare Part B any time while you are covered under the group health plan
- to enroll in Medicare Part B during the eight-month period beginning the month your group coverage ends, or the month employment ends, whichever is first

By enrolling in Part B while you are still covered by your group health plan (or during that first month that you aren't covered), you will have the opportunity to have your Medicare coverage begin either the first day of the month you enroll, or to delay the coverage until the first day of any of the following three months. By enrolling in any of the other seven months of your special enrollment period, your coverage will begin the first day of the month following your enrollment.

It's important to note that if your group coverage ends, or if your employment ends, during your initial enrollment period, you will not be granted a special enrollment period. This is because Medicare will assume that you will enroll as you would normally. The special enrollment period is designed to benefit only those who don't use their initial enrollment period because they have continuing health care coverage through their employer.

Should you not take advantage of your special enrollment period, you will have to wait to enroll until the next general enrollment period begins. By enrolling then, you will be subject to the 10-percent surcharge, as you would have been under normal circumstances. The privilege afforded to you is only done so during the eight-month special enrollment period, or while your group health coverage is in force.

People who are receiving social security disability benefits and are covered under their employer's group health plan, or a family member's group health plan, also have the special enrollment period and premium rights that are extended to those workers and spouses over the age of 65.

Special Enrollment Period and Medigap Insurance

When considering whether or not to enroll in Medicare Part B coverage, you will need to think about how it will affect your eligibility for Medigap insurance policies. If you enroll in Part B at or after age 65, you will trigger a one-time "Medigap open enrollment period." But if you enroll in Part B while still covered by a group health plan, you may not need a Medigap policy. Your group health plan would be the primary payer for any health or medical bill claims, while Medicare would be the secondary payer. After your group plan coverage ends, you may find that you need a Medigap policy, but are unable to purchase one because your open enrollment period has expired.

Therefore, it may be advisable to delay enrolling in Part B until your employer-provided group health plan is about to end, because you will be able to optimize your health coverage. During the open enrollment period, you will be able to purchase any Medigap plan from any company at the most favorable prices available for your age group, all without having to worry about being turned down. The insurance company cannot refuse you coverage or charge you more than any other open enrollment applicants for that particular policy. Of course, the different Medigap plans will vary in premium range by what extra coverage is being offered. This also means that any health problems or preexisting conditions will not be used to withhold any coverage from you.

Medicare Managed Health Care Plans

When we discuss Medicare, we are referring to the government-run program, which is also referred to as Original Medicare. There are other options available, too. Some people have found that they can enjoy additional benefits and lower costs by joining a managed care plan. People most commonly use health maintenance organizations, or HMOs. However, there are also preferred provider plans (PPOs), private fee for services (PFFSs), and others. (See Table 13.7 for a comparison.) These Medicare managed plans must provide the medical and hospital services that Medicare covers.

Medicare managed plans operate in much the same way as an employer's managed health plan would. You usually have to see a doctor within the plan's network of physicians and receive services from within the network, as well. And, generally, neither Medicare nor the managed care plan will pay for services that are obtained from outside the network, unless it is emergency care or urgent care needed while outside the network (coverage area).

Although you may take part in the managed care plan, you must be enrolled in Medicare Part B and continue to pay the annual premium. However, the plans may provide more coverage than Medicare would alone. For instance, some plans may offer coverage for hearing exams, eyeglasses, prescription drugs, and other services. You will need to refer to the plan description to determine exactly what your Medicare managed care plan offers.

Other Health Coverage and Medicare

If you have private health coverage, you will need to determine how your Medicare coverage will fit in with it. Just like Medicare doesn't cover every expense, neither will your private plan. Plus, you may have your spouse or other dependents on your private plan. Their coverage will be affected by any decision you make regarding your own coverage. It's very important to not cancel any coverage before your Medicare coverage begins.

If your health coverage comes from a Department of Defense program, your coverage will change, or possibly end, once you are eligible for Medicare. By contacting either the Defense Department or a military health benefits advisor, you will know how to proceed and whether you should enroll in Medicare Part B. For those people with health coverage from the Indian Health Service, Department of Veterans Affairs, or a state medical assistance program, you will need to contact those offices to determine if enrolling in Medicare would be beneficial to you or not.

MEDICAID

We really can't go into much depth when talking about Medicaid because it is a state-run program, and therefore, the rules are different in each state. Medicaid offers public assistance with health care for those who can't afford it on their own. It's a welfare health care system. To determine if you are eligible for Medicaid, you will have to contact your state's Medicaid office. Medicaid is financed by both the federal government, as well as state governments.

Unlike Medicare, Medicaid will pay for extended care in a skilled nursing care facility and other services. There is typically no copayment or deductibles that the covered person would have to pay, either. Those people who receive Supplemental Security Income (SSI) are automatically eligible for Medicaid. SSI is a federal program that guarantees a minimum monthly income to those 65 and older who are blind or disabled and have limited income and assets.

There are many rules surrounding Medicaid, of which the "spend down rule" is the most well-known. In order to qualify for Medicaid, you must spend down your assets until they are under a specified limit. You must also not have a large monthly income, but again, these limits are all set by the individual states. There are cases where people will qualify for Medicaid even though their incomes may be higher than the approved limit, but their medical expenses are so tremendous that they reduce the net income to meet state requirements.

Because of the way the system is set up, becoming eligible for Medicaid shouldn't be a goal. By being reliant on the government to take care of your health costs, you will have to sacrifice your financial freedom, as well as be subject to decreased choices for your health care. Having them pay your costs means playing by their rules. But, by taking responsibility for your own health care and long-term care coverage, you will be in a better position to dictate what care you want, which doctor you go see, and other important matters.

Table 13.7   Knowing Your Options with Medicare

Medicare options	What you receive	Things to remember
Original Medicare— *Received directly from the government.*	Coverage for care from most doctors and hospitals in the country. Limited out-of-pocket costs if you have Medicare supplemental insurance (Medigap).	No coverage for most prescription drugs, hearing aids, or vision care. May be subject to high out-of-pocket expenses if you don't have any Medigap insurance, which may be expensive.
Medicare HMO and Medicare PSO— *Offered by a private health plan.*	Coverage for care at a lower cost than other Medicare options if you use network doctors and follow plan rules. Often some prescription drug coverage and other additional benefits are available. Medigap not needed.	Care typically only covered with primary care doctor or plan approval, except in emergencies. Generally, no coverage for routine care when you are away from home. CAUTION: Plan may raise premiums, cut benefits or discontinue Medicare coverage.

Table 13.7 (*Continued*)

Medicare options	What you receive	Things to remember
Medicare PPO— *Offered by a private health plan.*	Similar to HMOs, except some coverage for care from nonnetwork providers and direct access to specialists.	Full coverage only from network providers. Same caution as above.
Medicare PFFS— *Offered by a private health plan.*	Coverage for care from most doctors and hospitals in the country.	Monthly premiums and out-of-pocket expenses may be very high Same caution as above.
Medicare MSA— *Offered by a private health plan.*	Coverage for care only after you pay deductible (may be as much as $6000). If not much health care is needed, extra money can be freed up to use on health care when needed.	If you get sick, there will be a very high out-of-pocket expense due to deductible (as much as $6000) before coverage begins. Same caution as above.

WHERE DO YOU WANT YOUR MONEY TO TAKE YOU TODAY?

T he main financial concern that most people have these days is, "Will I have enough money to retire?" It's a very good question. And, all other things considered, your retirement should be your most pressing financial issue. Although you may want to help pay for your child's or grandchild's education, you shouldn't do it at the sacrifice of your own future comfort. Taking care of your retirement money and your future is the most important thing to consider.

Retirement planning would be very easy if we all held crystal balls that foretold our future. How long will we live? What will inflation be like in 20 years? Will I have any major illnesses that may eat up my retirement money? If we knew the answers to those questions, preparing for our retirement would be a snap. Unfortunately, what the future holds is very cloudy. Therefore, we must plan for our retirement more diligently. This is one reason why retirement planning is so closely tied to personal financial planning. The process would be incomplete, at best, without some form of retirement planning. Because retirement planning impacts both your future and current lives, it is the most influential part of financial planning.

With the stock market downturn of 2000–2002 and the economic recession, people are experiencing the first real market decline since the 1973–1974 bear market. We've seen massive sell-offs of stock and mutual funds by individual investors who have gotten scared and pulled all their money out of the market. Yes, it's scary to lose money, especially when it's your retirement fund, but is that the smart thing to do? Would you be better off keeping your retirement funds invested in stocks and bonds, or in money market instruments? And, what is a suitable way to hold your retirement money? Throughout this chapter, we look at the various retirement accounts and discuss the pros and cons of each. We also talk about ways to enhance your portfolio value once you have retired and are taking distributions from your accounts as income so that you don't outlive your money. Just as an increase in life expectancy has an impact on the social security system, it will also have an impact on your retirement funds.

So now the question becomes, where do you want to start? We've outlined savings, how to save, and different types of investment vehicles in which to invest your money. In my opinion, having an emergency fund is far more important than building up your nest egg for retirement. That way, if you have extra money to use for an emergency, you won't have to tap into your retirement accounts. However, once you have built up a sufficient cash reserve (or if you already have one), you should turn your attention to your retirement plans.

Look back at the list of goals you made. Did you list specific things that you wanted to do or have once you were retired? If you didn't, please consider what your retirement goals are. Once you have identified what you want to do when you are retired, we can start making realistic predictions about how much you need to save. For instance, if you want to do a lot of overseas traveling, it's important to plan for that now, so you can have that extra money included in your retirement accounts. If you don't plan for those contingencies now, it may be harder to pull them off once you have retired. The last thing I want to hear from clients is that they want to do something, but can't because although they have the time, they don't have the money!

After you determine how much money you will need to live on (and play with) during retirement, the final step is to take action on your plans. Although there is computer software that can help you estimate your retirement needs, it can't help you save. That's something you will have to do on your own. And, as we discussed in Chapter 3, it's the hardest step. However, don't let fear or procrastination set you back.

THE HISTORY OF RETIREMENT

The notion of retirement really didn't have a big impact on America until after World War II. At that point, people would give 30 to 40 years of their lives to one company, who in return, would pay workers good salaries and generous pensions once they stopped working. In that way, companies were very paternalistic toward their employees. The employees were also very dedicated to their employers. Working until you were 65, quitting, and then enjoying your pension income was the common thing to do. People looked forward to the time when the company that they had worked so hard for would begin to take care of them.

But, during the later stages of the twentieth century, that notion became radicalized. No longer were these companies taking care of the workers who had dedicated their lives to them. More people were finding that they no longer wanted to be chained to their desks. Although they were good at their jobs, they weren't being fulfilled, plus, they had the financial security to know that they didn't need their jobs anymore. Working until age 65 became the dinosaur of retirement planning.

For those who still want to retire completely, that option still exists. It is also a very popular choice for many people, especially those who are nearing retirement. For others, though, the idea of retirement, of ceasing to work, isn't a very ideal option at all. To stop working, for many, meant the onset of boredom, and later, depression. This is why many people find that they are busier in retirement than they ever were during their actual working lives! I have many clients come in to see me who say that between spending time with their children and grandchildren, visiting with friends, volunteering, and other activities, they have found that they have no time to themselves! But, I've not heard one complaint about that because they are doing what they love to do, rather than working.

Another popular life change revolves around changing careers. I have many clients who retire from a large corporation, only to become independent contractors for those same companies making more money than they did as employees. The advent of the independent contractor really came to center stage during the 1990s. All the independent contractors I have met have told me that they wouldn't change their status to employee for anything. This way, things get done on their own timetables. And isn't that what people ultimately want: to control their own destiny?

Still others are moving from their high-paying corporate jobs, to lower-paying, more fulfilling jobs during their 50s. These people then find that they can continue working at their less-stressful jobs well into their 70s. All of this results from not having to rely on their larger paycheck. While this may not seem like something you can feasibly afford to do, it may be something to aspire to. By deciding on what your goals are, you will be able to realize them much easier than if you don't.

THE BIGGEST HAZARDS OF RETIREMENT PLANNING

Setting goals is easy; following through on them is more difficult. Remember what I said about setting big goals and little goals? Many times, I've found that people set their sights too high, only to see themselves fall short of their goals. It's not because they failed, entirely, to reach these goals; it's because they didn't break down their goals, and became overwhelmed. Smaller hills are easier to climb than very tall mountains. Therefore, break down your large mountainous dream into smaller, more attainable foothills. By doing this, you'll be more apt to follow through on your goals and reach them. Another hint is to make sure that your larger goals are also realistic. While having $5 million set aside for retirement is a very nice idea, is that how much you really need? Or, do you need less, more like $1 million? Taking a realistic look at your goals and your needs will also help you achieve these goals.

There are other pitfalls of retirement planning, including starting late, investing too conservatively, and investing too little. While one of these is enough to stunt the growth of your retirement fund, a combination of all three will kill it. I've always followed the adage that it's never *too* late to start. While that's true, the later you start, the more you will have to put away for retirement. That's because you will be closer to retiring then, than if you had started earlier. It's amazing how many people will come to me and tell me that they want to retire in 10 or 15 years, and yet, they have done next to nothing about investing money for their retirement. Sometimes it becomes an unpleasant fact that they will have to work longer than they want to simply because they don't have the means necessary to retire.

However, there is the flip side to that. I've had many people in their 20s and early 30s, sometimes single people and sometimes couples, come in with retirement accounts that are already blossoming. For me, that's a wonderful feeling, because I know that these people already have the discipline to save. I won't have to try and inspire them to save. It's also impressive because for most people in that age bracket, there are other things that consume their money, be it a new house, children, or student loans. It's so easy to put off saving for tomorrow when there are bills due today. That's why I advocate paying yourself first.

What I'm trying to say is don't put off until tomorrow what you can do today. Start saving money for your retirement. Open an IRA and invest the maximum amount of $3000 per year. Open a Roth IRA so you can enjoy the tax-free income once you start to take money out. Do you find that you sometimes have extra money at the end of the month? Invest it, rather than spend it. You may not want to, you may not even like it, but you'll find that it will benefit you more later than it will now.

Another problem is that many people are investing their money too conservatively, often in bank CDs or money market funds that are paying less than seven percent. With the uncertainty in the market, it's understandable to want to be more cautious with your money. Certainly, I would never encourage anyone to speculate with their retirement money; it's too important. However, investing too conservatively may hurt you just as much as being too risky. Wise people may decide to take a fair bit of risk with their money. They know that by investing too conservatively, their money isn't going to keep up with inflation, thus, lowering the buying power of their money.

When you invest your money, you want it to be working as hard for you as you did for it, right? By socking it away in a CD or money market fund (or worse yet, a savings account), your money isn't working very hard for you at all. It's almost just sitting there, waiting for you to come get it. But, investing the money with a little bit more risk may result in your money working harder for you. Again, you just have to be realistic. To want to average 10 percent a year may not be unrealistic. To want 20 percent or more per year is unrealistic. Just invest your money according to how much risk you are comfortable taking, keeping in mind that not all years are rosy and your account may lose some value.

Then there is investing too little money, meaning too little overall, not in increments that are too little. Generally, there is no such thing as too little, unless you are hitting single-digit numbers. For instance, $5 per week is too little. That is only $260 per year But, if you can invest $50 per week ($2600 per year), that's much better. The more money you can invest at one time, the better, because then all that money will be able to start working for you. But, truly, any amount is better than nothing.

Investing too little over the long term won't help you too much. That's why investing as much as you are comfortable with, and starting as early as you can, are so important. It's so easy to procrastinate, but to do that will mean that you don't value your retirement. You could be retired for 10, 20, or even 30 years of your life. Don't you want to be able to enjoy it as much as possible?

These dangers become even greater when you consider the implications of compound earnings, which magnifies these mistakes. Compound interest can turn a small investment into a much larger investment over time. That's why it's really important to invest your money early, as well as take some risk. Compound interest at 6 percent doesn't sound too bad, but what if you could get compound interest at 10 percent? Sounds much better doesn't it? Especially if you consider that increasing the interest rate by 4 percent could mean doubling or tripling your money. For example, the difference between investing $1 at 5 percent and investing $1 at 10 percent for 30 years is $13.13 ($17.449 − $4.322).

This assumes that everyone can handle higher-risk investments, when the truth is that there are some people who cannot tolerate the risk involved with certain investments. If you find that you really can't sleep at night because you are worried about your money, then you do need to have it invested more conservatively. However, your choice then becomes putting it in something like a bank CD (which is also insured up to $100,000 per investor) or a savings account. Obviously, since both investments are very low risk, you will need to put your money in the bank CD because it yields a higher interest rate than the savings account would. Also, since you will be utilizing lower-paying investments, you will need to invest more than you would otherwise. Therefore, if you were going to invest $1500 per year in higher-risk investments, you'll need to invest more than that, say $3000, simply because the money is going into lower-paying investments.

All things considered, try to invest as much as possible in an investment vehicle that has the highest potential return that you are comfortable with. And, while it's never too late to start, if you haven't yet begun to save for your retirement, do it now! The earlier you begin, the more money you will be able to amass before you retire. You may also find that you'll be able to retire sooner than you had anticipated.

ESTIMATING YOUR RETIREMENT NEEDS

Once you have set your goals and you have started to form a clear picture of what you would like to do during your retirement, you need to figure out how much money you will need to live on. If only that was all there was! Unfortunately, our economy isn't static, and will be subject to many fluctuations between now and when you begin your retirement. That means that not only do we not know how the stock markets will perform, but we also don't know what kind of inflation we will face over the next few years. It could be that inflation is rather stagnant, or we could see a period of high inflation. Regardless, you need to make sure that you are prepared for your retirement. Although the future is characterized by so much uncertainty, that's no excuse for putting off retirement planning.

There are a couple of ways to estimate your needs. The first is a more expense-driven method, while the second is a needs-and-wants method. The expense-driven method asks you to estimate the percentage of your current expenses that you will have during retirement. When I use this method for retirement planning, I generally say that the expense percentage will not change; I use 100 percent. My reasoning is that although some expenses will go away, others will replace them. In fact, you may find that you are spending more in retirement than you did while you were working.

For example, Jeff and Mary Client are concerned about their retirement. They want to approach their planning from an expense point of view. They have itemized all their current expenses (on a monthly basis) and find that they are spending $72,000 per year. That includes helping their son with his college tuition, roughly $4000 per year. They also contribute to an IRA for both of them, $6000 at current limits. They would like to retire in 10 years. At that time, they won't be spending the $4000 for their son's tuition, nor will they be putting $6000 into IRAs for both of them. Their expenses will drop by at least $10,000 per year. However, Jeff and Mary have said they would like to start traveling at that time because they haven't had much time to do any traveling yet. They would like to take at least two trips per year and are excited about traveling abroad.

Jeff estimates that their other expenses will remain the same. Their house is already paid off, as are their cars. Their main expenses are all discretionary, which they think will remain about the same, but may increase since they will have more time. So, although their expenses will appear to drop by $10,000, they will probably increase, especially once inflation is considered. Therefore, Jeff and Mary think that spending $72,000 per year during retirement will be an accurate figure.

For some people, though, estimating the percentage of their *current* expenses will not yield an accurate analysis. That's where the needs-and-wants method comes in. Rather than compare the current level of expenses with what will be estimated for retirement, this approach goes into the future to calculate how much annual income the clients will need in order to keep the standard of living that they want. It also takes inflation into consideration, and will calculate how much the clients need to save between now and when they plan to retire.

Should conditions or expectations change (i.e., retirement date changes, clients receive a large inheritance, inflation is much greater than anticipated), it will be necessary to update the model to reflect an accurate and realistic forecast for the clients. Depending on what the updated analysis says, you may need to adjust your savings and investments to help you reach your goals.

FUNDING YOUR RETIREMENT

Once you've figured out how much money you will need to fund your retirement, the question becomes, "Where will that money come from?" To answer this, you will need to estimate what your annual income will be during retirement. Currently, the two main sources of retirement income are social security and employer-sponsored pension plans. However, unless you will be retiring in the very near future (20 years or fewer), you may not be able to rely on social security as a guaranteed income stream. But what about pensions? These days people are changing jobs more frequently, which causes them to have smaller pensions, or no pensions at all. Plus, companies are phasing out pensions to help cut costs. What I've found is that most people cannot count on pensions. And, unless the Social Security Administration figures out how to continue funding the social security trust funds, people won't be able to rely on that, either. See Figure 14.1) In fact, many people in their 20s and 30s don't even believe that Social Security will be around for them when they want to retire. This means that people have to rely on themselves more and more for their retirements.

Let's assume that social security will be there for Jeff and Mary Client. Since they both work, they will both be entitled to their own retirement benefits, rather than having one receive worker's retirement benefits and the other receive spousal benefits. Assuming that they will receive about $15,000 per year in retirement benefits, with annual expenses of $72,000, they will need at least $57,000 (in today's dollars; inflation will push that figure higher) per year to help fund their retirement, assuming no other sources of income. Once inflation[1] is figured in (at a relatively high rate of five percent over 10 years), that $57,000 per year needed turns into $92,853 per year! (Annual expenses after inflation are $117,288.) Neither Jeff nor Mary believes that they will receive any type of retirement pension from their employers. Therefore, they will have to save this money themselves.

RETIREMENT NEEDS

$72,000	= annual expenses
$72,000 × 1.629 (5% inflation factor)	= $117,288
Annual expenses – Social Security =	
$72,000 − $15,000	= $57,000 (annual shortfall)
$57,000 × 1.629	= $92,853 per year
$92,853 ÷ 10%	= $928,530
Total needed	**= $928,530**

Jeff and Mary now know that they have an annual shortfall of nearly $93,000. In order to reach that goal, they will hypothesize their annual rate of return, so that they know how much they need to save on an annual basis. If we estimate a 10-percent annual return on Jeff's and Mary's money during retirement, we see that they need to save a total of $928,530 ($92,853 ÷ 10) before they retire in order to be able to live on $72,000 per year in today's dollars. Continuing with the 10-percent return, their nest egg will yield $92,853 per year to make up their shortfall. Plus, as long as the principal ($928,530) isn't touched, it will continue to generate this income for Jeff and Mary, and will eventually become part of their estate.

[1] Inflation factor found in *Personal Financial Planning*, Eighth Edition, by Lawrence J. Gitman and Michael D. Joehnk. Harcourt Brace College Publishers, 1999.

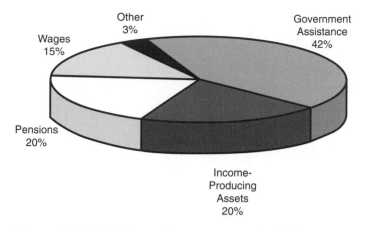

Figure 14.1 This illustration represents the different sources of retirement income. Notice how government assistance makes up the biggest portion right now. In years to come, we'll see a change in the overall percentages, as income-producing assets begin to make up a larger portion.

But, how much do they need to save on an annual basis to reach their goal? Jeff and Mary have decided that they don't want to count on a 10-percent return. Rather, they would like to decrease that to 8 percent. Using an interest factor of 14.487[2] (for 10 years at 8 percent), we see that Jeff and Mary will need to save $64,094 per year ($928,530 ÷ 14.487).(See Table 14.1)

WHERE TO INVEST?

The easiest part has been done. We've figured out how much is needed to cover the shortfall for Jeff's and Mary's retirement. But now they are faced with the hardest part: saving the money. As we discuss in Chapter 3, saving money is the hardest part to becoming wealthy. But it's the most vital part of retirement planning. Although knowing how much money you should be saving is an important component of retirement planning, actually saving the money is the most important. So if you are unsure of how much money you should be putting away, don't let that deter you from starting.

[2] Interest factor from *Personal Financial Planning*, Eighth Edition, by Lawrence J. Gitman and Michael D. Joehnk. Harcourt Brace College Publishers, 1999.

Table 14.1

Jeff and Mary Client	Date

I. Estimated Household Expenditures in Retirement	
A. Number of years until retirement	10
B. Current level of household expenditures	$72,000
C. Estimated retirement expenses (as a percentage of current)	100%
D. Estimated retirement expenses (B × C)	$72,000
II. Estimated Retirement Income	
E. Social Security income — annually	$15,000
F. Expected pension income — annually	$0
G. Other income	$0
H. Total annual retirement income (E + F + G)	$15,000
I. Excess (shortfall) of income	($57,000)
III. Inflation	
J. Estimated inflation rate	5%
K. Inflation factor	1.629
L. Inflation-adjusted shortfall (if necessary)	$92,853
IV. Funding the Shortfall	
M. Anticipated rate of return on assets during retirement	10%
N. Required amount needed (L/M)	$928,530
O. Anticipated rate of return on assets before retirement	8%
P. Compound interest factor	14.487
Q. Annual savings required to fund retirement	$64,094

* This is Jeff's and Mary's worksheet, which shows how much money they will need to fund their retirement. You may easily substitute your figures for theirs to come up with the amount of money you need to save for your retirement. This example is a one-time-only chart. Throughout your lifetime, these figures will need to be updated and reanalyzed.

There are many different types of accounts that you can use to help accumulate your retirement nest egg. The most common are employer-sponsored retirement accounts, such as 401(k)s, 403(b)s ,and 457 plans. There are retirement plans that are designed for self-employed people, like SEPs. Then you have the traditional IRAs and the Roth IRAs. One of the best features of retirement accounts is their tax-deferred earnings status. As discussed in Chapter 10, by investing money in accounts such as IRAs and 401(k)s, all your earnings may grow on a tax-deferred basis. This makes these accounts very attractive for all tax-paying people, not just those in high tax brackets.

For the novice investor, all these accounts and their different features and advantages may be overwhelming, but by increasing your knowledge, you will be better able to choose which type of account is right for you. Plus, a financial advisor will be able to guide you through the seas of the various types of retirement accounts.

EMPLOYER-SPONSORED RETIREMENT PLANS

There are two types of employer-sponsored retirement plans: basic and supplemental. The basic plan calls for automatic employee participation after a certain term of employment, such as one year. The supplemental plan is a voluntary program that enables employees to increase the amount of money being set aside for their retirements. Although the supplemental plans are the most common, we also touch on basic plans, so that you are familiar with them as well.

Basic Plans

Basic plans have participation requirements that employers institute to help keep their costs down. For the most part, employers have decreed that in order to be eligible for the retirement plans, you must meet at least age (such as 21) and years-of-service requirements. Often times, there is also an income-level requirement. This is because employers feel that there is a higher turnover ratio for those people who are newly hired and younger. To help keep their administrative costs low, they've sought to disallow those categories of employees from participating. Of course, the belief is that once those newly hired, younger people are with the company longer, they are more apt to stay, and so they merit the retirement plan.

Employer pension plans are a type of basic plan. However, you may find that you are expected to contribute to your own pension plan. There are both noncontributory and contributory pension plans.

Under the noncontributory type, the company will pay for the entire cost of an employee's benefits. But, under a contributory plan, both the employee and employer share the cost. More often than not, companies have instituted contributory plans, where the cost to the employee ranges between 3 and 10 percent of annual income. The employer then generally matches what the employee has put in.

But, what if you leave the company? The ability and willingness to change jobs, and even careers, is higher now than it ever has been. So what do you do when you have money in a contributory pension plan and you leave that company for another one? You are legally entitled to at least the amount of money that you put in, adjusted for any profit or loss. Whether you qualify for the amount that your employer contributed is determined by the company's policy. You can take the benefits as a lump-sum amount (it being taxable plus a 10-percent penalty if you are younger than $59^{1}/_{2}$), you can roll it over into an IRA, or you can take it as monthly income once you are retired. Of course, the amount that is transferred may be more or less than the initial investment.

Companies also have established vesting rules (which occur when employees have a nonforfeitable right to their pensions). This gives some employees an added incentive to work longer. Prior to 1974, companies usually had vesting rules that stated that the employees had to be employed at the company for at least 25 years, or they received no pension benefits. The Employee Retirement Income Security Act of 1974 (ERISA) helped fix that by regulating the amount of time that the companies could set for vesting. Those rules were again updated in 1986 with the Tax Reform Act, which greatly benefited employees. Now, employers must choose between two vesting schedules. The first is called cliff vesting, and dictates that an employee is fully vested after no more than 5 years of service, but the employee receives no vesting privileges until that time. Once you're fully vested, you have the right to all the money that has been paid in so far, yours and your employer's, again adjusted for any profit or loss. The second schedule is a graded schedule. At the minimum, you would begin vesting at your third year of employment at 20 percent. Each year, you would be vested by an additional 20 percent until you reached 100 percent after 7 years on the job. These rules apply to an employer's contributions. You are always 100-percent vested in any contribution you make on your behalf.

DEFINED BENEFITS VERSUS DEFINED CONTRIBUTION PLANS. The two most commonly used methods to calculate retirement benefits are the defined contribution and defined benefits plans. With the defined benefits plan, employees will know exactly how much they will receive in retirement benefits before they retire. This is because the way the benefits are paid out and calculated are expressly defined in the plan's provisions. This also means that no matter how well or poorly the underlying investments do, the employer must pay out the benefits. There will be no deviation from the formula. Usually, the formula includes the number of years of service and the amount of money the employee was making. For example, you worked for XYZ Company for 25 years. They based their defined benefits plan on the average of your final (and usually, highest) 3 years of income, which works out to $78,000. Their formula stipulates that you will receive three percent of your salary average for each of your years of service. Your *annual* benefit would be $58,500.

DEFINED BENEFITS ILLUSTRATION

Average salary for final three years	= $78,000
Percentage paid	= 3%
Years of service	= 25
Annual benefit = $78,000 × 25 × 3%	= $58,500

Under a defined contributions plan, the plan provisions detail the amount of contribution that the employee and employer must make. Then, at retirement, the employee is granted whatever monthly benefit those contributions will afford. While this type of plan also takes age, years of service, and income level into consideration, the most important factor is the investment return on the contributions. A defined contribution plan guarantees the employee nothing in the way of benefits except for what the fund managers have been able to obtain, which can lead to a lot of volatility. However, there is a standard that the fund managers must follow, so that the contributing employees don't find all their money gone at retirement.

As the employee, your main concern is the amount of money you will receive in the form of benefits once you have retired. Generally, a pension plan is considered good when employees receive between 70 and 80 percent of their net preretirement pay. However, ascertaining how much you will receive will become more difficult to do as more companies shy away from the defined benefits plan and towards the defined contribution plan. From an employer's perspective, the move is an easy decision because the economic future is unknown. Employers simply don't want to find themselves responsible for paying out benefits that they don't have the funds for. Unfortunately, for the employees, this means that you are required to take an additional part in your retirement funding.

TAX IMPLICATIONS. Employer-sponsored retirement plans are often referred to as qualified plans. This means that the plans qualify for important tax benefits under the Internal Revenue Code. For the employer, these benefits include a current tax deduction on the payments. For the employee, the benefits include deferral of income tax on the employer contributions. Finally, earnings accumulate on a tax-deferred basis. Most distributions from qualified plans are also eligible for tax-free rollovers to IRAs and other retirement plans.

> **Special note:** Some employees have decided to forego making their pension plans qualified. These nonqualified pension plans receive no special tax treatment, nor do any contributions made to them. Any contributions made by an employee to a contributory pension plan that is nonqualified is still fully taxable and treated as ordinary income received.

Supplemental Plans

Supplemental plans are voluntary for employees. These plans offer employees the chance to increase the amount of funds set aside for their retirements, as well as shelter some of their income from income tax. There are three types of supplemental plans: profit-sharing, thrift and savings, and salary reduction plans.

PROFIT-SHARING PLANS.   As the name implies, profit-sharing plans allow a company's employees to share in the company's earnings. Proponents of profit-sharing plans argue that these plans give an added incentive to employees to work harder. They reason that if the employees work harder, the firm will be more profitable, with the earnings flowing back into the employees' pockets. Whether or not this actually happens is unknown. However, both employees and employers like the benefits of this type of plan. For one, a profit-sharing plan may be tax qualified, and enjoy the same favorable tax treatment that a qualified pension or IRA would. Second, there is no contribution requirement for the employer. The company will simply contribute a percentage of its profits. Therefore, when there is a good year, the contribution may be larger than that of a poor-earnings year. A company will set certain minimum and maximum contribution percentages, so that the employees have a general idea of how big (or small) a given contribution will be.

Many times, a firm will contribute its own company's stock to an employee's profit-sharing plan. This doesn't mean, though, that an employee's contributions must be invested in that company's stock. Generally, there is a number of investment options, such as stock and bond funds.

When investing in your employer's company stock, there are some things to consider. First, if the company has a good year and is very profitable, you will benefit in two ways: Your employer's contribution may be greater, and the value of that stock may increase. However, heavily investing in your employer's company stock is generally frowned upon. While you may feel that your company is very strong, that doesn't mean that it will always remain that way. Should the company have a poor year, you may face a declining value in your profit-sharing plan, as well as uncertainty at work. If you can diversify your profit-sharing account's portfolio, you'll be better off in case something does happen.

Consider the predicament of the many employees of Enron Corporation. For the past few years, Enron's stock has been going strong. It's been trading in the $70–$80 range, hitting $89.625 on September

18, 2000. For those employees who had sunk a considerable portion of their retirement money in the company's stock, it looked like they had made a profitable decision. Unfortunately, things didn't stay so rosy. Enron's stock began to slide in February of 2001. Although it came back a little in April of that year, the stock price continued to go down. It hovered in the $50 range from March to early June of 2001, but things just got worse. By December of 2001, the stock price was less than $1 per share. Imagine your retirement money doing that. So think very carefully before you invest 100 percent of your retirement money in your company's stock. Investing a portion of your contribution, say 5 to 10 percent, is perfectly healthy. Plus, if your employer offers a match of your contribution with company stock, you really shouldn't add to that amount by investing your contribution in company stock. Even the best companies can have problems with their stock prices. You just don't want to be on the receiving end of these problems. By diversifying your retirement plan, you won't be.

Interestingly, nonprofit corporations can sponsor profit-sharing plans. At one time an employer could only make contributions to a profit-sharing plan if it had either current-year or prior-year retained profits. This was not a major limitation unless the employer had consistently been unprofitable. The profit requirement was eliminated from the Internal Revenue Code several years ago. It would be more precise to call these plans discretionary defined contribution plans, but the term profit-sharing plan has been used for many years.

THRIFT AND SAVINGS PLANS. Thrift and savings plans offer the same type of tax treatment that other types of qualified plans do, with one exception. Although any contributions made by the employer are not included in an employee's gross income for the year in which they were made, any contributions made by the employee are still counted in his or her gross income for that year. So any money you put into your thrift and savings account will still be considered as income, and you will face ordinary income tax on those amounts.

An employer who makes contributions to an employee's plan will do so in a set proportion of the employee's contribution up to a maximum percentage. The money contributed will then be deposited with a trustee, who will it them in various types of securities, such as stock and bond funds and the stock of the employing company. These plans also offer a much more liberal vesting period than other plans do. Typically, an employee is 100-percent vested in the employer's contributions as soon as the contribution is made. Thrift and savings plans also have looser policies regarding withdrawal of funds and cessation of participation. Be careful, though, because there is usually a waiting period to reenter the program once you have stopped participating.

For example, you participate in your company's thrift and savings program. Your annual salary is $60,000 and you put 10 percent, or $6000, per year into your plan. Your employer will match any contribution you make at 75¢ on the dollar up to 6 percent of your salary. Your employer's contribution to your plan would be $3600.

EMPLOYER'S THRIFT AND SAVINGS PLAN CONTRIBUTION

Employee's salary	– $60,000
Employee's contribution	**= $6,000**
Employer's contribution	= 75¢ for every $1 up to 6% of $60,000
75¢ × $6,000	= $4,500
6% of $60,000	= $3,600
Employer's contribution	**= $3,600**
Total contribution	**= $9,600**

Although the fact that an employee's contribution is counted as part of his or her annual income remains a disadvantage of the thrift and savings plans, if you have access to one at your work, I would advise that you participate. Most thrift and savings plans require the employer to make contributions on behalf of the employees, and the account will accumulate much faster since you won't be the only one contributing.

SALARY REDUCTION PLANS. The most common form of employer-sponsored retirement account is the salary reduction plan, or the 401(k). The term 401(k) refers to the IRS code that establishes these accounts. 401(k) plans are available to those employees in for-profit, private business. There are similar plans for people who work for public schools, universities, colleges, and nonprofit hospitals; these are known as 403(b) plans. Employees of state and local governments, as well as some tax-exempt organizations, will participate in 457 plans.

401(k) plans are a type of defined contribution plan, and as such, many employers will contribute to their employees' 401(k) accounts. Sometimes an employer will match 50¢ for every dollar contributed by the employee up to a certain percentage of salary, but sometimes an employer will match dollar for dollar up to a percentage of salary. Employer contributions are not counted as part of the employee's gross income, and so the employees aren't taxed on that until they begin to take distributions from their plans. Plus, any contribution made by an employee is taken out of the employee's gross income and sheltered until distributions begin. All earnings grow tax-deferred. Most employers offer a wide range of different types of investments that the employees may invest their 401(k) money in. The advantages to the 401(k) plans are quite beneficial to the employee. While the tax treatment for 403(b) and 457 participants is the same as for the 401(k), many employers do not match for 403(b) plans, and matching for 457 plan participants is almost nonexistent. (See Table 14.2)

Table 14.2   Contribution Limits for Salary Reduction Plans

Year	401(k)/403(b)/457 plans
2002	$11,000
2003	$12,000
2004	$13,000
2005	$14,000
2006	$15,000

403(b) plans are subject to a variety of special rules, and they are limited to investing in annuities and mutual funds. The plans are subject to fewer discrimination rules than 401(k) plans and are more flexible than 401(k) plans in many ways. Any salary reduction contributions you made to a 403(b) plan will reduce the contribution you make to a 401(k) plan. However, any contributions made to a 457 plan (beginning in the year 2002), do not limit the amount that may be contributed to a 401(k).

There are some other characteristics of 457 plans that should be considered. First, these plans don't offer the same safeguards that 401(k) and 403(b) plans do. Qualified plan assets are segregated from the employer's assets. If the employer becomes bankrupt, your benefits are still safe. Assets of governmental 457 plans must also be held in a separate trust for the participants' benefit. But a tax-exempt organization cannot set up a separate trust. For this reason, you should be very certain that your tax-exempt organization is financially sound before contributing to its 457 plan, Finally, assets in a 457 plan sponsored by tax-exempt organization cannot be rolled over to IRAs when you leave employment. A governmental 457 plan can be rolled over.

Let's consider how participating in a 401(k) can be beneficial, not just for planning for your retirement, but also for decreasing your current income tax due. John Client has been working for the same company for about 20 years. As a result, his salary is quite high, and so he feels that he can contribute the full amount ($11,000 for the year 2002) to his 401(k) plan at work. Unfortunately for John, his employer doesn't offer any type of match. With John's salary of $125,000, he finds that he is in the 30% (using year 2002 tables) tax bracket. By diverting $11,000 from his salary into his 401(k), he is saving himself $3300 in taxes ($11,000 × 30%) since he is reducing his income to $114,000. Therefore, it could be said that he is contributing $7800 to his 401(k) while the IRS is contributing $3300 because of the tax savings.

The more you are able to contribute, the faster your account will accumulate. Add in any match that your employer provides, and that will just increase the amount of saving going on for your retirement. Participating in a 401(k), 403(b), or 457 is an excellent way to beef up your retirement nest egg, while enjoying some tax savings in the meantime. Don't worry if your employer doesn't offer any matching contribution. Just because they may not match now, doesn't mean they won't match in the future.

All employer-sponsored retirement plans have the same tax treatment. Gains and interest accrue on a tax-deferred basis, and there are no taxes due until the participant begins to take distributions. At that time, the participant will face ordinary income tax on the portion withdrawn. However, there will be a 10-percent early-withdrawal penalty imposed for those people who are younger than $59^1/_2$.[3]

SMALL BUSINESSES AND SELF-EMPLOYED PEOPLE

Investing in a 401(k) or 403(b) may sound like a great idea, and if you have access to one at work, it is a tremendous way to increase your retirement nest egg. However, 401(k)s also pose a large cost to the employers who offer them. Because of that, many smaller businesses can't afford to establish 401(k)s at work for their employees. But that doesn't mean that the employees don't have any kind of retirement account to use. There are a few different types of plans that smaller businesses and self-employed workers can use that will offer them the same type of preferred tax treatment, as well as the encouragement to save money for retirement. We're talking about the SEP, SIMPLE, and Keogh plans. These plans are self-directed because they allow the employee, or self-employed worker, to choose exactly what the contributions are being invested in. While the employer who established the SEP and SIMPLE will choose the institution at which the plan is started, the employee will have the final say over which available investments will be used for all contributions. Depending upon where the plans are established, the employees could have quite a range of available choices.

SEP Plans
Employers may establish SEP (simplified employee pension) plans for their employees using either individual retirement arrangements (IRAs) or annuities that are individually owned by each employee.

---

[3] There are certain exceptions for this rule, notably the SEPP exception, which is discussed in a subsequent section.

These plans require less paperwork than the more recognizable types of retirement accounts, thus making them easier for small business owners and self-employed workers to establish and fund. The SEP is more attractive to smaller business owners, but, there is no current regulation stating how big or small a business must be in order to adopt an SEP. Any business could offer its employees the opportunity to contribute to a SEP if so desired.

SEP plans offer the same type of tax treatment for all contributions and distributions as other types of retirement accounts. Any contribution made by an employer on an employee's behalf won't be counted as part of that employee's current gross income, and the employer may write off the contribution as a company expense. The interest and gains of the account accrue tax-deferred, and the SEP owner won't have to pay any type of income tax on the account until distributions begin. Self-employed people who contribute to their own SEP may deduct their contributions on their tax returns. Technically speaking, SEP plans aren't considered qualified retirement plans, as 401(k)s are. Instead, they are classified as traditional IRAs that meet the tax law requirements to become SEPs.

Business owners who use the SEP for their employees may contribute up to the lesser of (a) 25 percent of the employee's compensation or (b) $40,000 (indexed in 2002). Other rules include immediate and 100-percent vesting for eligible employees of employer contributions, and contributions may be made any time before taxes are due. For example, you could make your SEP contribution for the year 2002 anytime before April 15, 2003. Employees may also withdraw any amount from their SEPs at any time. Because these are IRA accounts, they are owned and controlled by the individual employees, not the employer. However, SEP IRAs are also under the same rules as traditional IRAs. That means all distributions will be 100-percent taxable to the IRA owner, plus a 10-percent early-withdrawal penalty if the owner is younger than $59\frac{1}{2}$ years old.

SIMPLE Plans

The SIMPLE plan is relatively new, having been introduced in 1997. It comes in two forms: the SIMPLE IRA and the SIMPLE 401(k). SIMPLE plans allow eligible employees and self-employed workers to elect to receive their compensation or earned income as cash or to contribute them to their SIMPLE IRAs through a qualified salary reduction arrangement. The employer must then make a contribution to the employees' SIMPLE plans on either a matching (up to three percent of compensation) or nonelective (two percent of compensation) arrangement, no matter what elective the employee has chosen. If the employee has chosen to go with the salary reduction agreement, the employer will make the matching contribution, generally dollar for dollar up to three percent of compensation or $7000 (for the year 2002; see Table 14.3 for upcoming years). With the current limitations on deferral amounts, an employee whose employer sponsors a SIMPLE program could have as much as $14,000 deferred during the year 2002, as long as the employee earns $233,000 of compensation or more (3 percent of 233,000 is approximately $7000). Employer contributions are done on a tax-deferred basis to the employee. There is no tax due on the account until distributions have begun. Employees contributing to their SIMPLE IRAs on the salary reduction plan will do so on a pretax basis. As with traditional IRAs, the gains and interest will accrue tax- deferred. The same distribution rules apply. For those people taking money out of their SIMPLE prior to age $59^1/_2$, there will be a 10-percent early-withdrawal penalty. But SIMPLE owners face an additional early-withdrawal penalty in certain cases. If you were to open up and contribute to a SIMPLE plan, and *within* two years of doing this took distribution from the account, you would face a 25-percent early-withdrawal penalty, rather than the 10-percent penalty. After the first two years, the penalty will drop back down to 10 percent. You may roll over a SIMPLE IRA from one to another

Table 14.3   SIMPLE Plan Contribution Limits

Year	SIMPLE
2002	$7,000
2003	$8,000
2004	$9,000
2005	$10,000
2006	$10,000

with no penalty. You may also roll over the SIMPLE into a traditional IRA, provided the 25-percent penalty has disappeared.

Similar to SEP plans, SIMPLE IRAs are traditional IRAs that meet the stringent requirements for being a SIMPLE. Plan contributions must be made to the SIMPLE IRA, not to a traditional or a Roth IRA. Eligible employees and self-employed workers may make contributions that are either a percentage of expected compensation or a fixed dollar amount.

As with SEP plans, employees are immediately 100 percent vested in their employer's contributions to their SIMPLE accounts. They may take withdrawals at any time from the plan, bearing in mind the tax laws. If we compare SIMPLE and 401(k) feature by feature, the advantage almost always goes to the

---

Special note: With the recent tax law changes by Congress, new rules regarding employer-sponsored retirement plans have been instituted. They are:

- Annual additions to a participant's profit sharing or 401(k) account, including employee and employer contributions and allocated forfeitures, may be as high as $40,000 (or 100 percent of compensation, whichever is less)—this is up from $35,000 or 25 percent of compensation. The amount for 403(b) accounts is $35,000.

- A benefit of as much as $160,000 (or 100 percent of average compensation, whichever is less) may be provided for a defined pension plan benefit for years beginning after January 1, 2002—this is up from $140,000 and 100 percent of compensation.

- Plans may consider up to $200,000 of the participant's compensation when applying contribution limits—this is up from $170,000.

- Participants who are age 50 and older who have contributed the maximum amount are allowed to "catch up" and contribute more the their retirement plans. (See Table 14.4.)

401(k). 401(k) plans are better for two very important goals of small plan sponsors: maximizing contributions and skewing employer contributions. However, the SIMPLE IRA is still very attractive to employers who look for low-cost plan with few administrative burdens.

SIMPLE 401(k) plans are different from the SIMPLE IRAs because the employees don't own their individual accounts. The other requirements for a SIMPLE 401(k) are the same as for the SIMPLE IRA, however, the 401(k) must meet some additional requirements that are set forth for traditional 401(k)s.

Keogh Plans

Keogh plans have been around much longer than SIMPLEs, as they were established in 1962 as part of the Self-Employed Individuals Retirement Act. Historically, Keogh plan followed statutory provisions that governed partnerships and people who are self-employed. However, as discussed in Chapter 10, the only distinction that still exists is the manner in which self-employed individuals determine their income for the purpose of applying the above limitations.

Keogh defined contribution plans allow up to 20 percent of earned income or $40,000, whichever is less. So if you were to earn $20,000 per year doing some extra work that was considered self-employment work, you could start a Keogh with a $4000 contribution for that calendar year. Those who contribute to a Keogh will still be able to make their annual contributions to their traditional and Roth IRAs.

Keoghs are subject to the same tax treatment as other types of retirement accounts. Interest and gains are accrued on a tax-deferred basis. Any withdrawal made before age $59^1/_2$ will be subject to a 10- percent early-withdrawal penalty, and all withdrawals will be subject to ordinary income tax. Contributions made on an employee's behalf for an employee won't be counted as part of the employee's current taxable income, and any contributions made by an employee as part of a salary reduction agreement will be done on a before-tax basis.

Table 14.4. Allowable Catch-Up Limits

Year	401(k)/403(b)/457	SIMPLE
2002	$1,000	$500
2003	$2,000	$1,000
2004	$3,000	$1,500
2005	$4,000	$2,000
2006	$5,000	$2,500

INDIVIDUAL RETIREMENT ARRANGEMENTS

Most people are familiar with individual retirement arrangements, or IRAs. However, they may not be as familiar as they should be. An IRA is a powerful tool that will help you save money for your retirement, as well as shelter some of your money from taxes. Similarly, many people assume that an IRA is a specialized type of investment, perhaps a specific mutual fund or stock in which all IRA owners are invested. Not so. An IRA is strictly a type of account; it's a category of accounts, not a specific investment. In fact, an IRA can hold stocks, bonds, real estate, annuities, or any type of investment you can think of. The types of IRAs, including the traditional and the Roth, are designed to promote retirement saving. With the introduction of the Roth IRA in 1998, retirement saving got a real boost because the Roth offers specialized tax features that no other type of retirement account does. Until recently, the annual contribution limit was $2000. This really didn't allow the IRA accounts to show a great deal of growth over time, even with the bull market we experienced in the late 1990s. Now, Congress has agreed to increase the contribution limit, which will help those who contribute to IRAs to see a quicker increase in their savings.

Traditional IRAs

Traditional IRAs may be opened by anyone, regardless of whether the person has a retirement plan established at work. These IRAs are very common, and although they share some of the same characteristics as other IRAs and retirement accounts, they have one distinguishing mark about them. Traditional IRAs are tax deductible. That is, the contribution that you make to your IRA may be deducted from your income tax, which helps you save money on an annual basis, as long as you contribute to a traditional IRA every year. Each family member may have his or her own IRA, no matter how old that person is. However, he or she must have some sort of earned income.

   The only exception is that a nonworking spouse may have a traditional IRA account if the other spouse has some sort of earned income.

Special note: Those individuals who have contributed the maximum to their IRAs and are age 50 and older are allowed to "catch up" and contribute more to these accounts. See Table 14.5.

The other features of the traditional IRA are the same as for other types of IRAs. First, you may only contribute $3000 per year per person, right now. (See Table 14.5.) Second, there is a limit to the amount of money you can make per year and still be able to *deduct* the IRA contribution. You may still be able to make the contribution, just not deduct the amount, be it the full amount or a portion. (See Table 14.6.) Finally, all earnings and gains are accrued on a tax-deferred basis. No tax is paid on the earnings until any distributions are made.

Table 14.5.   IRA Contribution Limits

Year	Without Catch-Up	With Catch-Up
2002–2004	$3000	$3500
2005	$4000	$4500
2006–2007	$4000	$5000
2008 and after	$5000*	$6000

*This amount will be adjusted for inflation in $500 increments.

Once IRA distributions have begun, all the earnings and gains that the account(s) have accrued are counted as ordinary income. Your IRA will continue to have its gains accrue tax deferred as long as the account exists and has a value. As for withdrawals, any money taken out of an IRA is subject to tax. There will be a 10-percent early-withdrawal penalty for distributions made to those who are younger than $59^{1}/_{2}$ years old, with a few exceptions. The IRS typically allows people to take up to $10,000 out of their IRA penalty-free as long as the money will be used for a first-time home purchase or for qualifying education purposes. There is another exception that is discussed in a subsequent section. IRA owners are required to begin taking distributions from their IRAs once they reach $70^{1}/_{2}$ years old. These are called required minimum distributions (RMDs). The IRS has established a formula to determine how much you should take out depending on how old you are.

Nondeductible IRAs

Nondeductible IRAs are, in essence, no different than traditional IRAs, except that you can't take a tax deduction for your contribution. But that's it; everything else is the same. And there is no difference in the way your account will be handled. You will just not be able to deduct whatever money you put in; all contributions are made on an after-tax basis. Nondeductible IRAs are still limited by the amount of money you may contribute. Just because you can't deduct what you contribute doesn't mean that you can put in whatever amount you want. The limits outlined in Table 14.5 reflect those for nondeductible IRAs, as well. The rules regarding distributions and tax treatment are the same as they are for traditional IRAs.

Rollover IRAs

Many times when a client has retired, or changed jobs, we take the money out of his or her company's retirement plan and roll it over into an IRA. While you can roll over retirement plans and pensions into traditional IRAs, the government has established rollover IRAs in order to keep the money separate. Whether or not you utilize a rollover IRA is up to you. However, if you were to set up an SEPP program for yourself and didn't want to use any of the money that was in your job's retirement plan, or pension, you would want to keep that money separate. By rolling over your retirement plan money, you avoid the mandatory 20-percent tax withholding, as well as continue to enjoy tax-deferred investment growth.

Roth IRAs

Roth IRAs are the newest way to save money for retirement in an IRA. They are also the most powerful way. This is because the money that accrues in a Roth IRA is tax free. When you put money into a Roth IRA, you do so on an after-tax basis; you can't take any type of deduction for it. However, all the interest and other gains that build up the value of your account will not generate any type of taxes. When you begin to take distributions from your account, you will pay no taxes: no taxes on the gains, and no taxes on the money that you originally put in.

Let's consider Mike Smith. He establishes a Roth IRA for himself and puts $3000 in it. Over the years, he gradually adds to it. Many years pass, and Mike retires and wants to take some money out of the account. He goes through his statements and finds that he has invested $18,000 total (all after tax) of his own money. The account has grown to just more than $73,000. As Mike takes money out of his Roth IRA, he won't pay any tax on it. And as long as there is still money in the account, it will continue to grow tax free.

The Roth IRA isn't without its drawbacks, though. First, if you have an annual adjusted gross income of at least $150,000 (married filing jointly) or $95,000 (single filers), you won't be able to contribute the full amount to a Roth. The IRS has phased out contributions to Roth IRAs based on income levels. You won't be able to make a contribution at all once your income hits the $160,000 (married filing jointly) or $110,000 (single filers) level. Second, the account must have been open for at least five years, and the individual must be over the age of $59^1/_2$ when distributions are made for the tax-free provision to count. That means if you are 57 and establish a Roth IRA for yourself, you must wait until you are at least 62 before you can begin to make withdrawals. Otherwise, it's taxable.

As for regular withdrawals, the same rules apply as for the traditional IRAs. Besides the five-year rule, the only other exception is the required minimum distribution rule. Because the money that goes into a Roth IRA is after tax, and since the money that is withdrawn from a Roth is tax free, the IRS imposes no rule as to when the money must come out of the account. So you don't have to make any withdrawals from a Roth IRA until you are 90 if you want!

Converting to a Roth IRA

Many clients ask me about converting their traditional or rollover IRAs to Roth IRAs. They think that by converting, they will be able to take their money out of their existing IRAs tax free. However, it doesn't work like that. To convert a traditional or rollover IRA to a Roth IRA, you will need to pay the taxes due, just as if you had taken the entire amount out of the IRA. (SEP and SIMPLE IRAs may also be converted after two years.) Plus, if your AGI is more than $100,000, you are ineligible to convert. (Tax payers who file as married but filing separately are always ineligible to convert.) You don't think that the IRS will let you just convert and not pay any taxes, do you? If you think that you will benefit from the tax-free distributions, and you have the cash on hand to pay the taxes due, then converting may be a good idea. But, for most people, converting their traditional and rollover IRAs to Roth IRAs is just a poor idea, especially if you find that you have a substantial amount of money invested in IRAs.

Substantially Equal Periodic Payments

I mentioned before that there was an additional way to take distributions from your IRA prior to turning $59^1/_2$ without paying the 10-percent early-withdrawal penalty. The program called Substantially Equal Periodic Payments, or SEPP (not to be confused with SEP plans), will help you achieve this. The SEPP program is generally used by those individuals who have retire and have no source of income, but their retirement funds and are younger than $59^1/_2$. Because the person has retired, he or she is not earning any income. That person will also be too young to take money out of his or her retirement accounts without penalty, or to draw social security. But, he or she has to have some sort of income, right?

Essentially, SEPP works like this. After adding up the total value of your traditional IRAs (if you have rolled over your company's 401(k) plan into a rollover IRA, then you may keep that separate), a computer program will calculate the monthly amount that you may take from your accounts at a fixed percent, usually between five and nine percent. Remember to keep your Roth IRAs separate. By agreeing to take the SEPP-established amount as monthly withdrawals, you agree to the terms of the program. You must not alter the payment amount for five years, or until you are $59^{1}/_{2}$ years old, whichever comes last.

If you do change anything about your monthly dispersements, the entire amount you have taken will be subject to the 10-percent penalty tax. By abiding by the terms, you will avoid the penalty. Of course, whatever you take will be subject to regular income taxes. Therefore, if you are 57 and wish to participate in the SEPP program, you will have to take the same amount from your accounts until the five years (60 payments) are up. Likewise, if you began taking SEPP payments at age 52, you would have to continue until you were $59^{1}/_{2}$, or for seven-and-a-half years. However, if you were to die before the 60 payments were completed, the agreement dies with you. Your beneficiary wouldn't be required to complete the SEPP program. The SEPP program is especially useful if you have rolled over your 401(k) plan from work and would like just to live off of that while your other accounts continue to grow. You can opt to have the SEPP just use the value of your rollover accounts, instead of your traditional IRA accounts.

Plus, don't think that just because you are taking money out of your IRA, you must use it all. If you find that the monthly amount is too much income for you, and I have clients that have found that, you can always reinvest the money into a nonqualified (regular) account, where it can grow. You just can't receive more or less than what is specified by the SEPP calculation. But by diverting some of the unnecessary money into another account, you can help continue to grow your money so that if you need it later, it will be there.

> **Special note:** On October 3, 2002, the IRS released Revenue Ruling 2002-62 to help taxpayers preserve their retirement savings when there is an unexpected drop in the value of their retirement money. Those who began receiving fixed payments from their IRA or retirement plan under SEPP may now switch without penalty to a method of determining the amount of payments based on the value of their account as it changes from year to year.

GROWING YOUR MONEY DURING RETIREMENT

Many people have asked me how my clients continue to grow their assets even though they are taking money out as income on a monthly basis. It's simple, I tell them. It's all in the way their accounts are handled. Generally, the younger a person is, the more risk they want to take, which means investing their money in riskier investments. That doesn't mean that we are speculating with their money, but since they have a longer time before they are going to retire, they feel that they can invest in more growth and aggressive growth investments, which could provide them with greater growth over the long term. As my clients age, I move them from the riskier to the less-risky investments, keeping in mind their risk tolerance and goals. I've found that as we do this, the clients' money has continued to grow, just at a slower pace. I don't forsake the growth-oriented investments entirely, though. I'm just more apt to have more of the client's money invested in bonds and cash or fixed investments. Plus, I continue to monitor their risk tolerance, so that the investments they are involved with are in keeping with their feelings.

There's really no other secret than that. Of course, I always take my clients' risk tolerance into account as I am managing their money. As my clients get older, their portfolios should adapt to their changing needs. Some financial planners believe that if a client is older when he or she begins retirement planning, that the client needs to be invested more aggressively. To a certain extent that is true. However,

Table 14.6. Is My IRA Contribution Tax Deductible?

Modified AGI*	If you are covered by an employer-sponsored retirement plan and your tax filing status is:			If you are not covered by an employer-sponsored retirement plan and your tax filing status is:			
Income limits	Single Head of household	Married filing Jointly (even if your spouse isn't covered by plan at work) Qualifying widow(er)	Married filing separately	Married filing jointly (spouse has plan at work)	Single Head of Household	Married filing Jointly or separately (spouse has no plan at work)	Married filing separately (spouse has plan at work)
$0.01 to 10,000	Full deduction	Full deduction	Partial deduction	Full deduction			Partial deduction
$10,000.01 to $31,000	Full deduction	Full deduction	No deduction	Full deduction			No deduction
$31,000.01 to $41,000	Partial deduction	Full deduction	No deduction	Full deduction			No deduction
$41,000.01 to $51,000	No deduction	Full deduction	No deduction	Full deduction	Full deduction	Full deduction	No deduction

Table 14.6. Is My IRA Contribution Tax Deductible? *(continued)*

$51,000.01 to $61,000	No deduction	Partial deduction	No deduction	Full deduction	No deduction
$61,000.01 to $150,000	No deduction	No deduction	No deduction	Full deduction	No deduction
150,000.01 to $160,000	No deduction	No deduction	No deduction	Partial	No deduction
$160,000.01 and up	No deduction	No deduction	No deduction	No deduction	No deduction

*Modified adjusted gross income is the amount on line 14 on Form 1040A, and line 33 on Form 1040. Certain income and interest income exclusions apply.

you want to be careful that you aren't too aggressive, because just as quickly as your investments can go up in value, they can decline. If you ever feel that your advisors are suggesting that you should invest your money too aggressively, or if you are uncomfortable with the investments you are in, talk to them. If you don't think that they are listening or care, you may want to switch advisors.

RETIREMENT PLANNING AS A WHOLE

While retirement is just one stage in our lives, it really encompasses everything we do. Retirement planning should be our biggest concern, and first priority, when it comes to financial planning. Especially now that people are living longer, retirement may be a 30-year or 40-year period. This isn't something that should be taken lightly.

If you haven't thought about your retirement, now is the time to start. It's never too late to start, but the longer you put off your planning, the worse off you could be. I've yet to meet anyone who has told me that they wanted to retire early, but were unable to, and that that was a good thing. No one wants to retire any later than necessary. By saving and investing your money now, you stand a greater chance of fulfilling your retirement dreams. Sure, it takes a bit of discipline, but are things that come easily really worth having?*

* Reference for this chapter: *Planning For Retirement Needs*, Fifth Edition, by David A. Littell and Renn Beam Tacchino. The American College, 2001.

YOU CAN'T TAKE
IT WITH YOU

Many people that I have talked to assume that estate planning is strictly for the super wealthy. They also assume that since they aren't in that category, they don't need any help with their estate. However, anyone can benefit from some estate planning; some people need a more complex level of planning than others. Still, if you think you don't need estate planning, ask yourself these two questions. Do you have any possessions? Would you like to be in control of what happens to these possessions? If you answered "yes" to either of these questions, then you are a candidate for estate planning. Plus, the more work you do to increase your income and net worth, the more your heirs will benefit from an estate plan in the future.

There are many components to estate planning, including wills, trusts, and life insurance. Some will be more beneficial to you than others. Because there is no catch all to estate planning, we'll just be going over the basics. It's then up to you to meet with your financial advisor and attorney to draft a plan that is right for you.

What's in an estate? Many things, some of which you may not have even realized. First, everything that you own in your name, such as bank accounts, IRA accounts, your company's retirement benefits, and life insurance policies. Second, half of everything you own jointly with your spouse. This includes your home (unless you live in a community property state), investments, and bank accounts. Then, your share of anything you own in common, such as property you own with a business partner, is included. If you are the trustee or custodian for any trust or custodial accounts, they are included as part of your estate. And finally, everything that you own jointly with anyone except your spouse is included, unless there is proof that the other person helped pay for it.

All of these things combined will make up your estate. Once that figure is determined, the federal (and perhaps state) government will want a share. However, that's where estate planning comes in. Should you do nothing, the government can take up to 50 percent of your estate in taxes. Wouldn't you want your children, grandchildren, or other heirs to have your property and money rather than the government? In order to decide who gets what and to minimize estate taxes, you will need to ensure that you have done some work before you die. I know that death is not a favorite topic of conversation, but, a little foresight on your part will make your heirs' lives much easier down the road.

WHAT IS ESTATE PLANNING?

Minimizing estate taxes and transfer costs while providing the greatest possible financial security for your heirs and beneficiaries defines estate planning. This is a very goal-oriented portion of financial planning. One of the main challenges for estate planning is to achieve a high standard of living in your retirement plus preserving as much of your assets as possible to pass on to the next generation. As part of the inheritance maximization, estate planning tries to minimize the amount of estate taxes your beneficiaries will have to pay.

Excessive estate taxes pose a major problem to many estates, and in some cases, may even be eliminated!

Also included as part of estate planning are ensuring that your assets go where you want them to, simplifying the transfer of your assets to your beneficiaries, and minimizing family conflict. A death can do strange things to the surviving family. I have seen more than one family torn apart after the death of a loved one. By providing a plan that specifies where your assets are to go, you won't be making the executor of your estate the "bad guy." Family bitterness and jealousy are only two things that can be prevented by proper estate planning. You can also avoid leaving family members with financial insecurity and illiquid assets, leaving assets to minors who are incapable of handling them, and having improper distribution of your estate.

Estate planning can be as simple as a living trust and a will. Or, it can involve gifting and charitable remainder trusts. The more assets you have, the more important estate planning becomes. For those people with a high net worth, estate planning is especially important. But there are also a number of people who are in dire need of estate planning and may not even know it. Couples who are not married must do some estate planning, if they hope to provide for the surviving partner after the other's death. The courts will not take special consideration if these couples haven't put their desires into legal documents.

ESTATE TAXES

During the year 2001, Congress passed a large tax cut for the American people. As part of that legislation, they also overhauled the estate and gift taxes, making estate planning much easier for Americans, including eliminating the estate tax by the year 2010. Congress has also enacted a declining scale for the generation skipping tax (GST), concluding with its eventual repeal in the year 2010. However, the gift tax will be sticking around. While these taxes are being phased out and even eliminated, the new law has a sunset provision, just like the income tax portion of the tax cut. If Congress does not enact a new law upholding these changes during 2010, the tax laws will be restored to present conditions. That is, the GST and estate tax will be reinstituted in 2011.

But, until then, we will enjoy new, and lower, estate tax laws. Beginning in 2002, the top gift and estate tax rate will be 50 percent, which is down from 55 percent. Plus, the old five percent surtax (on cumulative transfers between $10 million and $17.184 million) will disappear. As time goes on, the top tax rate will continue to decline until 2010, when the estate tax disappears and the gift tax tops out at 35 percent.

Table 15.1   New Top Gift and Estate Tax Rates

Year	Rate
2002	50%
2003	49%
2004	48%
2005	47%
2006	46%
2007–2009	45%
2010	35%
2011 *	55%

While the estate tax rates continue to drop, the threshold at which the estate tax is imposed continues to go up. The maximum amount allowed without triggering estate taxes (the exclusion amount or unified credit) was $675,000 during 2001. The exclusion allowance means that you could give your beneficiaries up to $675,000 tax free. Anything above that amount was subject to an estate tax of between 37 and 55 percent. That rate was supposed to increase gradually until 2006, when it was scheduled to top out at $1 million. Now, the exclusion amount for the year 2002 is $1 million, increasing every year until 2009. Then the tax will be repealed in 2010. Unfortunately, many people don't understand that the estate tax will only be gone for just that one year. Barring any action from Congress, the estate tax will be reinstated in 2011 at the $1-million exclusion allowance.

*Under the new law's sunset provision, the old law will be reinstated unless Congress takes further action.

Table 15.2   New Exclusion Allowance Amounts

Year	New law	Old law
2002–2003	$1,000,000	$700,000
2004	$1,500,000	$850,000
2005	$1,500,000	$950,000
2006–2008	$2,000,000	$1,000,000
2009	$3,500,000	$1,000,000
2010	Law repealed	$1,000,000
2011*	$1,000,000	$1,000,000

As far as state taxes go, many states base their estate and inheritance taxes on the amount of the federal credit allowed for death taxes paid to a state. The new tax law not only modifies the credit, it also phases it out. Some states, including California and Florida, are prohibited by their state laws to enact an inheritance tax, but most states aren't. Whether the states will individually step in and enact their own inheritance taxes remains to be seen. But if they do, they will each be able to establish their own exemptions and tax rates, as well as define what can be taxed.

The first step to estate planning is to write your will. The next steps are all based on whether you and your financial planner think that you need any form of advanced estate planning. Remember, estate planning is not based on your need *now*; it's based on what your estate is estimated to be worth years from now. Perhaps a will is all you will need, especially if you believe that you will not live past the year 2010. But, you may find that you need much more than just a will.

DO I NEED A WILL?

As a matter of fact, yes, I would say you probably need a will. A will is the simplest way of transferring your property to someone else (your beneficiaries or heirs) after you die. It will also name the people (the executors) who you want to carry out your wishes. Most people

*Barring any further action from Congress, the estate taxes will be reinstated at their previous rates in 2011.

are advised to make out a will as soon as they have some sizable assets, but since "sizable" is a subjective term, I advise people to have a will if they feel that they have property that they would like to give to someone. Certainly by the time you have children, you should have a will, as you will be able to name your children's guardian in your will.

Special note: Many investment companies will ask that you name a beneficiary for your accounts when you open them up. Usually, you will be allowed to name as many beneficiaries as you want. For nonretirement accounts, ask that your account be a Transfer on Death account, which will allow you to place a beneficiary on it.

If you were to die without a will, you would be dying intestate. When you draw up a will, you reserve the right to decide how your property will be divided. By dying intestate, you are giving the courts the right to split up your property. This means that no matter what you promised people while you were living, the chances of those wishes being carried out are pretty slim.

Another problem for the beneficiaries of someone who has died intestate is that the courts will usually divide the property up according to living, lawful relatives in equal shares. You will lose control of your property, and it may wind up that your Aunt Bertha, who you intensely dislike, will receive a bulk of your estate, while your best friend since childhood receives nothing. Deathbed promises are not upheld in a court of law. And, if you die intestate without any heirs (in this case, family), your estate will pass to the state. The importance of a will shouldn't be overlooked. We have strived to have control over our property and assets while we are alive. Why should we give up that control after we have died?

If you already have a will, you may need to go back and review it. Many times, I have seen clients get divorced but never change their wills. If they were to die today, their ex-spouses would receive their assets. Plus, recently there have been a number of changes with the tax laws, especially regarding estate taxes. Wills should be reviewed every two to three years, unless something major (i.e., the birth of a child, or remarriage) occurs before that. If you haven't reviewed your will for a while, do so now.

Sometimes my clients don't want to leave certain family members any of their estates. Who you choose to leave an inheritance to is your decision, and if you feel that you want to disinherit someone, that's your choice. You can cut out any person, including immediate family members, simply by leaving them out of your will. You may want to specify in your will which people you don't want to inherit anything. This will make contesting your will much more difficult. Or, you can simply leave them just a few dollars. This will definitely get your point across.

As far as disinheriting spouses, ex-spouses, children, and grandchildren, the rules vary. For spouses that live in a community property state (Arizona, California, Idaho, Louisiana, Nevada, New Mexico, Texas, Washington, or Wisconsin), the law assumes that your spouse owns one-half of everything you both earned during your marriage. But by both of you signing a legal document that states which property belongs to which person, you will be able to decide where your assets go upon your death. In noncommunity property states, your spouse legally has the right to claim one-fourth to one-half of your estate, regardless of what your will states. However, this provision usually kicks in only if your spouse contests your will.

If you are worried that your ex-spouse may try to claim part of your estate after your death, don't be. Unless they have a claim against your estate prior to your death (i.e., a qualified domestic-relations order, a court order that awards a portion of your retirement or pension benefits to your ex-spouse), that person won't be able to lay claim to anything. But, it will also depend on how things were divided during the divorce.

Should you choose to disinherit any of your children or grandchildren, all you need to do is specify your wishes in your will. But just because you leave them out accidentally, doesn't mean that they won't receive anything from your will. Many states have laws that protect against accidental disinheritance. This way if you don't update your will, and you have had an additional grandchild or two enter the picture, they won't be left out. Legally, unless you say that your child or grandchild is not entitled to any of your estate, they are eligible to receive the same share as your other children and grand-children if they contest your will.

LIVING WILLS AND PROXIES

There are a few other estate planning tools that you should consider having. The first is a living will, which tells your doctors what your wishes are concerning life support. If you don't want to be kept alive by a life support machine, you will need this document; otherwise, your doctors are bound by their oath to do whatever it takes to keep you alive. Second, you may want a health care proxy or power of attorney. This will authorize someone you trust, usually a close fam-ily member, to make medical decisions for you in the event you are unable to communicate your wishes. Finally, you should consider a durable power of attorney, which will allow whomever you choose to make any kind of financial decision for you. If you have a trust, or plan to set one up, you may want a separate power of attorney section inside the trust. Some financial companies require that the durable power of attorney be stated within the trust and may not accept a sep-arate power of attorney. However, you may still name the same per-son as your power of attorney.

TRUSTS

I've heard many people say that by establishing a trust, you will elim-inate any estate taxes due. That is a false statement. However, trusts do simplify the transfer of your assets to your heirs, as well as estab-lish whatever guidelines you want. For example, if you want to leave your grandchildren each a sizable amount of money, but believe that they will be too young to manage the money by themselves, you can put the money into trust where it can stay until they are old enough (which is an age that you determine). Or, you can ensure that your assets don't pass directly to your family members by putting them into a trust.

Trusts are legal entities that function as corporations do. They may allow you to save on some estate taxes, as well as help minimize the amount of estate taxes paid. They allow you to continue to control your assets, both while you are living and after you have passed away. Plus, trusts can specify how the trust's money can be spent. There are different types of trusts, including revocable, irrevocable, living and bypass trusts.

In some instances, trusts can take the tax burden off of an individual, who may be in a higher tax bracket, and shift it to the trust, or its beneficiary. However, the government has sought to limit the amount of tax savings that can occur through trusts. For instance, the beneficiary of certain types of trusts must be at least 14 years of age, or else the income is taxed at the grantor's (person who transfers the property into the trust) tax bracket. But, trusts may allow for a significant estate tax savings by removing the property out of the grantor's estate, much to the benefit of future generations, without incurring any federal estate taxes.

While setting up a trust, you will need to select who you will want to be your trustees. A trustee acts for the trust, and will be required to make any decisions regarding the trust. Many times, I have seen where it is advised that trustees be from a corporate setting (i.e., a trust company or bank that has been authorized to oversee the trust), but I feel that these third parties won't understand your family and your wishes. It's true that a trustee needs to be able to make impartial decisions, should have sound business knowledge, and should have some skill in investment and/or trust management. But it's also important to have a family connection to your trust. Corporate trustees may charge a very high maintenance fee for their services, all the while not doing anything to benefit the trust. If you have a family member who is experienced with investments and business, and you trust that person, have him or her act as a trustee. If you don't have anyone that has the experience, consider having a corporate trustee and a family member act as cotrustees, so that one cannot make all the decisions.

Revocable and Irrevocable Trusts

When the grantor wishes to retain control over the assets placed in the trust, as well as the right to change, amend or even terminate the trust, the grantor creates a revocable trust. However, if that person wishes to waive those rights, he or she may create an irrevocable trust. In an irrevocable trust, the grantor not only gives up the right to the property in the trust, he or she also relinquishes the right to any income produced from those assets. Plus, if any of the grantor's circumstances change, that person will be unable to alter the trust in any way.

Living Trusts

Living trusts may be either revocable or irrevocable, and are established during the grantor's lifetime. In a revocable living trust, the grantor retains the rights to the property that is placed inside the trust, as if the grantor were still the owner in name of all the assets. The grantor is then taxed on any income that is produced by the trust's assets. The major advantages to revocable living trusts are (1) the management continuity and the income stream are guaranteed to last beyond the death of the grantor, (2) any assets that have been placed in the trust won't have to go through the probate process since the trust will continue to survive after the grantor has died, (3) the trustee is responsible for all management and investment decisions, and (4) all aspects of the living trust, including the amount of assets within the trust are private. Unlike the probate process, which is a matter of public record, the trust documents, named trustees and, all other parts of the trust will remain a private matter even after the death of the grantor. Disadvantages include the cost to set up the trust, as well as any management fees charged by the trustee. Plus, since the grantor still has control over the trust's assets, they are included as part of the grantor's estate, and may be subject to estate taxes upon the grantor's death.

The advantages to setting up an irrevocable living trust are the same as for the revocable living trusts. Irrevocable trusts may also help reduce the amount of taxes paid by the grantor, since the property is not only removed from the grantor's estate, any income from the assets is also removed. However, the disadvantages of an irrevocable living trust outnumber those of a revocable trust. First, the grantor loses the right to his or her property placed in the trust plus any income generated by these assets. Second, the grantor will not be able to make any changes to the trust, nor rescind it, once it has been established. Third, the grantor may be subject to gift tax on the assets placed in the trust, depending upon the assets' value. And finally, the grantor will still be responsible for any fees charged to set up the trust, and perhaps, some management fees charged by the trustee. Usually, though, the trustee is paid directly from the trust.

Bypass Trusts

Bypass trusts are also known as marital or A/B trusts. Married couples who have an extensive net worth, and therefore need all the unified credit they can get, establish them. Bypass trusts divide a couple's assets so that each of them may claim the maximum unified credit ($1 million in 2002 and increasing until 2010 when it is repealed). A bypass trust will help reduce, or even eliminate, estate taxes by passing the trust's assets directly to the heirs, and thus, bypassing the surviving spouse's estate. Normally, when one spouse dies, he or she bequeaths the entire estate to the other spouse. The surviving spouse doesn't need to worry about estate taxes because assets inherited from a spouse aren't subject to estate taxes. But, the deceased spouse hasn't used their unified credit. When the surviving spouse dies, the beneficiaries will only be able to apply one unified credit, making the rest of the assets subject to estate taxes.

One way to make sure that the bypass trusts work is to make sure that each spouse has enough assets to maximize the benefit of the unified credit. Sometimes this means retitling assets that are in one spouse's name to the other spouse's trust. One spouse may give the other spouse an unlimited amount of money without triggering any gift tax. So, if you find that your spouse has less money in his or her name, and his or her trust, give your spouce some of yours. The point of establishing bypass trusts is to maximize the unified credit for each of you.

For example, Matthew and Cynthia Client have a joint gross estate of $5 million. Both of them are in good health now, but are in their early 80s. Matthew has been worried that if one of them were to die soon, their estate would be hit with enormous estate taxes. They would like to establish A/B trusts to help reduce the amount of taxes their children will have to pay on their estate. Upon dividing their assets, Matthew discovers that he only has about $1.2 million in assets in his name, while Cynthia has $3.8 million. Since they want their trusts to be as equal as possible, Cynthia gives Matthew $1.3 million worth of assets, which he places into his trust. Now they both have trusts worth $2.5 million. Plus, they incurred no gift tax because they are married. As long as their assets don't appreciate very rapidly, and providing they live past the year 2008, their heirs won't be subject to a large amount of estate taxes. And, if they both were to pass away in the year 2010, none of their estate would be taxed.

Irrevocable Life Insurance Trusts

These are established to be the owner of your life insurance policy. Once you have passed away, the death benefit is paid to the trust and doesn't become part of your estate. The proceeds can then be used to pay whatever estate taxes are due, or can be invested, with the interest going to benefit your heirs. This type of trust is best suited for those who have very large estates that would be subject to estate taxes.

Charitable Remainder Trust

This type of trust benefits the charity, or charities, of your choice. There are two major benefits to this trust. First, you (and possibly, your beneficiaries) can receive an annual income from the interest generated by the assets in the trust. Second, you can receive a tax deduction for the assets that you give each year to the trust. Then, after you (or your beneficiaries) pass away, the charity gets the principal.

There are other types of trusts, but these are the most commonly used and referred to. You may now know what type of trust you think you need, if any, but, no book can take the place of actually meeting with your attorney and financial advisor to determine what you need and what you should do. Be sure to consult with them prior to making these decisions.

WHY YOU SHOULDN'T OWN YOUR OWN LIFE INSURANCE POLICY

Perhaps the biggest estate-planning mistake I see is people owning their own life insurance policies. Many people assume, and rightly so, that by taking out an insurance policy on themselves, they are creating a liquid asset for their heirs to pay any estate taxes. This is an admirable sentiment; and it will work that way. However, that doesn't mean that you want to actually own the policy. If you have a large estate and own your own life insurance policy, you will only be making your estate larger when you die. This is why, although the government has decreed that life insurance policy benefits may pass to the beneficiaries tax free, the death benefit will be included as part of the estate of the policy owner.

For example, Alice and Tom Client have a joint net worth of $8 million. They have split up their estate into two bypass trusts, so each estate is worth $4 million. However, they are both pretty sure that they won't live long enough to see the repeal of the estate tax in 2010. Therefore, their beneficiaries will have to pay some estate taxes when either one (or both) of them dies. Tom takes out a life insurance policy on himself for $750,000. While he's not sure how much his estate taxes will be, he feels comfortable that the death benefit from the insurance policy will cover most, if not all, of the taxes due. Alice also takes out a $750,000 policy on herself. Both Alice and Tom own their own policies. If Tom were to die today, only $1 million of his estate would pass to his heirs tax free. The remaining $3 million will be taxed.[1] Plus, since he is the owner of his insurance policy, his estate has now increased by $750,000 overnight, making his total gross estate worth $3,750,000! If Alice were also to die right now, her estate would be the same. Their beneficiaries would have to pay estate taxes on her $3.75 million. They would have the two death benefits of $750,000 each, but would have to come up with the remaining tax money on their own or directly from the estates.

Tom's estate	= $4 million
Tom's death benefit	= $750,000
If Tom were to die today (2002):	
Tom's exclusion allowance	= $1 million
Tom's taxable estate	**= $3 million + death benefit**
	= $3.75 million

[1]This example is a very simple calculation (assuming no costs and the maximum allowed tax credit) only designed to show the effects of owning your own life insurance policy. It's not designed to be an actual example of what a couple would pay in estate taxes.

Alice's estate	= $4 million
Alice's death benefit	= $750,000
If Alice were to die today (2002):	
Alice's exclusion allowance	= $1 million
Alice's taxable estate	**= $3 million + death benefit**
	= $3.75 million

Now, if Tom and Alice were to die at the same time, their heirs would have to pay estate taxes on the two estates combined. That would mean a total taxable estate of $7.5 million. If Tom and Alice's estates were to fall into the top estate tax bracket (50 percent in 2002), their heirs would be responsible for $2.42 million in taxes. The beneficiaries would have the combined death benefits of $1.5 million to help pay the taxes, but they would be left to come up with $920,000 on their own.

Combined estates

Tom's taxable estate	= $3.75 million
Alice's taxable estate	= $3.75 million
Estate taxes due—Tom	= $1.21 million (roughly)
Estate taxes due—Alice	= $1.21 million (roughly)
Combined taxes due	= $2.42 million
Combined death benefit	= $1.5 million
Additional needed	**= $920,000**

But, if neither Tom nor Alice owned their insurance policies, their taxable estates would not include the death benefit. So continuing with our example, both Tom's and Alice's taxable estates would be $3 million apiece. If they were both to die at the same time, and assuming top tax rates, the estate tax due would be $1.56 million. Their heirs would only have to come up with $6000 for the rest of the taxes.

Tom's taxable estate	= $3 million
Alice's taxable estate	= $3 million
Estate taxes due—Tom	= $753,000 (roughly)
Estate taxes due—Alice	= $753,000 (roughly)
Death benefits	= $1.5 million

One of the best ways to have your life insurance policy, but not actually own it yourself, is to have one of your heirs own the policy. If you have children, you could ask one of them to own the policy, which would cover your life and name all the beneficiaries you wanted. In order to pay for the policy, you could then gift that child the money necessary to pay the premiums (up to the maximum gift allowance per year), which would not only help provide liquidity at your death, but would also help lower the amount of your estate through your annual gifts. Plus, depending on how long the policy is in force, your total premiums paid will be much less than the death benefit.

Another way not to own your own insurance policy is to have your trust own it. We have already discussed the irrevocable life insurance trust, but by placing your insurance policy within your trust, you remove it from your estate, which will lower your taxable estate at your death.

SECOND-TO-DIE POLICIES

Perhaps your combined estate with your spouse isn't very large, or you would like to use the marital credit when you pass away. If you leave your estate to your spouse when you die, you will be losing out on your ability to use the exclusion allowance for your part of your estate. This could mean that your heirs will have to pay a large amount in estate taxes when your spouse dies. By purchasing a second-to-die life insurance policy, you will help combat a potential large tax bill. A second-to-die, or survivorship life, policy covers both your and your spouse's lives. However, no death benefit is paid until the second spouse dies. Therefore, if you and your spouse have a policy, and you die first, your spouse won't receive any death benefit. But, upon your spouse's death, your beneficiaries will receive the death benefit.

If you are considering this type of policy, make sure the policy has a provision to split the policy into two separate life plans, one for each of the lives insured, which will cover an amount equal to one-half of the original death benefit. This helps in case of a divorce, further changes in estate tax law, or changes in your estate situation.

STEP-UP IN BASIS

Many of my clients plan on leaving their beneficiaries shares of stock. This is one good way to help your heirs reduce the amount of money they pay in capital gains taxes because of the step-up in basis law. The step-up in basis rule was also affected by the new tax laws that were enacted in 2001, but for most people, it won't be a big issue.

Under the old rules, any inheritance of stock or another asset would allow the recipient to scoot around the capital gains tax because the original tax basis for the asset would be wiped out. For instance, you inherited 1000 shares of XYZ stock from your father. He originally paid $10 per share (or $10,000). When you inherit the stock, it is worth $90,000. Had your father sold the stock, he would have been taxed on the gain of $80,000 at the long-term capital gains rate of 20 percent. His tax due would have been $16,000. But you inherit the stock instead. Your basis in the stock is the value when he died, or $90,000. If you were to sell the stock for $90,000, you wouldn't have to pay any capital gains tax. But if you were to wait, and you sold the stock when it was worth $95,000, you would be taxed on the gain of $5000.

Father's tax basis for 1000 shares	= $10,000
Value of stock at father's death	= $90,000
Your tax basis in stock	= $90,000
Sell stock for $90,000	= no tax due
Sell stock for $95,000	= tax due on $5000 gain

Now, the new step-up in basis rules say that those rules are limited to transfers of $1.3 million for each taxpayer. Plus, an additional transfer of $3 million will be allowed for the surviving spouse. Any inheritance in excess of those limits will not have any step-up in basis. So if you inherit stock worth $2 million, with an original basis of $500,000, and you sold the stock for $2 million, you would be taxed on a gain of $200,000. The original basis does matter once the inheritance is in excess of $1.3 million, unlike under the previous rules, where the original basis didn't matter at all.

Inheritance worth	= $2 million
Original basis	= $500,000
Total basis	= $1.8 million
Sell stock	= $2 million
Gain	**= $200,000**

ESTATE PLANNING FOR UNMARRIED AND GAY AND LESBIAN COUPLES

Up to this point, we've discussed estate planning from the point of view of a married couple. But that doesn't mean that unmarried or gay and lesbian couples aren't privy to the same kind of estate planning. In fact, the opposite is true. Estate planning becomes even more important if you aren't married, but share your life with someone. Both unmarried straight and gay couples don't benefit from the same protection under the law that married couples do.

First, when you die, your property will pass to others in one of four ways:

- automatically through joint ownership (bank accounts, house, etc.)
- by designation of a beneficiary (IRAs, life insurance)
- under the terms of a trust
- under the probate laws

If you haven't made arrangements to have your property and assets pass to your beneficiaries through any of the first three methods, your property will automatically pass through probate. By having a legal will, you will avoid having the courts decide who receives your assets. If you don't, you will lose control of who receives your estate. If you were to die intestate, the law first considers that the assets go to the spouse. If there is no spouse, then they flow to any children. If there are no children, then the assets go to the parents; if there are no parents, then they go to the grandparents, and so on. As I've stated before, the law doesn't allow any leniency for close friends or your favorite charity to inherit your assets. You need to make that sure you put your wishes in writing. For gay and lesbian relationships, Vermont is the only state that recognizes the surviving partner in intestacy laws.

You need to consider that, by law, whoever is listed on the title to any property is considered the legal owner, unless there is a legal agreement that states otherwise. If you die, your partner (unlike your spouse) won't have any legal right to your property if that person wasn't registered as a legal owner. Your partner would have to establish that he or she was legally part owner of the property, and thus, entitled to it after your death. Most states won't accept a verbal agreement to that effect, they'll only take it in writing.

Special note: Be careful of how you are titling your assets. Many times, unmarried gay and straight couples will want to show how committed they are to their relationships by putting their partner's name on their accounts. However, if those accounts are valued at more than $11,000, your loving gesture may be considered a gift, and you could be subject to paying gift tax. There are ways to get around any potential gift tax that your CPA can help you explore.

A will may not be sufficient on its own, though. You may find that you will need a trust. If that's the case, you will have the same options that married couples do. You want to be sure that your partner is taken care of if you pass away.

Estate planning is vital, no matter how big or small your estate is. You've worked too hard to increase your net worth, save for your retirement, etc., to see a large portion of your money go to the government. I've yet to meet any people that say they are so excited to die because then the government will finally be able to collect all that money from their estate. Actually, that's a rather ridiculous statement, isn't it? But, for many people, that's what happens. Failing to do proper estate planning will have no effect on you during your life, but it will have a dramatic effect on the lives of your spouse, children, and other heirs.

FINANCIAL TERMS

Adjusted gross income   The amount of income remaining after subtracting any adjustments to income (like tax deductions) from income. This figure is used for calculating whether you are eligible for certain tax-related items.

Amortization   Reducing the principal of a loan by regular payments

Annuity   A contract between an insurance company and an individual in which the company agrees to provide income, which may be fixed or variable in amount, for a specified period of time in exchange for a stipulated amount of money.

Asset   Anything owned that has monetary value.

Asset allocation   The process of determining what proportions of your portfolio holdings are to be invested in the various asset classes.

Beneficiary   The person who receives the death benefit of an insurance policy. Beneficiaries are also those named by account owners as the people who will receive the account once the owner dies and those who will benefit from assets placed in a trust. Also known as an heir.

Capital gains   Gain realized through the sale or exchange of capital assets, such as securities or real estate.

Cash reserve   Money that is available to meet expenses that were not planned for in a budget. Commonly, the suggested level of cash reserve equals three to six months of cash expenses, but the size of a cash reserve can vary based on family income, job stability, current debts, amount of insurance deductibles and risk tolerance.

Cash surrender value   The amount of money payable to an investor in exchange for a life insurance policy or annuity that has not yet matured.

Coinsurance   A part of an insurance policy that designates how much coverage the insurance company will provide and how much out-of-pocket costs the insured will pay for medical costs. For example, an insurance company may stipulate they will pay 80 percent of covered expenses, and the insured will have to pay for the remaining 20 percent. That 20 percent is referred to as the copayment.

Death benefit   The amount payable under a life insurance policy upon the death of the insured. The proceeds consist of the face amount of the contract, plus accumulated dividends (if any), plus amounts payable on riders, less any money owed to the life insurance company on the policy in the form of loans and loan interest.

Decreasing term insurance   A form of term insurance where the death benefit decreases over the life of the policy.

Defined benefits plan   An employer-sponsored pension plan where the formula for calculating benefits is defined in the plan provisions. An employee would then be able to calculate how much retirement income they would receive from this plan.

Defined contribution plan   An employer-sponsored pension plan that dictates the contribution amounts that must be made by both the employee and employer, while making no guarantees about the size of the retirement benefits.

Disability insurance   A form of insurance that replaces a person's income after he or she has suffered an injury or accident that prevents that person from working and earning a living. Disability insurance comes in both short-term and long-term form.

Discretionary income   The difference between income and expenses. It is money that you have to invest to help you reach your financial goals.

Dollar-cost averaging Investing a fixed dollar amount at regular intervals. When prices are low, your investment purchases more shares. When prices rise, you purchase fewer shares. Over time, the average cost of your shares will usually be lower than the average price of those shares. Such a plan doesn't assure a profit and does not protect against losses in a declining market. However, over longer periods of time it can be an effective means of accumulating shares.

Elimination period The amount of time an insured person must wait before their insurance benefits begin. During this time, the insured must pay for his or her own care in the case of long-term care or medical bills. In relation to disability insurance, the insured would receive no income from the policy during the elimination period. Also referred to as a waiting period.

Equity Value of a person's ownership in real property or securities. For instance, current market value of a home, less the principal remaining on its mortgage, is the equity of that property.

Expenditures Money spent on living expenses and to purchase assets, pay taxes, and pay off debt; bills.

Face amount The amount of the death benefit for insurance policies. This is also called the face value of the policy.

Government obligations Instruments of the U.S. government's public debt. Examples are Treasury bills, notes, bonds, savings bonds, and retirement plan bonds. These are fully backed by the U.S. government.

Grantor A person who transfers his or her own property to trust ownership.

Gross estate All assets, including personal, business, and investment assets, retirement benefits, and life insurance policies that are owned by a person at the time of death, before being reduced by payment of estate settlement expenses.

Individual retirement arrangement (IRA) A type of retirement account which grows on a tax-deferred basis. The owner may take a tax deduction for any contributions he or she makes to the account. When distributions begin, that person is then taxed at his or her ordinary income rate on the whole amount withdrawn. IRAs can be any type of investment vehicle, including annuities.

Inflation risk The risk created by the reduced purchasing power of the dollar; your dollar will purchase fewer goods in the future than it will today.

Insolvency The financial state in which net worth is less than zero.

Insured   The person who is covered by an insurance policy. The insured doesn't necessarily have to be the owner of the policy, but he or she can be. For estate planning purposes, the insured shouldn't be the policy owner.

Itemized deductions   Personal expenditures that can be deducted from adjusted gross income to determine taxable income.

Joint tenancy   A form of co-ownership that provides that each joint tenant has undivided interest in the whole property. When one joint tenant dies, this interest passes to the surviving joint tenant or tenants. The last surviving joint tenant obtains title to the entire property.

Keogh plan   A retirement account to which self-employed people may make pretax contributions of either $40,000 or 20 percent of annual earned income, whichever is less. The principal grows on a tax-deferred basis.

Level term insurance   A form of term insurance in which the amount of coverage remains the same throughout the entire life of the policy.

Liabilities   Debts or anything owed to another person or party. Liabilities include credit card balances, mortgages, auto loans, etc.

Long-term care insurance   A form of insurance that pays for the costs associated with nursing homes, in-home care and other types of long-term care.

Margin   A partial payment on investment units, the remainder of which is loaned by the brokerage firm. When investors buy on margin, they hope prices will go up fast enough to cover the loan, thereby increasing buying power. If prices drop, however, losses increase.

Medicaid   A state-run public assistance program for those people unable to provide for their own medical bills.

Medicare   A federally sponsored health plan to help offset medical costs for people over the age of 65, disabled people, and those who suffer from permanent kidney failure.

Mutual fund   A mutual fund pools the dollars of many people, and undertakes to invest those dollars more productively than individuals could for themselves.

Net worth   The difference between the total value of all assets and the total value of all liabilities.

Nonqualified   This term describes certain types of investment accounts in which the principal is invested after tax and the gains are currently taxable to the account holder.

Personal financial advisor   One who helps individuals in an ongoing process to arrange and coordinate their personal and financial affairs to enable the individuals to achieve their objectives.

Personal property   Generally, any property other than real estate.

Policyholder   The owner of an insurance policy. This person may or may not be the person covered by the policy.

Portfolio   All assets held by a mutual fund at any specific time, and thus, held by the shareholders. Also, the total investments held by an individual.

Preexisting condition   Any physical or mental impairment that a person has at the time that he or she is applying for an insurance policy. Some policies, if approved, will then exclude any coverage related to that impairment.

Principal   The amount of money that is financed, borrowed, or invested.

Qualified retirement plan   A plan sponsored by an employer to provide retirement benefits for employees, that meets certain regulatory requirements. The employer may deduct contributions to the plan, and the employees do not include benefits in their taxable income until received, usually after they have retired. Also, this term refers to the type of accounts that receive beneficial tax treatment by the government, such as IRAs.

Roth IRA   A type of IRA in which the principal grows tax-deferred and all withdrawals may be made tax free.

Security   An investment of money in a common enterprise with the expectation of profit from the effort of others.

Standard deduction   A fixed deduction that depends on the taxpayer's filing status, age, and vision. A taxpayer who doesn't have sufficient itemized deductions can take this.

Tenancy in common   A form of co-ownership. Upon the death of a co-owner, interest passes to the estate and not the surviving owner or owners.

Term insurance   A form of insurance that provides a "no frills" approach to protection. Term insurance only provides a death benefit. There is neither an accumulation of cash value, nor an increase in the death benefit due to investment choices. Insurance coverage only lasts as long as the specified term, unless the policyholder chooses to renew his or her policy.

Thrift and savings plan   A retirement plan granted by an employer to supplement pension benefits, as well as other types of benefits, in which the employer makes a contribution in proportion to what the employee contributes.

Trust   A legal arrangement by which title to property is given to one party who manages it for the benefit of a beneficiary or beneficiaries.

Trustee   The person or persons who act on behalf of a trust.

Unified gifts/transfers to minors The Uniform Gifts to Minors Act (UGMA) and Uniform Transfers to Minors Act (UTMA) are state laws that enable gifts to be made to minors. An adult is designated a "custodian" of the property. The minor, however, is the owner of the property, pays taxes on the earning generated by the property, and has an unrestricted right to use it upon the age at which the custodianship terminates (usually 18 or 21, depending upon the state).

Universal life insurance A combination of term insurance and an investment account. The investment account grows at a specified interest rate, which in turn goes towards the purchase of death protection. Universal life differs from whole life in that the premium is split between administration fees and the investment account.

Variable universal life insurance Life insurance where the death benefit is, for the most part, tied to the results of the separate investments that support the policy's payment obligations.

Vesting An employee's nonforfeitable rights to receive the pension benefits, or other retirement account benefits, based on his or her own and the employer's contributions.

Wealth The total value of all items owned by an individual, such as bonds, stocks, bank accounts, home, and automobile.

Whole life insurance A type of life insurance that provides a cash value that goes along with the insurance coverage and death protection. This type of policy covers an individual for his or her entire life unless the policy is surrendered prior to the insured's death.

Yield The current cash income produced by an investment. For example, bonds provide income in the form of interest, and stocks in the form of dividends.

INDEX

ABOUT THE AUTHOR

Charles C. Zhang, CFP™, ChFC, CLU, CMFC, CFS, is a Senior Financial Advisor-Advanced Advisor Group with American Express Financial Advisors, one of the nation's leading financial planning companies. He has won many awards in the company and in the industry. He has been acknowledged as one of the premier financial planners in the country by *Worth, Ticker* and *Financial Planning* magazines. In 2001, he received the President's Recognition Award from American Express Financial Advisors for demonstrating the provision of high-quality advice to the clients.

Charles holds some of the most prestigious designations and degrees in the industry. He has earned these designations: CERTIFIED FINANCIAL PLANNER™, Chartered Financial Consultant, Chartered Life Underwriter, Chartered Mutual Fund Consultant and Certified Fund Specialist, and also holds master degrees in economics and finance. Charles is an adjunct professor of finance at Western Michigan University.

Lynn L. Chen-Zhang, CFP™, CPA is a financial advisor with American Express Financial Advisors. Prior to joining American Express Financial Advisors, she was a Certified Public Accountant (CPA) with one of the "big five" CPA firms. Lynn has a master's degree in accountancy. She specializes in income tax planning and employee stock option planning.